Power and Politics in the Book of Judges

Power and Politics in the Book of Judges

Men and Women of Valor

John C. Yoder

Fortress Press
Minneapolis

POWER AND POLITICS IN THE BOOK OF JUDGES

Men and Women of Valor

Copyright © 2015 Fortress Press. All rights reserved. Except for brief quotations in critical articles or reviews, no part of this book may be reproduced in any manner without prior written permission from the publisher. Visit http://www.augsburgfortress.org/copyrights/ or write to Permissions, Augsburg Fortress, Box 1209, Minneapolis, MN 55440.

Cover design: Joe Reinke

Cover image: *Deborah Praises Jael*, Gustave Doré

Library of Congress Cataloging-in-Publication Data is available

Print ISBN: 978-1-4514-9642-0

eBook ISBN: 978-1-4514-9662-8

The paper used in this publication meets the minimum requirements of American National Standard for Information Sciences — Permanence of Paper for Printed Library Materials, ANSI Z329.48-1984.

Manufactured in the U.S.A.

This book was produced using PressBooks.com, and PDF rendering was done by PrinceXML.

To Millard Lind, who introduced me to the study of the Hebrew Bible

Contents

	Acknowledgements	ix
	Preface	xi
1.	Introduction and Overview	1
2.	Power and Knowledge	45
3.	Power and Trust	79
4.	Power and Honor	115
5.	Power and Wealth	165
6.	Conclusions and Reflections	207
	Methodological Appendix	227
	Bibliography	235
	Index of Names and Subjects	247
	Index of Scripture References	269

Acknowledgements

This book would not have been possible without the support and advice of my former Whitworth University colleague Scott Starbuck, an exacting language teacher and a perceptive Hebrew Bible scholar. Not only did he give detailed attention to each page of my manuscript, for my benefit he also adjusted his Hebrew exegesis class to focus on the Book of Judges. Will Kynes, who was teaching Old Testament studies at Cambridge University, provided very helpful suggestions that have improved every chapter of the book. Perry Yoder, at Anabaptist Mennonite Biblical Seminary, offered critical guidance at the beginning of the project. Carolyn Sharp at Yale and Corliss Slack at Whitworth read sections of the work at various stages of its completion. Daniel Farrer, a Whitworth University history student, provided assistance in double-checking the Hebrew words and their transliterations. Gail Fielding and Nancy Bunker of the Whitworth University library were helpful at every stage of this effort. The staff at Fortress Press—Neil Elliott, Marissa Wold, and Mark Nussberger—were wonderful editors with whom to work. I am grateful to Whitworth University for supporting this work with a sabbatical leave and with a research grant from Whitworth's Weyerhaeuser Center for Faith and Learning. I would also like to thank my Whitworth political science colleagues for encouraging me even though I ventured off in a research direction that seemed somewhat far afield. Of course, I alone am responsible for any shortcomings in the book.

Preface

I began this study of Judges because of my long-standing interest in patron-client politics and because the material in Judges is an attractive and underused source of comparative data on that topic. I was also drawn to Judges because, as a person of faith, I am haunted by the fact that while the heroes in the book thought and acted in ways moderns would consider deeply immoral, they are often presented by religious people as spiritual champions. Finally, as a pacifist and former director of the Whitworth University peace studies program, I am challenged by people who sometimes justify the use of force by referencing the Hebrew Bible, especially stories in Judges.

Power and Politics in the Book of Judges: Men and Women of Valor is a book about political culture and political behavior. In the Hebrew Bible, the male protagonists in Judges were identified as "men of valor" or "mighty men." Ambitious, and at times ruthless, they would be labeled chiefs, strongmen, patrimonial leaders, or even warlords in today's world. Although the sixth-century BCE Deuteronomistic editor portrayed them as moral champions and called them judges, the original bardic storytellers and the men of valor themselves were preoccupied with the problem of gaining and maintaining political power.

My study considers the variety of strategies the men and women of valor used to gain and consolidate power. Certainly the use of violence, the redistribution of patronage, and the control of the labor and reproductive capacity of subordinates were among their key political tools. However, the central argument of my book is that these individuals relied on other political resources that carried less risk of depleting their wealth or requiring constant exercise of force. The main body of my book devotes a chapter to each of the following strategies used by the men of valor in their pursuit of power: 1) mobilizing and dispensing indigenous knowledge, 2) cultivating a reputation for being uncommonly reliable, 3) presenting themselves as honorable (consequential), and 4) positioning themselves as skillful mediators between the realms of earth and heaven. Each chapter builds on important theories from political science, anthropology, sociology, and economics. Throughout the book, I deal with the political implications of the tension between Yhwh and Baal and the way powerful strongmen in Judges used their association with Yhwh to advance their political, economic, or military agenda. I also give attention to the messengers of Yhwh, most likely I will argue itinerant politico-religious agitators, who mobilized ambitious political leaders by promoting Yhwh as a deity with unparalleled temporal and supernatural power.

In writing this book, I have been influenced by my understanding of African society, especially African political culture. My first encounter with Africa was as a volunteer teaching secondary school in the Congo, a country ruled by the ruthless patrimonial strongman Mobutu Sese Seko. Later, when conducting field research in Congo, I encountered many benevolent traditional chiefs who exercised their patrimonial duties in a way that promoted the well-being of their communities. Over the course of my five decades of involvement in Africa I have had many opportunities to study the continent's peoples

PREFACE

and political systems. Besides writing about politics in Congo, Liberia, Dahomey, and Buganda, my on-the-ground experiences include lecturing in universities in Liberia, Kenya, Ghana, and Tanzania, leading student study groups to Liberia, Kenya, Tanzania, and South Africa, and serving as a consultant or election monitor in several West African countries. Throughout my career, I have been impressed by the pervasiveness and perseverance of patron-client politics in Africa as well as in other parts of the world distant in both time and place. I have been especially mindful of the similarities between the political strategies and values of traditional Africa and those of ancient Israel.

Drawing on my understanding of Africa, my book on Judges references religious, social, and political practices from the African continent. I do this for two reasons. First, the people in northeast Africa are part of a larger Semitic cultural and linguistic world which includes not only Egypt, the Horn of Africa, and North Africa, but also Syria-Palestine and the Arabian Peninsula. Through Egypt and the Red Sea corridor, trade goods, people, and ideas flowed between Syria-Palestine and sub-Saharan Africa. As a result, some practices and values were shared. Consequently, an understanding of Africa can contribute to a better understanding of ancient Israel. The rich potential of this avenue of investigation has never been adequately explored. Second, even when there is no connection between an idea or action in Africa and Syria-Palestine, the fact that a farmer, pastoralist, diviner, storyteller, merchant, or strongman in pre-industrial Africa engaged in a certain activity demonstrates that it would be possible for humans elsewhere to follow a similar pattern. This observation does not constitute proof, but it does support the formulation of plausible hypotheses. While the strategies of a diviner in Liberia cannot be used as evidence of how a seer in early Israel might have conducted business, the practices in Liberia prove that such an approach *can* be employed. While myths and legends of people in Central Africa have no direct bearing on the tales in Judges, the fact that African stories contain clichés based on fantasy but are filled with political and social meaning should alert one to the possibility that stories in Judges might use the same literary tool.

Because my book on Judges has four primary audiences—political scientists, historians, Hebrew Bible specialists, and general readers—I tried to balance the need to provide sufficient background information with the realization that some of that material will be regarded as common knowledge by others. People unfamiliar with the content of the book of Judges are advised to take the time to read through this short book in the Hebrew Bible before considering my own analysis. While any modern rendering will do, my recommendation would be to read Susan Niditch's literal translation, which captures the feel of the original Hebrew text.[1]

---

1. Susan Niditch, *Judges: A Commentary* (Louisville: Westminster, 2008), 213–81. In the main body of her commentary, Niditch also provides a more literary translation.

1

Introduction and Overview

The Judges as Political Patrons

When a messenger of Yhwh first encountered Gideon, the messenger greeted him saying, "Yhwh is with you, valiant mighty man" (*gibbôr heḥāyil* – גבור החיל) (Judg. 6:12).[1] With these words, the messenger identified Gideon as a member of an elite class wielding extensive military, political, and economic power. The messenger did not address Gideon as a religious leader or identify him as a magistrate. Had the messenger been a modern political scientist, not a peripatetic prophet, he might have called Gideon a patrimonial leader or patron. Other terms that come to mind for the contemporary reader are strongman, big man, boss, or even warlord. Gideon was but one of many commanding figures, most of them warriors or heads of prominent houses, who exercised authority in ancient Syria-Palestine. In part, the power of these individuals was based on their

---

1. The term גבור (*gibbôr*) means "man of valor" while the term חיל (*ḥayil*) can be translated as "strong man" or "prosperous man." Unless otherwise noted, throughout this book, all translations from Judges are my own. All other biblical references are taken from the RSV.

ability to mobilize followers, followers who were not just fighters or producers, but who were people with unusual temporal or supernatural knowledge. The power of the great men and women of valor also rested on their reputation for reliability, their claim to honor, and their great wealth. These individuals are the focus of the Hebrew Bible's book of Judges.

Although the heroes in the book of Judges were first and foremost political figures, to my knowledge they have never been the object of sustained study by a political scientist. Past scholarship on premonarchic Israel has been dominated by biblical scholars, historians, sociologists, and literary specialists.[2] In looking at politics in the centuries before the monarchy, they have chronicled the competition among the Israelites, Canaanites, and Philistines. They have looked at the process of tribal unification that ended in national solidarity. They have studied the consolidation of political authority as Israel transitioned from a decentralized polity to a centralized monarchy. While these scholars have done much to illuminate the Early Iron Age, the time period described in the book of Judges, their focus has not been primarily on the inner workings and intellectual foundation of political dealings in that era.[3]

An exception is Niels Peter Lemche, who argues that ancient Israel was governed by the rules and values of patron-client politics. Loyalty and deference were the glue holding the structure together. Patrons offered protection for people seeking justice and security

---

2. For two discussions of methodology emphasizing historians, anthropologists, archeologists, sociologists, and literature experts, see Mark Smith, *The Early History of God: Yahweh and Other Deities in Ancient Israel*, 2nd ed. (Grand Rapids, MI: Eerdmans, 2002), and Anthony J. Frendo, *Pre-Exilic Israel, the Hebrew Bible, and Archeology* (New York: T&T Clark, 2011). Conspicuously absent in both books is any reference to political scientists. Political theorist Michael Walzer does look at Judges, but relatively superficially. Walzer, who is more concerned about the theme of covenant, regards Judges as a transitional book. See Michael Walzer, *In God's Shadow: Politics in the Hebrew Bible* (New Haven: Yale University Press, 2012).
3. The Early Iron Age spanned the two centuries from 1200 to 1000 BCE.

while clients gave tribute and obedient support to the rulers. Even relationships enforced by threat and military power were cloaked in the language of family, friendship, and devotion. Frequently, political arrangements were sealed by vows of loyalty spoken in formal ceremonial settings.[4] While Lemche offers a valuable heuristic overview of patronage, he does not provide a detailed description of the internal dynamics of the patron-client relationship, nor does he attempt an in-depth analysis of political culture, the set of underlying values that shape all political behavior.

The goal of my book is to take on that task. The study will investigate the political resources available to powerful men and women in premonarchic Israel, consider the political strategies they employed, and describe the political culture that guided their actions. The analysis of early Israelite political strategies, political resources, and political culture is based on the fact that the men and women depicted in the book of Judges were deeply engaged in—even preoccupied with—temporal political power. In spite of this reality, except for the work of Max Weber, virtually all scholarly studies of premonarchic Israel regard the characters in Judges as religious figures, thus people preoccupied with the relationship between the world of humans and the world of the supernatural. However, the heroes portrayed in Judges did not think of themselves as religious functionaries or as dispensers of legal rulings. Of course, like everyone else in the ancient Near East, they took religion into account. But they regarded religion as a tool to be used for political advantage, not as a set of guidelines for encouraging ethical behavior or for promoting social justice.[5] Some of them did settle disputes and

---

4. Niels Peter Lemche, "Kings and Clients: On Loyalty between the Ruler and the Ruled in Ancient Israel," *Semeia* 66 (1994): 119–32. Lemche, whose main interest is in the time of the monarchy, begins his article by comparing ancient patrons to Mafia godfathers who demanded absolute loyalty in return for powerful protection. Lemche laments the fact that biblical scholarship has focused on family instead of larger community governance.

enforce common law. But those actions were just part of their work as heads of great houses and as patrons of larger communities. The main interest of the men and women of valor was not in religious faithfulness nor in the details of law; rather, their concern was maximizing political power. Their quest for power is richly documented in the praise names, oral histories, legends, and fictional tales contained in the book of Judges. These accounts reflect the strong men's and women's ideas about patronage politics, their strategies for political survival, and the challenges they faced in the pursuit of power.

The lives of the men and women of valor in Judges have been hidden by distance in time, cultural dissimilarity, and the fragility of the chain of transmission between original actions and eventual written descriptions. In fact, historical minimalists, rightly skeptical of an overly literalistic reading of the Hebrew Bible, despair of finding any useful data in the accounts claiming to illuminate the time of the judges.[6] But, the real cause of their obscurity may have more to

---

5. At least not ethics and justice as understood by later Hebrew thinkers. At this point, it may be useful to offer working definitions of politics and religion. Politics deals with the use of power, the power to exercise control through the use of force and violence and the power to determine the distribution of economic and social resources. Politics is also about community decision making, whether decisions made by an autocrat or by the people as a whole. Religion focuses on the relationship between the world of humans and the domain of the supernatural. That relationship can be one in which people try to submit to divine will through ethical behavior or it can be one in which people attempt to manipulate the connection for their social, economic, or political advantage.

6. Although a majority of scholars believe that the stories contained in the main body of the book (Judg. 3:7–15:20) reflect very old oral histories, folktales, and legends about battles and governance, a number of researchers suggest that the entire book may be a much later literary invention. P. Deryn Guest, who points out that there is no independent confirmation for any of the material in Judges, argues that a later "creative writer ... deliberately contrived (a) literary work ... intentionally designed to fill a 'gap' period between the conquest and the ... monarchy." Noting that all scholars acknowledge the strong hand of a later editor, Guest posits that it is but a small step between editing and creating "*de novo.*" Guest, "Can Judges Survive without Sources? Challenging the Consensus," *JSOT* 78 (1998): 58–59. Although less radical than Guest, Marc Brettler argues that the stories in Judges were selected and refashioned to address concerns of the monarchic period or later. According to Brettler, the stories in Judges were created as foreshadowings of a centuries' long conflict between the house of Saul and the house of David. Brettler, "The Book of Judges: Literature as Politics," *Journal of*

do with our perspectives as moderns and postmoderns. Of course it is difficult to reconstruct the life and thought of people so far away in time and place, but that is a challenge familiar, even welcome, to any scholar trying to enter into distant worlds. The real reason why premonarchic leaders are so little known today is that their true nature and identity are embarrassments to those of us living in the shadow of the Enlightenment. We do not know who they are because we cannot accept them for who they truly were. We are offended by their crude religious rituals, their unscientific trust in the power of magic and divination, their easy recourse to brutality, their glorification of treachery and duplicity, and their shocking abuse of women. And, as Lemche notes, the patron-client values undergirding their political activities have been marginalized, even criminalized, in our times.[7]

Because the figures in Judges are unacceptable companions for people espousing contemporary Western values, they have been ignored or, worse yet, recreated in a way that is less jarring for

---

Biblical Literature 108, no. 3 (1989): 395–418. Other representative skeptics about the historicity of Judges are G. W. Ahlstrom, *The History of Ancient Palestine from the Paleolithic Period to Alexander's Conquest*, JSOTSup 146 (Sheffield: JSOT Press, 1993); and Niels Peter Lemche, *Ancient Israel: A New History of Israelite Society*, The Biblical Seminar 5 (Sheffield: JSOT Press, 1988). Minimalists have also challenged the historical reliability of the far more abundantly documented period of the early kings. See D. M. Gunn, *The Story of King David: Genre and Interpretation*, JSOTSup 6 (Sheffield: JSOT Press, 1978); and Gary N. Knoppers, "The Vanishing Solomon: The Disappearance of the United Monarchy from Recent Histories of Ancient Israel," *Journal of Biblical Literature* 116, no. 1 (1997): 19–44. In his book analyzing strategies for reconstructing the past (*Pre-Exilic Israel*), Anthony J. Frendo gives more weight to the historical value of biblical texts, even those lacking independent confirmation. Frendo argues that texts are no more unreliable than the artifacts or icons uncovered by archeologists. All three—texts, artifacts, and icons—offer a window onto the past and all three reflect political or theological biases. For a succinct and balanced review of the dispute about historicity, see Ziony Zevit, "Three Debates about Bible and Archeology," *Biblica* 83, no. 1 (2002): 1–27.

7. Lemche, "Kings and Clients," 122. Ironically, theologically conservative interpreters of Judges, people who regard many of the "judges" as champions of faith, have much in common with the far more liberal minimalists. Neither accepts the original tales as reliable. While the minimalists regard the heroic stories as later literary creations, theologically conservative exegetes filter the tales through the eyes of the much later post-seventh-century Deuteronomistic writers who recast the accounts in ways that would not have been recognized by the original storytellers.

modern sensibilities.⁸ Few readers who are church- or synagogue-goers have ever heard a sermon about Ehud, the hero who assassinated his sovereign Eglon, perhaps while the latter was sitting on his commode. Even if they did hear such a talk, almost certainly it omitted the claim that feces spewed forth from the gaping sword wound in Eglon's enormous belly or the possibility that Ehud escaped to the exterior of the palace by squeezing through the hole in Eglon's toilet seat.⁹ It is equally doubtful that many moderns have listened to a religious exposition extolling the virtues of casting lots to render legal judgments and determine guilt or innocence, or that they have been made aware that indispensable features of the ephod, a special garment worn by early spiritual leaders, were the two pockets holding the Urim and Thummim, stones used by a diviner to discover God's will.¹⁰ In addition, moderns would be surprised to learn that, instead of condemning Jephthah for sacrificing his only daughter, the book of Judges presents him as a principled hero. Also, people living today would find it difficult to accept the fact that the Ephraimite householder described in Judges 19 was willing to trade the honor of his virgin daughters for the safety of his stranger-guest and that his act was described as a culturally acceptable strategy.

---

8. One example of a fanciful recreation can be seen in the work of Martin Noth. Based on no evidence whatsoever from Syria-Palestine, but only on parallels from ancient Greece, he posited the existence of a well-organized twelve-tribe league which he named the amphictyony. Arguing from silence, Noth claimed that the absence of any explicit reference to the amphictyony demonstrated that the organization was so deeply engrained in Hebrew political and religious life that biblical writers saw no need to describe its structure or function. Going further, Noth argued that the so-called "minor judges" of Judges 10 and 12 were elected guardians and proclaimers of "divine law." The fact that divine law is never mentioned in Judges undermines such a claim. See Martin Noth, *The History of Israel* (New York: Harper, 1958), 85–102.

9. See Victor H. Matthews, *Judges and Ruth* (Cambridge: Cambridge University Press, 2004), 60; and Baruch Halpern, "The Assassination of Eglon: The First Locked-Room Murder Mystery," *Bible Review* 4, no. 6 (1988): 33–44.

10. The term *ephod* can also refer to a statue used for divination.

INTRODUCTION AND OVERVIEW

Generally, these and other uncomfortable details are disregarded by modern Christians and Jews.

When they are not simply ignored, oftentimes the narratives in Judges are rewritten to fit our more refined values. Instead of a brutal warlord celebrated by the praise name Hacker, Gideon is portrayed as an individual of commendable monotheistic zeal.[11] Samson is recalled as a champion, albeit a tad imprudent, endowed with great strength from Yhwh, not as a man lauded for his sexual appetite, his eagerness to exact revenge, and his propensity to take foolish risks. Jael is portrayed as a woman faithful to Yhwh, not as a seductress who symbolically rapes the lover-prey she puts to death. Jephthah becomes a miscalculating and heartless father, not an admirable promise keeper.

Lest it be assumed that only pious Jewish and Christian exegetes have inflicted intellectual violence on the men and women in Judges (perhaps a just reward for their unhesitating resort to bloodshed), more secular thinkers also have damaged them, either by dismissal or transformation. For example, the protagonists in Judges can become mere illustrations supporting prevailing literary theories. As a result, their stories are subject to dissection or revision. In an effort to force Ehud into the desired literary persona, that of a physically handicapped man who turns a shortcoming (his reputed left-handedness) into an advantage (the ability to draw a sword from an unexpected hiding place), commentators downplay the obvious reading that as a "left-handed Benjaminite" he was a member of an elite ambidextrous fighting force trained to wield a weapon equally well with either hand.[12] Modern deconstructionists, building on the notion of literary malleability and the opinion that text is about

---

11. The root word underlying Gideon's name (גדע) signifies "hacking, hewing, or cutting off." In the Hebrew Bible, the object of the hacking can be as varied as an arm, a staff, trees, a beard, bars of iron, or the horns of an altar.
12. For a discussion of ambidextrous Benjaminite warriors, see chapter 3, "Power and Trust."

contestation, draw scholarship even further from the proposition that the narratives in Judges can generate useful data about ancient times.[13] Although often yielding brilliant insight into underlying messages or concealed meanings, deconstructionists sometimes force the text of Judges in directions its original narrators or editors would not have understood or supported.[14] Ironically, although many modern scholars have little faith that at the narrative level ancient texts can describe the premonarchic period with any reliability, those same analysts have boundless confidence in their own ability to wrest hidden meanings from subtle turns of phrases, variations in the declension of nouns and verbs, the choice and placement of words in sentences, or even the absence of information in an account.

Modern social scientists who have studied Judges tend to downplay the importance of individual heroes, the main focus of the book. Beginning with Max Weber in 1923, twentieth-century researchers approached the book of Judges using the tools of history, economics, and anthropology. Some scholars described premonarchic Israel as a segmentary lineage system in which kin groups competed to

---

13. Mark Smith says that these approaches, which deemphasize the study of language and cultural context, result in a "sustained disassociation of the study of biblical literature from Israelite history" (*Early History of God*, xxv–xxvi).
14. One of the best postmodern literary expositions of Judges is that of Mieke Bal, *Death and Dissymmetry: The Politics of Coherence in the Book of Judges* (Chicago: University of Chicago Press, 1988). Bal focuses on the hidden, even suppressed, accounts of violence against women and the efforts to reshape the kin system from matrilineal to patrilineal. However, Bal is less concerned about analyzing the explicit message of the stories in Judges. Other works are less successful. In his extraordinarily detailed work, *The Rhetoric of the Book of Judges* (Leiden: E. J. Brill, 1996), Robert O'Connell argues that the author/editor of Judges was preoccupied with establishing the preeminence of the southern tribe of Judah and that the writer wanted to show the theme of social and religious disintegration that would be solved only by the appointment of a king. As J. Cheryl Exum has pointed out, O'Connell's argument is intricate to the point of artificiality. Exum, review of Robert H. O'Connell, *The Rhetoric of the Book of Judges*, in *Catholic Biblical Quarterly* 60 (1999): 537–38. Taking deconstructionism to its logical extreme and also trying to salvage historical meaning from distant texts, Jacobus Marais argues that the material in the book of Judges is a compilation of opinions placed in juxtaposition. Thus Marais turns the editor of Judges into a twentieth-century perspectivalist. According to Marais, any attempt to retrieve the actual past, beyond uncovering an ancient literary debate about the past, is futile. See his *Representation in Old Testament Narrative Texts* (Leiden: E. J. Brill, 1998).

monopolize land, labor, and leadership. Others examined the political forms in Israel as they evolved from charismatic and tribal to institutional and monarchical. Scholars with a Marxist bent combed the text of Judges and other "historical" books to uncover evidence of an egalitarian Israelite peasant revolution against oppressive Canaanite city-states.[15] While these approaches take seriously the actual structures, trends, and events of history, they tend to focus on macro-level realities. In doing so, they risk reducing the men and women of valor to lineage metonyms or ciphers for economic and class conflict. Except perhaps for Weber, none give much attention to the way that individual political leaders may have operated, much less thought, in the late second millennium BCE.

Biblical Sources about the Men and Women of Valor

An analysis of politics in the era before the monarchy should consider how the political leaders of the time were regarded in the Bible. This analysis logically begins with an overview of the sources that claim to describe that period in time. Three of the sources are contained in the book of Judges itself. In describing these three literary traditions, I rely heavily on the work of Susan Niditch, who summarizes and simplifies the contributions of previous scholarship. Without becoming overly entangled in the minutiae of source and text criticism, Niditch provides an appropriately comprehensive big picture.[16]

---

15. Relying on anthropologists such as Ronald Cohen, Colin Renfrew, and Elman Service, James W. Flanagan sees Israel's early history as the story of a transition from segmentary tribe to chiefdom to kingship. See James W. Flanagan, *David's Social Drama: A Hologram of Israel's Early Iron Age* (Sheffield: The Almond Press, 1988); and Flanagan, "Chiefs in Israel," *Journal for the Study of the Old Testament* 20 (1981): 47–73. The best-known Marxist approach is that of Norman K. Gottwald, *The Tribes of Yahweh: A Sociology of the Religion of Liberated Israel, 1250-1050 B.C.E.* (Maryknoll, NY: Orbis Books, 1979). Susan Niditch seems to dismiss Gottwald's claim as not being applicable to the book of Judges. See Susan Niditch, *Judges* (Louisville: Westminster, 2008), 58.

The earliest and most extensive accounts of the men and women of valor, accounts contained in the main body of the book of Judges (3:15–16:31), are tales of individual warrior heroes living in what later became the northern kingdom of Israel. Niditch labels these as "epic-bardic" stories.[17] First popularized within specific regions of Palestine, the stories likely circulated as separate accounts. This epic-bardic material includes historical recollections and legends, folktales, poems or victory songs, a fable, and taunts. While some of the stories may be grounded in historical reality, other tales are more fanciful, reminiscent of Homeric recitations. In any event, most scholars regard the accounts of people such as Deborah, Gideon, Abimelech, Jephthah, and Samson as among the oldest stories in the Bible. These bardic narratives maintain much of their early robust and unvarnished character. Even when they cannot be trusted to provide an accurate record of actual individuals and events, because of their age they open a unique and reliable literary window onto the political perceptions, values, and activities of Israel prior to the emergence of the monarchy. In these accounts the main characters are remembered as extraordinary political leaders who operated in turbulent times. The stories concentrate on raw power, the stuff of politics. The attempt to monopolize force and violence, the distribution of resources, and the process of decision making, all central to any discussion of politics, preoccupied the leaders described in the epic-bardic accounts in Judges. Eventually, the bardic tales were assembled into a single narrative that now makes up Judges 3 through 16.[18]

16. In discussing how the book of Judges was compiled over a period of many centuries, Niditch does not stray far from the work of Robert G. Boling, *Judges: A New Translation with Introduction and Commentary*, Anchor Bible 6A (Garden City, NY: Doubleday, 1975), 29–38.
17. Niditch, *Judges*, 9–10. As Niditch notes, the brief account of Othniel in Judg. 3:7–11 and the introduction to the story of Ehud in Judg. 3:12–14 are Deuteronomistic insertions and should not be attributed to the epic-bardic storyteller (ibid., 56–57).
18. Judges 3–16 also features other material. For example, Judg. 10:1–5 and 12:7–15 contain a list of so-called minor judges, men said to have led Israel. The brief accounts of their lives include the number of years they supposedly "judged," where they lived, where they were buried, and

Although the stories were stitched together centuries after their initial creation, it is impossible to conceal the fact that they were originally unrelated. While a later editor's annotations suggest that the men and women in Judges ruled consecutively and that they controlled all of Israel for several hundred years, the stories have neither geographical unity nor chronological continuity. Even taking into account the fictional tale of Samson, there are only six major figures in the bardic collection. None of these leaders claimed sovereignty over more than their own region and none had any official connection with any other leader.[19] Almost certainly, there would have been scores of such localized accounts about heroic men and women living in premonarchic Israel. Therefore the narratives in Judges should be read as somewhat random serendipitous glimpses into the political thought and life of the time.[20]

Any attempt to explain why the six stories in Judges survived is highly speculative.[21] However, 2 Samuel provides independent

---

perhaps a mention of their wealth and a reference to the sons and daughters of their house. For a discussion of these men see Alan J. Hauser, "The 'Minor Judges': A Re-Evaluation," *Journal of Biblical Literature* 94 (1975): 190–200. Hauser persuasively challenges Martin Noth's contention that the "minor judges" were legal officials administering justice while the "major judges" were military leaders. Hauser contends that the names of the "minor judges" represent a separate list of military leaders. Because the list also included Jephthah, the Deuteronomistic editor inserted the material into the epic-bardic series of stories. In addition, the story of Samson and Delilah (Judges 16) appears to have been added somewhat later. The evidence for this is that the Deuteronomistic editor offered two conclusions to the Samson account, one at the end of chapter 15, another at the end of chapter 16.

19. The only exception might be Abimelech who claimed Gideon as his father. However, Abimelech's base of operation was many kilometers away from Gideon's town of Ophrah. Furthermore, although Gideon was a strong champion of Yhwh, the word "Yhwh" never appears in the Abimelech narrative. The only deities mentioned are El and Baal. The most that can be drawn from this evidence is that Abimelech perhaps was aware of Gideon and that he may have attempted to strengthen himself by claiming a fictive tie to the renowned warrior.

20. While six stories may not seem much for a period lasting several hundred years, in comparison to what is known about other people and places from that time, these are extraordinarily rich sources.

21. In a personal communication, Scott Starbuck suggests that the tales might have been gathered together during the time Israelite monarchs were seeking to consolidate their rule. In addition to using military power, forced labor, and patronage to expand their authority, kings might have tried to win the support of regional big men from the north by honoring heroic figures

evidence that some of the epic-bardic tales were well-known and valued during the first years of the monarchy.[22] The story of King David and Bathsheba in 2 Samuel 11 specifically mentions both Jerubbaal (Gideon) and his putative son Abimelech (11:21).[23] According to 2 Samuel, scheming to conceal his love affair with Bathsheba, David instructed his commander Joab to position Bathsheba's husband, Uriah, in the front line of battle. Following David's orders, Joab withdrew, isolating Uriah, who was killed (2 Sam. 11:14–17). Later, Joab commented on the dangers of approaching the wall of a city under siege. Joab specifically recalled that Abimelech, the son of Jerubbaal, had been killed because he recklessly got too close to the wall of a town under attack and that a mere woman standing on the wall threw an upper millstone that took his life (2 Sam. 11:19–21; cf. Judg. 9:50–54). This detailed reference in 2 Samuel indicates that tales from Judges were circulated in the tenth century and may have been used to instruct warriors about prudent conduct in battle.

Sometime, perhaps in the late 600s or early 500s BCE, an editor or editors took the epic-bardic stories and added a Yhwhistic religious commentary, which Niditch labels the "Voice of the Theologian." This commentary reflected the ideals of the Deuteronomic school of thought that flowered during the time of King Josiah (ca. 640–609 BCE).[24] According to 2 Kings 22, the book of the law (Deuteronomy)

---

of the tribal era. The epic-bardic accounts eventually may have been committed to writing on individual clay tablets that were stored in the royal archives at Israel's capital, Samaria. The tales then could have made their way to Judah after the fall of Israel in 722/21 BCE.

22. In 2 Samuel we have evidence of an explicit and very early independent reference to two of the most important epic-bardic tales in Judges. The story in 2 Samuel 11 predates both the Deuteronomistic writer's theological editorials and the humanist redactor's literary additions by hundreds of years. The parallel version in 1 Chronicles 19 omits the salacious and iniquitous details about David's dealings with Bathsheba and Uriah, details that cast the iconic King David in a negative light.

23. In 2 Sam. 11:21, Jerubbaal is called Jerubbesheth (with "besheth" connoting "shame"). This may be a later gloss intended to dishonor the deity Baal.

was discovered by the high priest in ca. 622 BCE. The finding then led to a religious revival spearheaded by Josiah. Several generations after Josiah, an editor(s)—whom moderns refer to as the Deuteronomistic Historian—compiled the books of Judges, Samuel, and Kings as commentaries on how well Israel adhered to the laws of Deuteronomy.

As Norman Gottwald says, although doing very little to remold the original epic-bardic material in Judges, the Deuteronomistic Historian added annotations that serve as formulaic "clamps" around the individual stories and around the collection as a whole.[25] True to the Deuteronomic ideal, the clamps focus on covenantal faithfulness and unfaithfulness. This pattern is first introduced in Judg. 2:1–5, which tells the story of a messenger of Yhwh, who reminded the people that Yhwh graciously delivered the people of Israel from Egypt and brought them into a new land. Through the messenger, the Deuteronomistic text further recalls that Yhwh made an eternal covenant with Israel and that, in return, Israel was ordered never to cut a covenant with the inhabitants of the land. However, according to the editor(s), the people of Israel were not faithful. They did not pull down the altars of the original evil inhabitants, nor did they listen to the voice of Yhwh. As a result, Yhwh did not drive out the indigenous tribes who, along with their gods, continued to be a trap for Israel. At this point, reports the Deuteronomistic Historian, the

---

24. The term "Deuteronomic" refers to the content and ideals of the book of Deuteronomy. "Deuteronomistic" refers to subsequent interpretations and applications of Deuteronomy. The later editor might have been one individual or a group of people representing a Deuteronomistic school of thought. There also is no way of knowing if the editor assembled separate stories or if they had been previously joined into a single narrative. During the exile, followers of the Deuteronomistic school made further amendments and additions. For a summary of the scholarly debate about the Deuteronomic/Deuteronomistic writer(s) see Roy Heller, *Power, Politics, and Prophecy: The Character of Samuel and the Deuteronomistic Evaluation of Prophecy* (London: T & T Clark International, 2006), 17–19. See also Niditch, *Judges*, 11.
25. Gottwald, *Tribes of Yahweh*, 150. These annotations are especially evident in the stories of Othniel (3:7-9 and 3:11), Ehud (3:12, 3:15a, and 3:30), Deborah and Barak (4:1-3a and 5:31b), Gideon (6:1 and 8:28), Jephthah (10:6-7 and 12:7), and Samson (13:1, 15:20, and 16:31b).

sons of Israel cried out and wept. This prologue to the subsequent collection of heroic stories summarizes the key Deuteronomic themes of Yhwh's blessings, Yhwh's covenant with Israel, Israel's apostasy, the hardship of punishment, Israel's grief and repentance, and Yhwh sending a deliverer.

The Deuteronomistic collector(s)/editor(s) added these thematic clamps to each and every story of the political champions in the book of Judges. Because they were attached so artificially and in such a standardized manner, they are easily detected even by the casual reader. However, as can be seen in the last lines of chapter 2 and the first lines of chapter 3, the Deuteronomistic editor(s) had difficulty applying the rubric of blessing, covenant, apostasy, punishment, repentance, cry for help, and salvation (blessing) to stories originally composed with a completely unrelated message. The result was occasional inconsistency. While at the end of chapter 2 the editorial additions attribute the lack of success in expelling Israel's enemies from the land to Israel's unfaithfulness, in chapter 3 the writer offers a different explanation. The second hypothesis is that Yhwh allowed Israel's foes to remain because he did not want Israel to forget the art of war (Judg. 3:1–2).[26]

Although the Deuteronomistic writings claim to reflect the principles of Deuteronomy, there are obvious deep contradictions between the two.[27] In Deuteronomy the role of the monarch is dramatically limited; in the later writings of the Deuteronomistic Historian the powers of the sovereign are exalted. Restrictions on

---

26. Elsewhere, the Deuteronomistic Historian offers yet a third explanation for the presence of other peoples in the land. In Deut. 7:22 the historian opines that Yhwh did not allow the Israelites to eliminate the previous inhabitants quickly and completely because he feared a newly empty land would be overrun by wild animals.
27. See Bernard Levinson, "The Reconceptualization of Kingship in Deuteronomy and the Deuteronomistic History's Transformation of Torah," *Vetus Testamentum* 51, no. 4 (2001): 511–34; and Gary N. Knoppers, "Rethinking the Relationship between Deuteronomy and the Deuteronomistic History," *Catholic Biblical Quarterly* 63, no. 3 (2001): 393–415.

royal authority are most explicit in Deut 17:14–20, known as the law of the king. This passage enjoins the king from building a large military (having many horses), from selling people into foreign bondage in exchange for horses, from multiplying the number of his wives, and from acquiring great personal wealth (stores of gold and silver).[28] Deuteronomy 17:14–20 also states that the king must be one of the people (not a person of foreign origin), and not seek to be elevated above his "brethren." Furthermore, by commanding the king to copy, read, and keep the law, the text subordinates the ruler to covenant directives and to the Levitical priests who safeguard the Torah. Later, Deuteronomy 20 places even warfare under the control of the priests. Bernard Levinson, who regards Deuteronomy as an idealistic, even utopian composition that was never implemented, also points out that Deuteronomy removes the king from the judicial system and takes away the king's right to forgive debts and restore land to original owners.[29] In short, Deuteronomy denies the king power over the military, the judiciary, and the cultus, restricts his ability to acquire wealth in wives and money, undercuts his freedom to express noblesse oblige (by cancelling debt and redistributing land), and prohibits him from claiming superior status over the people. The result is that all the tools of power—military, financial, judicial, cultic, patronage, and honorific—are neutralized.

As Levinson notes, the Deuteronomistic Historian, while claiming allegiance to Deuteronomy, subverts the book's central message by celebrating kingly powers. In contrast to Deuteronomy, the books of Samuel and Kings, both compiled by the Deuteronomistic Historian, portray Israelite monarchs as dominant political, military, cultic, and judicial leaders. Kings are praised for their wealth, virility, and majesty. Furthermore, the historian argues that Israel's fortunes are

---

28. Having multiple wives was not only a measure of wealth, but also an important diplomatic tool.
29. Levinson, "Reconceptualization of Kingship," 529–31.

wholly dependent on the faithfulness or unfaithfulness of the royal leader. Thus Josiah is portrayed as the pivotal figure in implementing the tenets of the newly discovered Deuteronomic law while the high priest is described as a somewhat secondary actor.[30]

Assuming Levinson is correct, it is easy to understand why the Deuteronomistic Historian did not rewrite the heroic tales in Judges. The charismatic men of valor foreshadowed the qualities that the Deuteronomistic Historian admired in a monarch. Audacious fighters, unrestrained by laws and bureaucrats, not subordinated to priests or the Torah, and distinguished as men of scrupulousness, wealth, and power, the protagonists in Judges represented qualities the Deuteronomistic writer valued in successful leaders. The Deuteronomistic Historian's only obvious modification to the tales about ancient men and women of valor was contained in the theological clamps that introduced the theme of covenant fidelity or infidelity. But, consistent with other Deuteronomistic writings, even this modification enhanced the standing of individual leaders, whose actions were said to have determined the fate of the entire nation. For the Deuteronomistic writer(s), the heroes in Judges were welcome political and religious liberators sent by Yhwh to rescue a beleaguered people.

For the most part, the Deuteronomistic writer looks favorably upon the so-called judges. However, consciously or unconsciously, the editorial remarks question the effectiveness of the militant big men and women in Judges. While not directly criticizing the judges as individuals, the Deuteronomistic Historian repeatedly asserts that the Israelite people were constantly attacked by powerful and predatory neighbors, both near and distant. Midianites from the south, Moabites from the east, Canaanites from the lowlands, and Philistines from the coast plundered, demanded tribute, took slaves,

---

30. Ibid., 532–34.

and humiliated the Israelite people. Even though the Deuteronomistic Historian observes that the judge-deliverers regularly rose up to provide relief, the writer explicitly notes that peace did not outlast the lifetime of an individual leader. Thus the editor characterizes the period of the judges as a time of political turmoil. Like modern political scientists, who prefer stable centralized states over short-lived patron-client polities, the Deuteronomistic Historian doubts the long-term value of individual heroic leaders.

In part as a result of the Deuteronomistic Historian's editorial comments, the men and women in Judges were transformed into institutionalized officeholders. While the epic-bardic storyteller had used the words "mighty" and "valor" to describe the early leaders, the Deuteronomistic editor(s) introduced the terms "judge" (šōpēṭ – שפט) and "deliverer" (môšiaʿ – מושיע).[31] By choosing the more bureaucratic and institutional word שפט, the Deuteronomistic interpreter has tempted modern readers to regard the men and women of valor as official functionaries at the head of established territories rather than as individual champions managing precarious patron-client polities. Because of the way the Psalms, prophetic literature, and the New Testament interpreted Judges, even the term מושיע has assumed a more regal connotation.

Building on the Deuteronomistic editor's annotated collection of heroic stories, another writer compiled the final layer of the book of Judges. The time and purpose of this addition are in more dispute than is the case for the epic-bardic accounts or the Deuteronomistic writer's amendments. Sometime after the fall of Jerusalem in 587 BCE, an author whom Susan Niditch labels the "Voice of the Humanist" added chapters 1 and 17–21.[32] Perhaps living in exile in Babylon, the

---

31. In describing Othniel, the Deuteronomistic text of Judg. 3:9–10 provides the first reference to these terms. The Hebrew word שפט, commonly rendered "to judge," is more accurately translated as "to govern" or "to rule." The epic-bardic storyteller never uses the word "judge" when describing a human being.

humanist provided chapter 1 as a prologue bridging the time between Joshua and the heroes in Judges. Drawing heavily from the book of Joshua, the humanist lists the ten tribes of Israel, indicates whom they fought and where they settled, and identifies the indigenous peoples who remained in the land. Unlike the Deuteronomistic writer, the humanist offers no theological explanation for any of the victories or defeats. Although the humanist asserts that the sons of Israel cast lots to determine which tribe should go first to fight the Canaanites, that Yhwh gave the Canaanites into the hand of Israel, and that Yhwh was with Israel, there is no mention of covenant, apostasy, punishment, repentance, or divine compassion. The humanist says nothing more than any other ancient social or political commentator would have said or thought. Even non-Israelites would have attributed success or failure to divine involvement and every non-Israelite would have consulted a divinity before going to battle. Most strikingly, and unlike the bardic storyteller, the humanist gives little attention to any individual hero. The one exception is the story of Caleb, Othniel, and Achsah in Judg. 1:12–15, an account borrowed word for word from Josh. 15:16–19.

The humanist's most distinctive contribution comes in chapters 17–21, chapters that conclude the book's final version. These chapters continue the nontheological and nonheroic tenor of chapter 1. To some extent, the humanist betrays an agnostic attitude toward the heroes of the past.[33] They are distant figures whose remoteness allows the humanist literary space to add stories making a plea for tribal

32. Niditch, *Judges*, 11–13. The following discussion of Judges 1 and 17–21 relies heavily on Niditch. Of the three dominant traditions in Judges, the humanist voice represented in chapters 1 and 17–21 is the most difficult to identify and date. Judges 18:30 refers to the fall of the northern kingdom, which took place in 722 BCE. Therefore, the humanist wrote no earlier than that date and perhaps a century or more later. Fortunately, the precise identity of the humanist is not critical for the main findings of my book.
33. Many commentators have pointed out the bias against Benjamin (Saul's tribe) and Dan in chapters 17–21. For example, see Gregory Mobley, "Judges," in *The Oxford Encyclopedia of the Books of the Bible*, ed. Michael D. Coogan (New York: Oxford University Press, 2011), 1:516.

unity and for generosity toward Levite religious functionaries.[34] Only one important person, Micah, who is definitely not a man of respected valor, a judge, or a rescuing champion, is mentioned by name. All the other protagonists are unnamed, presented as symbols of honorable or dishonorable behavior. Like chapter 1, the final section of Judges is preoccupied with the unity of the nation of Israel, a concern notably lacking in the bardic tales. Furthermore, in contrast to the sometimes disjointed and repetitive bardic stories, the humanist's accounts are carefully crafted, unified narratives suggesting literary sophistication. Perhaps composed as historical fiction, they point to the political and social concerns of educated Israelites who were living long after the time of the original men and women of valor and even after the time of the monarchy.[35] The humanist writer is keenly aware of the transitory nature of power and of the lurking danger of intertribal conflict. For the humanist, premonarchic times were distant, an age when there was no king. According to Niditch, the reoccurring phrase, "In those days there was no king in Israel; a man did what was right in his own eyes," is not so much a negative statement about an ancient era as it is a statement of regret that in the humanist's time Israel no longer had either a king or a nation.[36]

---

34. After the fall of the northern kingdom, many unemployed Levites sought refuge in the south. In the tale of the Levite and his concubine (Judges 19), the storyteller condemns inhospitality toward wandering Levites. However, that message is compromised by the story of Micah (Judges 18), which portrays displaced Levites as mercenary and untrustworthy.
35. In this respect, the humanist is writing roughly in the same time period and genre as the author of the book of Ruth. See Frederic W. Bush, *Ruth, Esther* (Dallas: Word, 1996). Bush notes that Ruth is written in a Hebrew style representative of the postmonarchic period. In his commentary, Victor Matthews says Ruth is a "tightly written, composite tale dating to the beginning of the postexilic period" (*Judges and Ruth*, 209). Agreeing with this perspective, Niditch writes that the worldview of the humanist is "congruent with those of some Persian or early Hellenistic period biblical writers" (*Judges*, 12). Ezra, Nehemiah, Jonah, and 3 Isaiah also may be relatively contemporaneous.
36. Niditch, *Judges*, 13.

Although the humanist's record may not be a reliable source for reconstructing premonarchic Israel, these writings prove there was a continuing interest in that time and that many of the key values evident in the epic accounts of the bardic storyteller persisted hundreds of years after the lives of the early leaders.[37] The reliance on divination, the importance of hospitality, the centrality of contractual reliability, the significance of honor, and the value of women as economic and political commodities all continued even after the monarchy had come and gone.

Other Hebrew Bible material offers insights about Israelite attitudes toward the big men and women, who lived in the thirteenth through the eleventh centuries BCE. Written during the period of the monarchy, Psalm 83 refers to threats from Israel's neighbors and also from the Neo-Assyrian Empire.[38] At a time when the very existence of Israel seemed in doubt, the writer calls on Yhwh to deliver Israel by destroying her foes as he had done during the time of the men and women of valor. Specifically recalling the battles of Gideon, Barak, and Deborah, the lyricist begs Yhwh to turn Israel's enemies into dust, burn them with fire, fill them with shame, terrify them, and cause them to perish in disgrace like the Canaanite and Midianite enemies many years earlier. Thus the victories and acts of vengeance described in the book of Judges are recalled with admiration and longing.[39]

---

37. Niditch says it is impossible to determine if the humanist relied on much older stories or if the accounts were written as historical fiction (ibid., 11–12).
38. Revived by Tiglath-pileser III (745–727 BCE), the Neo-Assyrian Empire was a model of military and bureaucratic efficiency. Instead of merely taking plunder and tribute, Tiglath-pileser permanently annexed vast territories. The Assyrian king was known for executing or deporting conquered peoples and also incorporating them into his vast army. For Tiglath-pileser's relation to eighth-century Israel see John Bright, *A History of Israel* (Philadelphia: Westminster Press, 1959), 253–54.
39. Like the references to Gideon and Abimelech in the story of David and Bathsheba (2 Samuel 11), Psalm 83 provides an independent verification that the heroes in Judges 3–16 were well-known during the time of the monarchy.

Psalm 106, likely composed during the exile, offers a negative perspective on the time described in Judges. Written at a low point in the political life of the Israelite people, the song attempts to explain the defeat and destruction of the nation. Using theological language, the psalmist attributes the many problems of the past to a lack of religious faithfulness. Describing a cycle of apostasy and deliverance, Psalm 106 refers to the evils of serving idols and of engaging in human sacrifice, specifically the sacrifice of sons and daughters. Such practices, asserts the writer, polluted the land with blood. As will be noted below, the use of idols and other tools of divination and devotion was a common practice for political leaders during the time prior to the monarchy. Furthermore, a willingness to sacrifice one's child in order to uphold an oath to Yhwh was regarded as a sign of extraordinary courage and strength on the part of a big man. By the time of the exile, these values had changed, at least among some.

The Christian New Testament includes two references to Judges. In Acts 13:20 Paul mentions the characters in Judges, identifying them as judges (κριτὰς), a word from the legal realm, and describing then as given by God.[40] The Letter to the Hebrews contains a more extensive citation. Lauding the great heroes of faith, men and women like Moses, Abraham, Sarah, and Rahab who had been obedient to God, the writer of Hebrews goes on to list the central figures in Judges—Gideon, Barak, Samson, and Jephthah—as well as Samuel and David. These individuals are credited with having "conquered kingdoms, enforced justice, received promises, stopped the mouths of lions, [and] quenched raging fire." They are said to have "escaped the edge of the sword, won strength out of weakness, became mighty in war, put foreign armies to flight" (Heb. 11:32–34.[41] The comments

---

40. The word κριτής (sing.) refers to an official rendering a legal decision or one having the ability to discern. A related word is the term κριτήριον, meaning "law court." The English words "critic" and "criterion" are derived from the two Greek words.

by Paul and the author of Hebrews are evidence that more than one thousand years after their stories had originally been told, the premonarchic heroes in Judges were extolled by the first-century CE Jewish and Christian communities as leaders given by God and as examples of faithful obedience.

Patron-Client Politics

As Max Weber noted in *Ancient Judaism*, the men and women described in the book of Judges were not judges who rendered judicial decisions. Rather, they were charismatic patrimonial political leaders similar to the big men and women in other premodern societies.[42] Weber was correct to contend that much of the energy responsible for Israel's political evolution came from the dynamic leadership of these figures. Drawing on the status of their lineage, the attraction of their strength and boldness, and the lure of their liberality, the "judges" built constituencies of support and moved Israel along the continuum from tribe to kingdom. Through bravery, cunning, deceit, threat, cruelty, magical powers, oracular insights, dispute resolution, claims of supernatural endorsement, the shrewd management of tribute and spoils, and a reputation for honor and reliability, the mighty men of valor exercised control over the Israelite people and their elders. In so doing, they laid the foundation for the tenth-century monarchy and they profoundly shaped the development of the Yhwhist religion.[43]

41. It may be significant that Abimelech, the one protagonist in the epic-bardic tales never identified as a partisan of Yhwh, is not included in the list.
42. Weber, *Ancient Judaism*, trans. and ed. Hans H. Gerth and Don Martindale (New York: Free Press, 1952), 11–12. For a more recent parallel to Weber, see James W. Flanagan, "Chiefs in Israel." While Flanagan's study deals with Saul, David, and Solomon, he looks at the role of powerful leaders in moving Israel toward statehood.
43. As will be noted in the final chapter, I believe the strategies and characteristics exhibited by the early leaders had a powerful impact on the subsequent development of government (the monarchs were exceptionally successful mighty men), ethnic and national awareness (the activities of the early heroes provided a shared collection of stories about heroes, battles, and

Building on Weber and relying on textual and archeological evidence, J. David Schloen argues that the metaphor of a patriarchal household shaped all relationships in the second-millennium ancient Near East.[44] The mores of a patriarchal family provided structure and served as a template for behavior at each level of society. Patrimonial relationships, based on loyalty, deference, and mutual responsibility, guided social, political, legal, economic, and religious intercourse. From the most humble families to magnificent royal courts, the simple domestic concept of parental control and concern bound together family heads and their dependents, owners and slaves, cities and subordinate rural areas, and kings and subjects. According to Schloen, a "decentralized hierarchy of households nested one into another" and incorporated every person, community, and region.[45] At the apex of society, the leader was regarded as a father, his officials assumed the role of subordinate kin, and his subjects thought of themselves as dependents within a family.[46]

While the relationships in the patrimonial household and in the larger political sphere were based on clearly defined social and legal expectations, in theory the relationships were also sustained by deep personal loyalty and love. Discussing the concept of covenant in the Hebrew Bible and in the ancient Near East, Bill Arnold emphasizes both the objective dimensions of conduct and the subjective dimensions of emotion characterizing the relationships between

enemies that could be used to create a unified story of the past), and religious beliefs, especially concepts about Yhwh (memories of the men and women of valor influenced later ideas about covenant faithfulness, divine power, divine discretion, and divine deliverance).

44. J. David Schloen, *The House of the Father as Fact and Symbol: Patrimonialism in Ugarit and the Ancient Near East* (Winona Lake, IN: Eisenbrauns, 2002). Although Schloen focuses on Ugarit, his study deals with many surrounding societies, including premonarchic Israel.
45. Schloen, *House of the Father*, 65. See also 283–87.
46. Applying Weber's concept of a traditional patrimonial household model to Syria-Palestine, Schloen notes that officials did not have specialized roles. A subordinate would serve in multiple capacities such as military leader, police official, tax collector, judicial officer, agricultural manager, and head of a house. These duties would be carried out simultaneously. Furthermore, there was no distinction between public and private spheres (ibid., 284–85).

covenant partners. Without rejecting the conclusions of earlier scholars, who accentuated the objective contractual legal expectations for proper covenant conduct, Arnold points out that covenants in the Hebrew Bible also stressed the subjective qualities of affection and personal loyalty. This emotional component of covenants can be seen in the initial love between David and Saul, the enduring love between David and Jonathan, and the imagery of conjugal love in the writings of Hosea and Jeremiah.[47]

Although Schloen and Arnold suggest that in its idealized form the patrimonial social unit was bound together by "love and justice," in reality a patrimonial community, whether that of a small intergenerational family, a prominent house, or an extensive polity, relied on multiple strategies to ensure loyalty and continuity.[48] The redistribution of material goods and the use or threat of coercion would have been some of the instruments of control employed by fathers, town elders, and powerful patrons such as those described in the book of Judges. However, a leader's honor, reputation for consistency, ability to render wise legal judgments, and capacity to access the realm of the supernatural were equally important tools to gain and maintain legitimacy. The strength and persistence of any social unit, from family to kingdom, depended on the leader's ability to exercise these tools effectively and efficiently. In looking at political power, Max Weber distinguished between charismatic

---

47. Bill T. Arnold, "The Love-Fear Antinomy in Deuteronomy," *Vetus Testamentum* 61 (2011): 551–69. Arnold builds on and revises a seminal essay by William L. Moran, "The Ancient Near Eastern Background of the Love of God in Deuteronomy," *Catholic Biblical Quarterly* 25 (1963): 77–87. See also Susan Ackerman, "The Personal is Political: Covenantal and Affectionate Love (*'āhēb, 'ahăbâ*) in the Hebrew Bible," *Vetus Testamentum* 52 (2002): 437–58; Moshe Weinfeld, "The Common Heritage of Covenantal Traditions in the Ancient World," in *I Trattati nel Mondo Antico: Forma, Ideologia, Funzione*, Saggi di storia antica 2, ed. Luciano Canfora, Mario Liverani, and Carlo Zaccagnini (Roma: "L'Erma" di Bretschneider, 1990), 175–91; and Jacqueline E. Lapsley, "Feeling Our Way: Love for God in Deuteronomy," *Catholic Biblical Quarterly* 65 (2003): 350–69.
48. Schloen, *House of the Father*, 13. Schloen's analysis may place undue emphasis on the integrated, harmonious nature of the patrimonial relationships.

and traditional patrimonial political systems. Although both operated according to many of the same principles, leaders in traditional systems generally expected to transfer their authority to the next generation without serious challenge. Charismatic authority, more dependent on an individual leader's personal qualities, was much more fragile. However, all patrimonial political systems, whether charismatic or traditional, relied on clients' loyalty for their survival and were at constant risk of collapse or decay if not properly managed.

Premonarchic Israel

Because of antiquity, because of cultural diversity, because archeological records are sparse, and because of differing methodological and theological approaches, the history of Early Iron Age Israel is a subject of great debate.[49] In the following overview, I try to summarize commonly held views about premonarchic times without getting overly entangled in the deep weeds of academic disputes. Some readers familiar with the literature will disagree with my portrayal of the scholarly consensus and all readers should be aware that virtually every statement I make has been contested by more than one reputable researcher. Readers also should keep in mind Anthony Frendo's warning that even generally accepted interpretations should not be confused with fact.[50]

---

49. For more detail about premonarchic Israel see the following: William G. Dever, *What Did the Biblical Writers Know and When Did They Know It? What Archaeology Can Tell Us about the Reality of Ancient Israel* (Grand Rapids, MI: Eerdmans, 2001); Frank S. Frick, *The Formation of the State in Ancient Israel: A Survey of Models and Theories*, Social World of Biblical Antiquity 4 (Sheffield, UK: Almond, 1985); Gottwald, *Tribes of Yahweh*; Lawrence E. Stager, "Forging an Identity: The Emergence of Ancient Israel," in *The Oxford History of the Biblical World*, ed. Michael D. Coogan (New York: Oxford University Press, 1998), 90–131; and Jonathan M. Golden, *Ancient Canaan and Israel: An Introduction* (Oxford: Oxford University Press, 2004). For a discussion of religion in the Early Iron Age, see Smith, *Early History of God*, and Frank Moore Cross, *Canaanite Myth and Hebrew Epic: Essays in the History of the Religion of Israel* (Cambridge, MA: Harvard University Press, 1973).

Before the time described in the book of Judges, the Egyptian empire exerted feudal control over the city-states located in Syria-Palestine.[51] The Amarna tablets, correspondence to the Egyptian capital from Canaanite vassals in the mid-1300s BCE, reveal that Egypt relied on local rulers to extract taxes, corvée, slaves, and plunder from the region.[52] In addition to imposing indirect rule over the area, Egypt maintained a military presence in the land in order to provide a buffer zone against powerful states to the north and east. The Amarna records indicate a good deal of social and political discord in the region as unruly vassals competed among themselves and as they faced unrest from a group of renegades labeled Apiru.[53] With the waning of Egyptian influence in the late fourteenth century, insecurity may have increased as the heads of city-states fought against each other, as some peasants and bonded workers resorted to banditry, and as Apiru mercenaries left the employ of the city-states to became freelance brigands.

In spite of political changes, the economy of the region displayed much continuity over a number of centuries. Wheat and barley were the main dietary staples; olives provided cooking oil; grapes were processed into wine; and sheep, goats, and poultry were used for their meat, milk, eggs, feathers, hides, and wool. Although these crops and animals could be found throughout the area, lighter rainfall

---

50. Frendo, *Pre-Exilic Israel*, 102.
51. Although feudalism is similar to patrimonial systems, scholars generally note that feudalism depends more on formal contracts while patrimonialism primarily relies on familial sentiments.
52. For translations of the Amarna correspondence, see William L. Moran, ed. and trans., *The Amarna Letters* (Baltimore: Johns Hopkins University Press, 1992). See also James B. Pritchard, ed., *Ancient Near Eastern Texts Relating to the Old Testament* (Princeton: Princeton University Press, 1969), 483–90.
53. Most scholars see a connection between the words "Apiru" and "Hebrew." The Apiru appear as mercenaries, renegade peasants, hostile outside interlopers, and as rival city-state rulers. Norman Gottwald suggests that the Apiru label could be used to denigrate any individual or group challenging the status quo. Thus powerful vassals accused each other of being Apiru. In any case, the frequent references to Apiru demonstrate a degree of political and social instability in the time period preceding the rise of the judges (Gottwald, *Tribes of Yahweh*, 401–9).

in the wooded hill country and in the south resulted in lower concentrations of people in those regions than on the coastal plains and interior valleys. In the more fertile and more densely populated areas, Canaanite rulers maintained economic control by organizing dependent workers on large estates, by conscripting peasants for corvée, and by taxing independent farmers living in the villages surrounding the walled cities. Over time, through the use of terraces and cisterns and by clearing away trees, free farmers and escaped serfs were able to settle more of the hill country where they established small, unwalled communities. Except for the absence of a defensive wall and public structures such as a temple or administrative building, such settlements did not differ greatly from the somewhat larger fortified towns. Some of the walled cities and rural settlements served as places of refuge where an individual could take temporary shelter from an angry pursuer seeking revenge.

From the south and east of the hill country, pastoralists moved in and out to take advantage of changing rainfall patterns related to the seasons. During the dry and fallow period between April and September, herders grazed their animals in the agricultural areas where the dung and other animal products would have been welcomed by the sedentary farmers. At this time, the various groups exchanged trade items, folk stories, recollections about genealogies, political commentaries, and religious concepts and rituals. Other transitory peoples brought additional economic, ethnic, and cultural variety. Midianite caravans moving through the area were the sources of ideas and exotic trade goods. Related to the Midianites, the Kenites, a landless group of metalworkers from the south, were regarded with some suspicion and also were welcomed because of their esoteric and essential knowledge. Described in the Bible as descendants of Cain, they traveled widely making and repairing tools and trinkets. Messengers of Yhwh, itinerant religious specialists, also played an important role during the premonarchic period because of their value to political big men who managed shrines or who needed divine power and oracular advice.[54]

Scholars generally agree that the Israelite people, who came to regard themselves as a separate ethnic group, and the indigenous Canaanites actually emerged from the same stock. Speaking the same language, cultivating the same crops, eating the same foods, building the same type of houses, worshiping the same gods (El, Baal, and Asherah), and celebrating the same agricultural festivals, the Canaanites and Israelites living in Syria-Palestine originally were members of a single cultural complex.[55] Frank Moore Cross notes that the language and images of theophany in early Israel borrowed heavily from the theophany of Baal.[56] Another example of cultural sharing in early Israel is that Hebrew poetry was both linguistically and literarily dependent on Canaanite precedents. Cross points out that the poetic meter of the earliest Hebrew poetry, for example the Song of Deborah in Judges 5, is typical of Ugaritic (Canaanite) epic style.[57] In his study of the Psalms, Mitchell Dahood shows how Hebrew songwriters appropriated Ugaritic odes to the gods as the basis for hymns praising both Yhwh and Israelite monarchs.[58]

---

54. In contrast to the messengers of Yhwh, the Levites (with claims of ties to Moses and Aaron) are not mentioned in the bardic tales. The later humanist writer, however, makes Levites central figures.
55. At least until 900 BCE, it is impossible to distinguish between Canaanites and Israelites based on archeological and linguistic evidence. Mark Smith notes that "Iron I Israel was largely Canaanite in culture.... Israel inherited local cultural traditions from the Late Bronze Age and its culture was largely continuous with the Canaanite culture of the coast and valleys during the Iron I period" (*Early History of God*, 27–28). As many scholars have noted, the name "Isra-el" honors El, the head of the Canaanite heavenly court. The people were not known as "Isra-ya." The implication is that the people embraced the worship of Yhwh sometime after they had solidified at least the rudiments of an ethnic identity. Anthony Frendo is more cautious when describing Israel's Canaanite roots. However, even he says that the vast majority of Israelites were of Canaanite origin. Frendo suggests that Hebrews from the south introduced the stories of the patriarchs and exodus. Coming into the hill country of Palestine they were then grafted into a much larger Canaanite group already known as Israel (*Pre-Exilic Israel*, 13).
56. Cross, *Canaanite Myth and Hebrew Epic*, 150.
57. Ibid., 115–16.

Because the process of cultural differentiation separating the Israelites from their neighbors was so gradual and took place over many generations, the people experiencing the change would have been unaware of the transition. Once the separation had reached the point where the existence of distinct and rival cultures was obvious, storytellers explained the differences through the medium of clichés about conflict and change. The martial clichés recorded in the book of Joshua attributed the dissimilarities and the tensions between the early Israelites and their neighbors to a series of battles, the Exodus cliché referred to an escape and epic journey, and clichés in Genesis and elsewhere suggested that cultural distinctions reflected long-ago sibling strife. While the travels, conquests, and family quarrels would be described by moderns as wanderings and struggles of the imagination, the concreteness of the symbolic images provided ancient people with a satisfactory explanation for how Israelite culture both replaced and remained in tension with the surrounding societies.[59]

58. Mitchell Dahood, SJ, *Psalms III: 101–150*, Anchor Bible 17A (Garden City, NY: Doubleday, 1970), xxii. Dahood sees a close relationship between Ugaritic texts from the fourteenth and thirteenth centuries BCE and early biblical poetry of the thirteenth and twelfth centuries. He says that the relationship is even more striking when looking at the psalms written mainly from the eleventh to sixth centuries BCE. In his three-volume commentary, Dahood argues that in many cases Hebrew poets simply replaced the name of a Canaanite deity or ruler with the name of Yhwh or a Hebrew king. While many scholars believe Dahood overemphasized the degree to which Ugaritic texts and language shaped Hebrew psalmody, a significant level of influence is undeniable. A modern parallel would be the way Friedrich Schiller's Romantic poem "Ode to Joy," which celebrated Greek mythology, was recycled by Beethoven in his Ninth Symphony (perhaps as a Masonic tribute), reused by Christians as the hymn "Joyful, Joyful We Adore Thee," appropriated by Nazi Germany, borrowed as the preindependence anthem of white-ruled Rhodesia, and made the "Anthem of Europe" by the European Union.
59. The use of clichés of war, travel, or family conflict to explain ethnic separation is a very common strategy among preindustrial peoples, who assume that dramatic events in the distant past must have been responsible for the differences they observe in the present. The image of battle suggests a more disruptive separation while tales of migration and sibling conflict acknowledge connection as well as distance. The now outdated debate as to whether the Israelites entered the land as disruptive conquerors or as peaceful migrant settlers actually grew out of the fact that the Israelites had competing perspectives about the past, rival interpretations expressed through contending clichés. While clichés should not be understood as literal descriptions of the past, there is room for common ground between scholars who interpret

The earliest known reference identifying the Israelites as a distinct group is from the Merneptah Stele, dated about 1207 BCE. The stele, which gives an account of Pharaoh Merneptah's victories in North Africa and Palestine, notes that in the course of battles in Canaan "the peoples of the tribes of Israel have been laid waste." The stele goes on to boast that all of Canaan had been pacified and had submitted to the power of the pharaoh.[60] Just how the Israelites mentioned in the stele came to be regarded as a separate ethnic grouping and how that grouping later grew into a community large and strong enough to establish a monarchy is subject to great debate. Ethnic identities are fluid. They can grow out of a people's recognition that they share a geographical region, a language, subsistence patterns, an outside threat, a central ruler, and a related set of social and religious beliefs, or that they trade and intermarry. In considering Israel in the light of traditional societies all over the world, it would be remarkable in the extreme if the people living in the Canaanite hill country had not claimed some type of ethnic identity. Just how that identity emerged may remain shrouded in the same mystery that obscures the origins of ethnic consciousness elsewhere in the world. While many traditional people regard their emergence as an act of divine intervention, the true miracle would be to find a people without an ethnic awareness.

The Israelites were surrounded by other Semitic peoples. The Edomites—living south of the Dead Sea and described as descendants

---

a story such as the exodus narrative as a pious fiction and those who believe there was an actual migration. Today, even more conservative scholars, who regard the story of the exodus as true, generally acknowledge that the account was introduced by a very small percentage of the people, who eventually became known as Israelites. The larger Israelite group then appropriated the saga as a cliché explaining their own social, economic, political, and religious situation. The stories in the books of Genesis, Exodus, and Joshua are similar to tales in African oral traditions about how ethnic groups came into existence. For a discussion of African clichés see Joseph C. Miller, *The African Past Speaks: Essays on Oral Tradition and History* (Folkestone, UK: Dawson, 1980), 24–31.

60. See Frank Frick, *A Journey through the Hebrew Scriptures* (New York: Harcourt Brace, 1995), 201–3; and Pritchard, *Ancient Near Eastern Texts*, 378.

of Esau—were regarded as a closely related, albeit somewhat hostile, people. Moab and Ammon were located east of the Jordan River. Along the Mediterranean coast to the north, the Phoenicians with their cities and ships were a more powerful and cosmopolitan people, whose roots also were Canaanite. Toward the end of the period described in Judges, non-Semitic seafaring peoples with ties to Cyprus and Greece settled on the southern and central coastal plains. Remembered as the Philistines, they posed a grave threat to the Israelite people. Nevertheless, some of these Sea Peoples were incorporated into Israel and became known as the tribe of Dan.

In the Late Bronze Age and Early Iron Age, hill country Israelites and their neighbors clustered in extended multigenerational households, known as the father's house (*bêt 'āb* – בת אב). The place of work and residence for Israelite families was a pillared, two-story building.[61] The low-ceiling ground floor was used for storage, food processing and crafts, and keeping animals. The upper floor, sometimes laid out around an open courtyard, provided dwelling space for human occupants.[62] Larger families, numbering ten people or more per household, included older parents, married sons and their children, unmarried daughters, servants, and poor kin. Although it was the ideal form, this multigenerational patrilineal family would often break down when its patriarch died and when older brothers established their own nuclear households. At any given time, only about one third of the households conformed to the ideal joint-family model while about two-thirds of the households included no more than five people.[63]

---

61. The pillared house had two rows of interior posts which supported an upper floor. Schloen and Stager believe the Israelite pillared house was a modification of a Canaanite structure which featured two solid interior walls instead of pillars (Schloen, *House of the Father*, 137).
62. Most houses contained less than seventy square meters (about five hundred square feet) of space (ibid., 147).
63. The information in this paragraph relies heavily on Schloen who summarizes and analyzes data generated by the most respected twentieth-century archeologists. Schloen says that the

Economically self-sufficient, families lived together in small village communities which generated a bit of surplus that they distributed to less fortunate relatives, sold to merchants, or offered as tribute to patrimonial political leaders who ruled much larger houses. Geographically proximate households regarded themselves as members of clans that generally numbered between one hundred and one hundred fifty people.[64] Guided by elders, Israelite clans were responsible for dispute resolution, legal decisions, land allocation, and defense against bandits and animal predators. Presumably the larger clan community gathered to celebrate marriages, conduct funerals, and observe festivals marking the harvests. These communities were characterized by some social disparity. Early legal codes indicate that slavery and pawnship were common and that wealthy men acquired more than their share of women.

The heroes described in Judges were heads of houses and clans. Their power was based on their ability to mobilize political support and material resources from members of those groups. Furthermore, the strategies they used to manage households were replicated in the methods they employed to rule more extensive domains. However, setting aside later extrapolations that reflect the perspective of people during the monarchy, there is no convincing evidence of any kind of central political or religious institutions unifying tribes, let alone an entire nation. Religious activity would have centered on household gods linked to family ancestors and to the cults of El (a benign father who reigned over a somewhat unruly heavenly court), of El's son

---

evidence points to a pattern that was relatively stable for centuries and that changed dramatically only with the social disruption brought by the end of the monarchy (ibid., 135–83).

64. According to Schloen, 70 percent of Israelite settlements occupied less than one third of a hectare of land, about the amount needed to build housing for 100 to 150 people. About 20 percent of the settlements were between one third and one hectare while only about 10 percent of the communities covered more than one hectare. Villages typically numbered between 100 and 150 people, in other words one clan, and contained about 20 households (ibid., 154–55).

Baal (a powerful and tumultuous god of war, fertility, and rain), and of Asherah (El's consort). Although the awareness and worship of the god Yhwh were also part of the religious landscape, oracles, necromancy, divining, sacrifices, images of metal or wood, blessings and curses, and oath-taking played important roles in the religious life of the hill country peoples who regarded themselves as Israelites. Among the elite, human sacrifice was practiced in times of dire crisis or at occasions expressing extraordinary gratitude to a deity.[65]

By the end of the period described in the book of Judges, Israel was not the same. Canaanite control over the hill country was being vigorously contested; small, isolated settlements and towns were increasingly united under aggressive big men who began imagining themselves as possible hereditary kings controlling extensive lands; and the worship of Yhwh as a powerful and jealous deity had become commonplace. What was responsible for these developments? Without denying the importance of gradual underlying social and economic forces, the following study will examine the role of the men and women of valor who were at the heart of the political and religious process that created the nation of Israel. Their stories are recounted in the book of Judges, which strongly asserts that these men and women, along with the religious specialists known as messengers of Yhwh, were the key actors during the premonarchic period.[66]

The Protagonists: Mighty Men and Women of Valor

As noted at the start of this chapter, the male protagonists in Judges were not actually judges, but mighty men of valor (גבור החיל).[67]

---

65. See Smith, *Early History of God*, 171–81. The topic of human sacrifice will be discussed in detail in chapter 5.
66. See the discussion about the messengers of Yhwh at the end of this chapter.
67. Only Deborah is actually said to have judged (שפטה). As will be seen in later chapters, her role was that of a seer, not a warrior/ruler.

Various forms of the roots גבר and חיל appear frequently in the Hebrew Bible. As a noun, חיל (*hyl*) can refer to a fortification, thus evoking a sense of unyielding defensive strength. In the Hebrew Scriptures the word is used to describe the ramparts of Thebes, Jerusalem, and Zion.[68] As a verb or adjective חיל suggests an enduring firm and strong action or quality.[69] Building on these meanings, חיל most often carries a military connotation, referring to an army, a warrior, or the strength of a horse. Second Samuel 11:16 indicates that the fiercest place on the battleground was occupied by valiant men. The armies of Assyria, the fighting men of Pharaoh, the soldiers of Jericho, and the warriors of Joshua are all described by the word חיל.[70] Although the primary meaning of the term suggests the resolute strength of a warrior, the word can be used to describe ability, efficiency, or trustworthiness in nonmilitary affairs. Moses selected able men (men of חיל) to assist him in governing while the pharaoh recruited able men from among the Hebrews to care for his cattle.[71] In addition, חיל is also associated with the security of wealth.[72]

Words based on the root גבר (*gbr*) also point to strength, but strength exercised more aggressively than defensively. As a verb, the word can mean the capacity to force, compel, or prevail over enemies. As an adjective, the word suggests boldness, pride, audaciousness, and might. A horse, a crocodile, a warrior, or the body

---

68. Nah. 3:8; Pss. 48:13; 122:7.
69. Job 20:21 refers to a prosperity that does not endure (is not strong) and Ps. 10:5 refers to the ways of the wicked, which are persistent. In Psalm 33:17 the adjectival form notes the strength of a horse.
70. There are dozens of passages where חיל is used to describe an army, generally foot soldiers in contrast to chariots or horsemen. A few of the passages are Exod. 14:9, 17, 28; Josh. 6:2; 10:7; Isa. 36:2.
71. Exod. 18:21 and 25; Gen. 47:6.
72. Some of the passages using the word to refer to wealth are Gen. 34:29; Num. 31:9; Deut. 8:17, 18; Isa. 8:4; 10:14; 30:6; Mic. 4:13; Jer. 15:13; Job 31:25; and Ps. 18:32, 39. Zechariah 14:14 explicitly lists gold, silver, and garments as examples of חיל.

of a man can all be described by the adjective גבורה. In Genesis, the Nephilim, superhuman children of gods and mortals, are called גברים. Similarly, Nimrod a fabled character in the mythical age of prodigious heroes, is described as the first גבור (mighty person) and as a גבור ציד (*gibbôr ṣayid*, mighty hunter).[73] Goliath, another figure of extraordinary might, is also identified as a גבור.[74] The name of the angel Gabriel (גבריאל), leader of God's heavenly army, is a combination of the word *gibbôr* and El. Although גבור can refer to a mighty army, a mighty king, mighty descendants, an angel, or a mighty deity, the word is used most often to describe a mighty warrior. Frequently, the words גבור and חיל are combined into a title, a title often translated as "man of valor." "Strong warrior," "firm warrior," or "valiant warrior" would also be appropriate renditions.

A survey of the many references to גבור החיל in the Hebrew Scriptures indicates that the men of valor were renowned as warriors, expert in the use of the shield and sword. First Chronicles 12:8 describes the men of valor as being swift as gazelles and having faces like lions. The reference to their physical appearance suggests long, flowing hair that was the mark of Israelite warriors.[75] Apparently, men of valor fought on foot, for they are commonly distinguished from men riding horses or driving chariots.[76] While highly regarded for their military might, a man of valor displayed other qualities. The young David, a man of valor, was skillful at playing music, prudent in speech, and handsome. In addition, it was said that he experienced divine approval because Yhwh was with him.[77] A man of

---

73. Gen. 6:4; 10:8–9.
74. 1 Sam. 17:51.
75. See Judg. 5:2. The Song of Deborah celebrates the flowing hair of self-sacrificing warriors (see Niditch, *Judges*, 70). Also, Samson the Nazirite famously had long locks, as did David's warrior son Absalom.
76. Exod. 14:9, 17, 28; 2 Kgs. 6:14–15.
77. 1 Sam. 16:18.

valor might also be industrious; Solomon, who admired the diligence of Jeroboam, a man of valor, placed him in charge of forced labor.

Although many men enjoyed the status of גבור חיל, the highest ranking among this group were individuals with considerable wealth and responsibility. When the king of Assyria demanded one thousand talents of silver from Menahem, the king of Israel, Menahem turned to his men of valor in order to raise the funds. Other references to the men of valor indicate that many were heads of houses, individuals whose names were well-known, and fathers of many offspring. From the Hebrew Bible we also see that men of valor were highly regarded for their exemplary character. The assistants Moses chose from among the men of valor were trustworthy people who respected Yhwh and hated bribery.[78] When Saul and his sons were killed, it was men of valor who risked their own lives to retrieve the bodies and give them a proper burial.[79] These brave and reliable men stand in sharp contrast to בני בליעל (*běnê bělîyaʿal*, sons of emptiness), disloyal men who were untrustworthy and worthless.[80]

Gideon was the first to be addressed as a man of valor in Judges, but he was not alone among Israel's mighty men of his time. An incident that took place later in Gideon's life indicates that he saw himself as but one of many such mighty men.[81] Preparing to execute two of his enemies he reminded them that they had killed a number of his own men at Tabor.[82] The dead men at Tabor were then described

---

78. Exod. 18:21, 25.
79. 1 Sam. 31:12.
80. 1 Sam. 10:26. The בני בליעל were the men who refused to recognize Saul. The word בלי can refer to the lack of water, lack of clothes (nakedness), or lack of knowledge.
81. These mighty men are somewhat of an embarrassment to biblical scholars who regard early Israel as an egalitarian society organized around respectable religious principles. Boling claims the mighty men were very rare (*Judges*, 111), and in his massive sociological study Gottwald hardly mentions them. Gottwald asserts that they became common only under the more hierarchical and oppressive monarchy (*Tribes of Yahweh*, 507).
82. The battle of Tabor receives no other mention in the story of Gideon. Failing to describe defeats was not uncommon.

as being just like Gideon, resembling the sons of a king—thus as Gideon's martial compatriots and social equals (his brothers, the sons of his mother).[83] In addition to Gideon, Jephthah, another prominent warrior big man in Judges, is specifically identified as a גבור (*gibbôr*) (Judg. 11:1). Although not labeled as *gibbôrîm*, the other big men described in the book of Judges certainly fall into that category. The left-handed warrior Ehud, Gideon's putative son Abimelech, and the great commander Barak have all the marks of the *gibbôrîm*. Judges 20:44 and 46 note that the tribe of Benjamin had numerous *gibbôrîm*, and the tribe of Dan is credited with five such individuals in Judg. 18:2. In addition, Samson's story should be thought of as describing the warrior qualities of a youthful man of valor.

Israel's ideal mighty man was David, who spent much of his life as a warrior mercenary. Prior to becoming a king, his career resembled that of the heroes in Judges. Assembling a group of subordinate mighty men, David was able to gain control of an entire kingdom. More than thirty of the mighty men serving under David are named in 2 Sam. 23:8–39. They are ranked according to their levels of responsibility and they are described as strong, valiant, and loyal individuals. Single-handedly killing large numbers of opposing warriors, fighting so doggedly that their swords stuck fast to their hands, slaying lions with their bare hands, and recklessly penetrating enemy lines just to fetch a drink of water for their thirsty commander are some of the deeds attributed to David's *gibbôrîm*.

As can be seen from descriptions of David's mighty men and from references elsewhere in the Hebrew Bible, leaders over subordinate mighty men rewarded their companies of fighters with promotions and booty and also with gifts of land, slaves, and women. In addition, the honor earned in battle would have been regarded as an important

---

83. Judg. 8:18–20.

prize. The very existence of the stories making up the book of Judges is evidence of how the power and valor of great warrior leaders were recalled and recounted. Holding together a group of competitive, impulsive, proud, courageous, demanding, and strong young followers—men enthralled by tales such as the legend of Samson—would have been a challenging task. A leader who demonstrated his success in that context would have been a logical candidate for more extensive responsibilities. It is, therefore, not surprising that Gideon harbored thoughts of becoming a king and that his putative son Abimelech attempted to put such aspirations into action.[84]

No female in Judges is explicitly labeled as a woman of valor (*'ēšet ḥayil* – אשת חיל), but many merit that title. Except for the stories of Ehud and Gideon, each epic-bardic saga features females who play important, even primary, roles. Achsah, Deborah, Jael, Sisera's mother, Delilah, and the woman who delivered the fatal blow to Abimelech are all strong women whose determination and/or warriorly qualities are recorded in the premonarchic tales contained in Judges. Their stories challenge any notion that all women were thought of as passive actors whose lives, ideas, and actions were completely controlled and constantly overshadowed by men.

Compiled more than five hundred years after the period depicted in Judges, Proverbs is the only book in the Hebrew Bible actually to use the term mighty woman (אשת חיל). Unfortunately, the phrase is diminished in translation. The RSV renders אשת חיל as "good wife" while the much earlier King James uses the words "virtuous woman." However, in Prov. 31:10–31, the אשת חיל is much more than a sexually pure and compliant spouse. The account in Proverbs 31 lists

---

84. Judg. 8:22–23. Even though the text explicitly states that the people, not Gideon, asked that he and his descendants rule as kings, Gideon may have initiated the request. Modern-day authoritarian leaders, who seek to extend their mandate, often justify their actions by claiming they are only acceding to popular demand, a demand they themselves create.

the economic and managerial marks of valor essential for the success of a great house, whether in premonarchic times or in the more cosmopolitan and urbanized postmonarchic era. The woman of valor in Proverbs 31 is an entrepreneur, household manager, landowner, vintner, philanthropist, and craftsperson. She is also described as strong, dignified, optimistic, confident, industrious, and kind. The passage in Proverbs concludes by saying that the woman of valor is honored by public praise and blessing in the city gates, lauded not for superficial charm and beauty, but for measurable accomplishments. Although Proverbs does not comment on the military attributes of valor, the leadership qualities in Proverbs are those that would have been attributed to illustrious men and women during the time of Judges.

The Messenger of Yhwh

While not nearly so prominent as the men and women of valor, another group of people in the book of Judges deserves mention. Appearing in the tales of Gideon and Samson, these enigmatic figures are known by the title messenger of Yhwh (מלאך יהוה – *mal'ak yhwh*) There are compelling similarities between the promises, admonitions, and actions of the messengers of Yhwh in Judges who appeared to Gideon and Samson's parents and in the account of Moses in Exodus 3. In each case, a mysterious and exotic individual appeared and disappeared suddenly and without explanation. In each case, the messenger promised power to an individual charged with fighting against an oppressor (the Midianites, the Philistines, or Pharaoh) and bringing deliverance. In each case, the power was explicitly linked to the deity Yhwh. In each case, the listener expressed doubt, reluctance, and even fear. In each case, the messenger was validated by a supernatural event (the miracle of

Gideon's fleece, the infertile woman becoming pregnant with Samson, and Moses's staff turning into a snake) and inexplicable pyrotechnics (a burning bush which was not destroyed, all-consuming flames for sacrifices ignited mysteriously). And, in each case, the recipient of the message went on to great deeds of triumph.

The commonalities in these stories suggest a pattern which has both a sociopolitical and a literary dimension. From a sociopolitical point of view, the messengers of Yhwh in Exodus and Judges appear to have been peripatetic agitators who dealt with strong, but marginalized, individuals, motivating and mobilizing them to strike out against political and ethnic enemies of the Hebrew people.[85] Seeming to appear out of nowhere, the messengers validated their words with spectacular demonstrations of magic, often involving fire. Given the similarity of their admonitions and modi operandi, it would appear that these agitators were part of a loosely organized company of revolutionary-minded individuals. From a literary perspective, it is likely that there was a shared tradition and a collection of somewhat standardized stories. The stories, perhaps created and preserved by the messengers themselves, might have become templates to guide their behavior and to gild their reputation. As the stories were told, the lines between reality, legend, and myth, as well as those between the human and divine worlds, would have blurred.[86]

---

85. Much of the scholarly discussion regarding the messenger of Yhwh has been driven by theological concerns about whether the messenger was a being separate from the deity. Thus the question deals with whether the messenger is to be regarded as Yhwh himself appearing in a theophany, as an angelic envoy, or a human agent claiming to act for the deity. See Rene A. Lopez, "Identifying the 'Angel of the Lord' in the Book of Judges: A Model for Reconsidering the Referent in Other Old Testament Loci," *Bulletin for Biblical Research* 20, no. 1 (2010): 1–18. Lopez correctly argues that the term messenger of Yhwh can refer to all three manifestations and that the Hebrew Bible describes multiple human messengers. Based on this conclusion, it then becomes possible to ask about the social structures in which the human messengers operated and the temporal functions they served.

Written hundreds of years after the epic-bardic stories were first committed to memory, the Deuteronomistic account in Judges begins with a tale of a messenger of Yhwh. In Judg. 2:1–5, the messenger condemns Israel for accommodating to Canaanite culture.[87] In this scene, the messenger spoke not just to one individual, but to all the sons of Israel gathered at Gilgal. Reminding the people of Yhwh's deliverance from Egypt, the messenger chastised the people for breaking the covenant they had once cut with their deity. According to the messenger, their sin was tolerating pagan altars and being lured by the gods of the local Canaanites. Weeping with remorse, the people offered a sacrifice to Yhwh and named the place Bochim (Weepers). Although less personal and more covenantal, the proclamation at Gilgal was consistent with the words of the messenger of Yhwh to Gideon and to Samson's parents.

The striking parallels between the Hebrew Bible's messenger of Yhwh and traditional diviners who instigated a revolt against German colonialism in early twentieth-century Tanganyika may help us understand the situation in ancient Israel more fully. Like the Midianites, the Philistines, or the pharaoh, the Germans greatly disrupted economic, social, and political life. Obligating Africans to build roads, grow cash crops, and earn money to pay a head tax, the Germans placed enormous pressure on the subsistence economy. Combined with a severe drought in 1905, the result was a serious food shortage. Like the messenger of Yhwh, who convinced Moses to challenge Egypt and Gideon to defy Baal, traditional African diviners loyal to the snake god Hongo promised supernatural power

---

86. In the case of Moses, one must ask if the story was projected back in time and attached to a heroic figure of the past or if groups associated with the Moses tradition introduced the actual practices and the literary genre into the land.
87. The literary technique used by the Deuteronomistic writer is similar to that used by the bardic-epic storyteller who inserted Jotham's fable into the story of Abimelech (Judg. 9:7–21). In each case the writer placed his or her words in the mouth of a third person.

(*maji* or magical water) that would protect Africans against German bullets. Although the leading spirit medium, Kinjikitile Ngwale, was executed in 1905, other itinerant mediums mobilized chiefs and warriors to continue what became known as the Maji Maji revolt. But unlike Gideon and Samson, who were given power enabling them to dishonor Baal and Dagon, Kinjikitile Ngwale did not succeed. His magic water did not turn bullets into water and Maji Maji did not lift the weight of oppression. The Germans remained in control and the two-year revolt (1905–7) took the lives of several hundred thousand Africans, who were killed in battle or died of famine. However, the uprising is remembered as one of the greatest threats to the European presence in East Africa.[88]

Methodology and Organization

The goal of this book is to describe the political values of premonarchic times. If, as the majority of scholars believe, the epic-bardic tales of Judges were created no later than the early monarchy, those narratives are rich sources for learning about how early Israelites *thought* leaders behaved, what they did to gain and hold power, and how a political system operated.[89] The stories of Deborah, Gideon, and Abimelech may not reveal much about the life of any actual individual, but they record what people hoped for and feared politically, how they conducted themselves in the public sphere, and the strategies they considered effective in governance.

The primary methodological tools and language in this book are those of social science, not theology. Borrowing anthropological, sociological, and politico-scientific theories about wealth, power,

---

88. See John Iliffe, "The Organization of the Maji Maji Rebellion," *Journal of African History* 8 (1967): 495–512; Thaddeus Sunseri, "Reinterpreting a Colonial Rebellion: Forestry and Social Control in German East Africa, 1874–1915," *Environmental History* 8, no. 3 (2003): 430–51.
89. As noted before, there is independent documentation from 2 Samuel that Israelite warriors were well aware of the heroes in Judges.

INTRODUCTION AND OVERVIEW

honor, and indigenous knowledge, this study applies those concepts to early Israelite society. As just seen, chapter 1 of the book summarizes commonly accepted understandings about late second-millennium Syro-Palestinian society and about how the book of Judges was built upon a collection of oral histories, legends, and folktales that were edited and supplemented by later writers. This chapter identifies the main characters in Judges not as religious or legal officials, but as men and women of valor operating within turbulent patron-client systems. The remaining chapters of the book examine how those men and women gained and consolidated power in patronage systems. The central argument is that they sought ways to rule that neither depleted their material resources nor required the constant exercise of force. Patrons who must frequently provide material rewards to clients or who must continually impose their will through violence risk exhausting their treasure and multiplying resentment to the point where it cannot be contained. The most successful valiant men and women in Judges found less expensive and less dangerous ways to maintain their power.

Building on the ideas of Jane Guyer, chapter 2 explains how the patron leaders used their control of indigenous knowledge, both temporal and supernatural, to enhance their authority. While studies of patron-client systems always emphasize the importance of mobilizing people for their ability to fight, work, or bear children, Judges offers many examples of leaders who collected people with intellectual expertise. Chapter 3 investigates the importance of having a reputation for constancy or reliability in order to hold power. Joel Migdal has noted that patron-client leaders are weakened because they are forced to delegate power and redistribute wealth in order to win and keep the loyalty of their subordinates. The book of Judges proposes an alternative strategy. Judges suggests that a leader who is renowned as utterly unswerving and absolutely faithful to contractual agreements can attract allies and neutralize enemies. But, as Hannah Arendt, Donald Shriver, and Miroslav Volf recognize, for society to survive, the rigidity of constancy must be tempered by clemency and compassion. Both the bardic stories of Jephthah and the humanist's tales of intertribal wars ponder that reality. Chapter 4 draws on the classic writings of Julian Pitt-Rivers, J. G. Peristiany, and Frank Stewart to consider how "big men and women" in Judges used honor as a way to exercise authority. Like the quality of reliability, honor can enhance power without drastically depleting resources or creating additional enemies. Even chapter 5, which looks at the use of wealth, suggests that effective individuals operating in a patronage system are able to manage material resources in a way that ensures more income than outflow. In an economic system relying on plunder, tribute, and gifting, men of valor in Judges added to their power and wealth by offering lavish and spectacular sacrificial gifts to Yhwh. Karl Polanyi's work on precapitalist economies, Macur Olson's descriptions of roving and stationary bandits, and Marcel Mauss's and Natalie Davis's writings on gifting were all instrumental in the development of chapter 5. Finally, building on Walter Brueggemann's thoughts about the dynamic and ongoing conversation between God and humans, chapter 6 concludes the book with a brief reflection on the enduring significance of the book of Judges. In all the chapters of this book, I owe a great debt to Susan Niditch. Her commentary on Judges and her study of war in the Hebrew Bible are models of careful scholarship and sensible interpretation.

2

Power and Knowledge

The Control of Knowledge

As prominent warriors, community leaders, and heads of houses, the men of valor in Judges managed subordinates, manipulated superiors, and dealt with enemies. As was true in other patronage systems, success depended on their ability to exercise force and distribute wealth. However, they also relied on other political resources. Knowledge mongers as well as pursuers of military power and material riches, the heroes in Judges valued information as much as physical strength, adeptness with patronage, or the ability to administer a great house. In exploring the question of how the mighty men of valor gained and held power, this chapter argues that the champions described in the book of Judges regarded knowledge as an indispensable tool for achieving that end. Some of that knowledge was dispensed by them personally; some was generated by others in their employ or under their control. Some of the knowledge was consumed by the men of valor themselves; some was reallocated as a form of patronage or even sold in order to generate income.

The knowledge pursued by men and women in Judges is what moderns label as indigenous knowledge.[1] Indigenous knowledge deals with both the temporal and supernatural worlds, worlds not sharply differentiated in pre-scientific societies. In the book of Judges, strongmen sought temporal knowledge about land rights, strategies for battle, the location of secret entrances in city walls, potential political conspiracies, and diplomatic history. They also collected information about who had wealth, who could be taxed, and who could be trusted. But even more important for people in the book of Judges was an understanding of the supernatural world. As anthropologist Harry G. West notes, people who acknowledge a supernatural realm seek to comprehend, gain access to, manipulate, and benefit from that world. Such insight, entrée, and control complement and enhance knowledge and actions in the temporal domain.[2] In the book of Judges, large oak trees, hills, temples, altars, sacred pillars, and sculpted stones provided physical points of access to the world of the supernatural. While ordinary individuals might have dealings with the paranormal, ritual experts were regarded as the most effective intermediaries between the worlds of the seen and the unseen. Seized in ecstasy, clothed in unique garments, and coiffed unconventionally, these spiritual specialists offered sacrifices and manipulated specialized implements of divination when serving as vessels of supernatural guidance.

---

1. The following UNESCO statement offers a good definition of indigenous knowledge: "Indigenous Knowledge (IK) can be broadly defined as the knowledge that an indigenous (local) community accumulates over generations of living in a particular environment. This definition encompasses all forms of knowledge—technologies, know-how skills, practices and beliefs—that enable the community to achieve stable livelihoods in their environment. A number of terms are used interchangeably to refer to the concept of IK, including Traditional Knowledge (TK), Indigenous Technical Knowledge (ITK), Local Knowledge (LK) and Indigenous Knowledge System (IKS)" (www.unep.org/ik/).
2. Harry G. West, *Ethnographic Sorcery* (Chicago: University of Chicago Press, 2007).

POWER AND KNOWLEDGE

In describing how leaders in premonarchic Israel used knowledge to build their fortunes, this chapter will borrow from the insights of cultural anthropologist Jane Guyer.[3] Looking at strongmen depicted in African legend, Guyer argues that political power is partially dependent on a leader's ability to mobilize knowledge. In assessing the importance of knowledge in traditional Africa, Guyer challenges the assumption that power is primarily linked to the control of people—wives, children, pawns, clients, and slaves—merely as producers and reproducers. According to Guyer, successful leaders assemble subordinates and associates for their intellectual attributes and specialized knowledge as much as for their strength to labor as farmers or porters, their physical prowess as fighters, their ability to bear children, or their membership in key kin groups. Thus Guyer calls on scholars to move beyond a static structuralist preoccupation with lineage or a materialistic Marxist emphasis on the control of surplus wealth. Although written to illuminate precolonial Africa, Guyer's essay opens up promising lines of inquiry for any preindustrial society. Her approach invites us to recognize the multifaceted character of indigenous knowledge and to consider the dynamic struggle to gain access to—monopolize, if possible—widely dispersed specialists whose intellect contributes to the political, economic, and social strength of a powerful town, prominent region, or influential leader.

In developing her argument, Guyer points out that knowledge, especially among preindustrial groups, is embodied in people. Such knowledge includes information about the behavior of animals, formulas to ensure fertility (of crops, animals, and humans), techniques to interpret dreams or visions, methods to settle disputes or identify wrongdoers, magical potions to harm enemies or help

---

3. Jane I. Guyer, "Wealth in People as Wealth in Knowledge: Accumulation and Composition in Equatorial Africa," *Journal of African History* 36 (1995): 91–120.

friends, strategies to win a battle, schemes to multiply wealth, ways to attract the favor of a lover, medicines for healing, and rituals to gain the favor of the gods. Although shrines, bits of writing, oracles and sayings, grave sites, sacred trees, and household idols may serve as mnemonic repositories of information, all of these tools require a living keeper or specialist who makes the knowledge accessible to the larger population.

Guyer emphasizes the fact that indigenous knowledge is idiosyncratic and particular. The sheer volume and range of information make it impossible for any single individual to master or remember it all. Furthermore, the living nature of knowledge makes it resistant to capture by one person or group. Subject to innovation, purchase or sale, borrowing, adaptation, experimentation, rejection, and obsolescence, this knowledge is never static. It continually adjusts in response to economic shifts, immigration, travel and trade, natural disasters, environmental modifications, political changes, and individual creativity.

According to Guyer, a successful big man or woman is one who can gather—Guyer uses the word "compose"—a diverse company of experts, whose knowledge enables the big person to preserve and multiply power. This knowledge can be leveraged by the big person to produce numerous offspring and to ward off disease and death. It can also be used to accumulate wealth, increase military prowess, and enhance one's reputation as a settler of disputes. However, given the personalized and multifaceted nature of information, the mobilization, control, and centralization of expert knowledge is a formidable task. Because indigenous knowledge cannot be captured by a static kin structure or a single religious institution, "compositional" success is tenuous. Not only may experts be ethnically and geographically distant, they may be outspoken, defiant, confrontational, and costly. Therefore, leaders must give constant attention to protecting their investment in the people, whose knowledge, not just labor, can be a key component of political power and wealth.

Guyer notes that in Africa the dynamic, innovative, and compositional nature of indigenous knowledge was nearly destroyed by colonialism which sought to restrict non-Western information and wisdom. Colonial authorities either deprecated or outlawed the use of traditional knowledge in all domains of life. As a result, long-held notions about education, the military, criminal justice, natural science, agriculture, politics, religion, the family, and medicine were cast aside by colonial officials. Under colonialism, the institutions supporting the exercise of indigenous knowledge were dismantled and many traditional experts who embodied the knowledge were exiled or killed. In addition, most of the remaining experts either became discouraged or lost their clients and patrons, who turned to "modern" sources of "truth."

Guyer's model, developed for Africa, can be used to explain the nature of politics in premonarchic Israel. Applying the model to the book of Judges reveals the central importance of knowledge for the exercise of power. Repeatedly in Judges we see prominent individuals attempting to capture and use knowledge in ways that increased their wealth, followers, territory, or stature. Occasionally, we see groups and individuals fail because rivals achieved superiority in the competition for information.

The Composition of Knowledge in Judges

The book of Judges invites the following questions: How did the mighty men of valor gain ascendancy? How did they maintain their hold on power? And what were the threats to their power? These questions cannot be resolved by reference to simple sociological, economic, or theological formulas. Jane Guyer's thesis invites us to consider the possibility that the strongmen depicted in the book of Judges were successful in part because they were able to "compose" knowledge. If the men of valor owed some of their success to the mobilization of information, we should find echoes of that fact in the vivid myths, legends, and histories of the book of Judges. However, when investigating the topic, we need to be aware that over the centuries, like the colonial authorities in Africa described by Guyer, political and religious partisans of a Yhwhist monarchy worked energetically to extinguish both the practice and memory of competing indigenous knowledge. This effort came to a peak during and after the reign of King Josiah in the late seventh century.[4] As seen in Deuteronomy, the judicial ideal for Josiah's time, non-Yhwhistic prophets or interpreters of dreams were to be put to death, even if they spoke the truth and even if their predictions came true (Deut. 13:1–5).

In spite of any politically or theologically induced amnesia intended to suppress the memory of heterodox ideas, the book of Judges is replete with references to indigenous knowledge and the ways powerful people used that knowledge. Many of those references are associated with oracular inquiry. In the second millennium, some of the most sophisticated intellectual activity took place at sites for divination. There, experts drew on tradition, experience, ritual, and the voice of the supernatural to offer advice and render decisions about vital issues facing their clients. Significantly, the first sentence in Judges contains the term "inquire" (šāʾal – שאל), an unmistakable reference to an oracular query.[5] That sentence, written by the humanist editor, is an appropriate introduction for the entire book.

---

4. For a discussion of this competition, see Morton Smith, *Palestinian Parties and Politics that Shaped the Old Testament* (London: SCM Press, 1987).
5. J. Alberto Soggin, *Judges: A Commentary* (Philadelphia: Westminster, 1981), 20. Soggin notes that when šāʾal (שאל) is associated with any deity, the reference is always to oracular activity.

Although in Judg. 1:1 the humanist writer refers to a military decision (determining which group should go first into war) and legitimizes only a single source for knowledge (Yhwh), the example is faithful to the spirit of a culture where the quest for knowledge was a preoccupation. Many other passages in Judges recall specific sites or physical objects associated with the process of gaining and divulging knowledge. Shrines, idols, altars, high places, distinctive garments for divination (ephod), charms, implements for casting lots (Urim and Thummim), sacrificial ceremonies to inquire of or thank a god, 'ăšērîm (sacred pillars representing the consort of Baal), temples (for example, the house of Baal of the covenant at Shechem), and especially sacred oak trees (where divining took place), all indicate that people in premonarchic Israel had myriad places and instruments to seek divine guidance and disseminate information.[6]

The explicitly emphasized popularity of divining sites operated by Deborah (Judg. 4:4–6), Gideon (Judg. 8:23–27), Micah (Judges 17), and the tribe of Dan (Judges 18) suggests that people from all walks of life frequented those places. From multiple stories and references in other books in the Hebrew Scriptures, it is clear that people received guidance in many areas of life. At the household level, they sought assistance in matters of marital fidelity, curing illness, and bearing and protecting children. When caring for animals and crops, they looked for advice about appropriate times for planting and harvesting and about ways of insuring the health and fertility of their flocks and herds. At other times, they wanted help in locating lost animals, resolving civil disputes, guaranteeing safety when traveling, and prospering in business.

---

6. Roy Heller discusses the various strategies for obtaining supernatural knowledge. He distinguishes between divination, in which a human being takes the initiative to acquire paranormal information, and prophecy, in which the human agent is a vehicle for a divinely instigated message. See Heller, *Power, Politics, and Prophecy: The Character of Samuel and the Deuteronomistic Evaluation of Prophecy* (London: T & T Clark International, 2006), 3–4.

While the sites and tools for seeking knowledge promised the backing of divine authority, words or signs from the ancestors or gods (including Yhwh) had to be mediated by human interpreters.[7] Although the mediums, shrine owners, or people who cast lots or used other divination techniques claimed to act only as unobstructed channels from the gods or ancestors, the human intermediary actually controlled the message. In the case of dispute resolution, a successful and respected intermediary would have drawn from a deep well of experience, intuition, understanding of social structures, knowledge of character, and memory of common law when rendering a decision. When offering advice about illness, a medium would have relied on a long practice of diagnosis and prescription.

An example from contemporary Africa illustrates how divining may have worked in ancient Israel. John Gay, an anthropologist with decades of experience living in Africa, relates the following story about a Liberian friend who suspected that the manager of her farm had stolen money. Although the manager denied wrongdoing, he agreed to a trial by ordeal. Gay writes,

> I was present as a witness. The ordeal man heated a cutlass red hot and announced that if applied to the leg of an innocent person no harm would be done, but that the guilty person would be burned. . . . He rubbed a liquid on the legs of the two parties [the accused and the accuser] and then on his own leg, seemingly the same liquid in all three cases. He applied the fiery red cutlass to his own leg first, and nothing happened. He reheated it and applied it to my friend's leg, and still nothing happened. I watched closely and could see that, in fact, her skin was depressed where the cutlass touched it. In short, he was not faking the physical contact of hot iron with flesh. He then turned to the accused person, applied the reheated iron, and at once the flesh sizzled and smoked. Guilt was established.[8]

---

7. First Samuel 28 describes in great detail how King Saul sought out a medium through whom he could consult the dead ancestor/seer Samuel.

8. John Gay, *Africa: A Dream Deferred* (Northridge, CA: New World African Press, 2004), 46.

POWER AND KNOWLEDGE

Gay continues by offering his own explanation of what had happened. He assumes that the "ordeal man" used subterfuge to make sure that only one participant was burned. But the real trick was deciding which party should be singled out for blame. In Gay's view, either the ordeal doctor had been paid to demonstrate guilt or he had determined—Gay suspected by psychological clues—that the man was culpable. It is also possible that blame was assigned according to social standing. In that case, the task of the ordeal doctor would have been to determine which of the litigants was of higher rank.

Gay's experience in modern Liberia suggests that while sleight of hand and adroit manipulation of physical implements are important, a diviner's experience and interpretive ability are the key ingredients in any trial by ordeal. The same would be true for other types of divination. Except in the most straightforward cases—for example, casting lots in cases parallel to those in which moderns would flip a coin or draw straws—the real voice in divination is that of the human in charge. While it takes training and insider understanding to conduct the physical steps of divination, the essential skill is far more complex and much more intellectual or psychological. This skill draws on an extensive store of indigenous knowledge.

In rendering their decisions, ancient Israel's diviners would have drawn on multiple facets of indigenous knowledge. Some of that knowledge concerned the techniques and implements that were the physical or formulaic manifestation of the process such as the specialized attire or coif that enhanced credibility and the verbal inflections and formulas associated with specific divination problems. Other components of knowledge were more subtle and cerebral. These included the capacity to read a person's character (intent, motivation, level of anxiety, and truthfulness), an understanding of practical solutions or strategies (for battle, for healing an illness, for overcoming infertility, for locating a lost animal, and for resolving a civil dispute), an ability to accurately assess social standing, and a knack for instilling confidence in the petitioner(s). All were crucial for successful divination. All required natural talent and all reflected specialized knowledge built upon careful training, extensive practice, and sound judgment. In short, good practitioners were highly qualified indigenous-knowledge professionals. Only several generations removed from the time depicted in Judges, the example of the child Samuel wearing a small linen ephod—the ritual garment with pockets for the Urim and Thummim, key implements of divination—and working under the supervision of the master diviner Eli suggests that preparation for professional life might begin as soon as a person could walk and talk (1 Sam. 2:18–20; 3:1).

Like their modern counterparts, not all ancient knowledge workers were honest. The Hebrew Bible contains multiple accusations about fraud and favoritism in the process of divination—for example, charges of malfeasance against both Eli's sons and Samuel's sons. A statement attributed to the seer Samuel indicates that integrity was a common concern for seers and diviners. In an address to the people of Israel, Samuel offered to submit to trial by ordeal should anyone accuse him of taking a bribe or judging unfairly (1 Sam. 12:3–5). When considering the matter of indigenous knowledge, the fact that fraud is mentioned is proof that people in Israel were well aware of the human element in the process of divination.[9]

---

9. Fraud on the part of diviners and prophets was a very real concern for ancient Near Eastern consumers of supernatural knowledge. See J. J. M. Roberts, "Does God Lie? Divine Deceit as a Theological Problem in Israelite Prophetic Literature," in *Congress Volume, Jerusalem 1986* (Leiden: E.J. Brill, 1988), 211–20. Roy Heller discusses the suspicion and uncertainty people had toward both diviners and prophets. Because divination was subject to error, even when practiced in good faith, diviners sometimes sought multiple readings to confirm their findings. Mediated through human words or actions, prophecy was considered to be more subjective. Therefore, prophets were even more suspect than diviners, who were regarded a bit more like objective spiritual technicians (*Power, Politics, and Prophecy*, 6–11). Deuteronomy 18:20–22 is another Hebrew Bible passage warning against false prophets.

While much of the knowledge noted in the book of Judges was related to divination, other types of knowledge or skill were more secular in nature. Specialized legal, historical, and geographical knowledge figure prominently in the narrative. For example, when the elders of Gilead hired the warrior/brigand Jephthah as their political leader and military commander, they invested him by means of a standard ritualized contract (Judg. 11:10). We must assume that unmentioned characters in the story were expert in the wording, conditions, and ceremonies involved in cementing an agreement between powerful and high-profile parties. Later, when attempting to negotiate with his rival, the king of the Ammonites, Jephthah sent messengers who displayed a detailed command of historical events and territorial borders. We may presume that the diplomatic history and geography recounted by these diplomats were expertly shaped to favor Jephthah's cause (Judg. 11:12–28). As with the covenant binding Jephthah and the elders of Gilead, the recitation of history and the references to previous agreements required specialized knowledge of legal procedures and agreements from the past. Both cases featured contending parties who sought to frame information in a way that best served their interests. The account of the strongman Abimelech also illustrates the complexity of political contracts. After prolonged negotiations, the citizens of Shechem entered into an agreement with Abimelech. Ratified at Shechem's sacred oak (Judg. 9:6), the contract gave Abimelech an exclusive right to collect duties on trade caravans passing through the region (Judg. 9:25).[10]

As might be expected from a book celebrating a warrior elite, much of the secular knowledge in the book of Judges is military in

---

10. Based on possible parallels with a covenant between David and the elders of Hebron, Abimelech's oath may have also contained the promise that he would rule with justice. For a discussion of David's covenant, see Scott Starbuck, *Court Oracles in the Psalms: The So-Called Royal Psalms in Their Ancient Near Eastern Context* (Atlanta, GA: Society of Biblical Literature, 1999), 192–95. I discuss this more fully in chapter 3.

nature. A brief account embedded in the book's editorial framework describes how the people of Israel recruited spies to secure insider information needed to defeat a walled city (Judg. 1:22–26). Judges also recalls how the big man Abimelech relied on intelligence collected by his deputy Zebul to identify the protagonists of a gathering rebellion (Judg. 9:30–31). When planning on how to counter a revolt at Shechem, Abimelech again turned to Zebul who suggested a strategy by which a small company of warriors would draw out the adversary by attacking and then falling back. Abimelech followed Zebul's advice. His staged retreat tricked the enemy into a reckless pursuit that ended with an ambush by forces Abimelech had hidden on both sides of the escape route (Judg. 9:32–45).[11]

The accounts in Judges indicate that supernatural and temporal knowledge were not regarded as sharply separate categories. The story of the strongman Barak emphasized the link between divination and military operations. Barak (a praise name meaning "Lightning") traveled a long distance seeking the advice of the prophetess-judge Deborah, who conducted her divination business under a sacred tree. Not only did Deborah tell Barak how to recruit his warriors, what battle strategy he should employ, and the times and places to attack, she also assured Barak that Yhwh himself had guaranteed success. This encouragement was either tempered or intensified by Deborah's taunt that a woman, not Barak himself, would earn credit for the triumph (Judg. 4:6–14). In another case, described centuries later by the humanist writer, fighters confronting the tribe of Benjamin "inquired of Yhwh" (the technical reference to divination) and were given specific counsel about when and where to do battle. Instructed to use an entrapment strategy similar to the one that led to Abimelech's success, the people of Israel then defeated the tribe of

---

11. Many African tales describe successful military campaigns that rely on this type of strategy. The famous Zulu leader Shaka used the method which has been called the "bull's horn" formation.

Benjamin. According to the story, even though the command to join the battle did not result in success initially, the oracular encouragement gave the attackers the resolve to continue the battle. The eventual outcome was a total rout of the Benjaminites (Judg. 20:18–46).

At the individual level, ancient Israelites thought information provided by a divine messenger or seer could enable a warrior to achieve great physical strength. Samson gained his powers by following a formula given to his mother by a messenger of Yhwh (Judg. 13:3).[12] Similar in nature to the fanciful story of Paul Bunyan, Samson's tale is a legendary construction intended to extol the qualities of a youthful warrior (*na'ar* – נער).[13] At a time when prowess in battle resulted in booty, honor, and women, one can only assume that aspiring warriors (or their kin) not only would have told and retold the story of Samson, but would have sought out rituals or medicines promising extraordinary strength. The story of Samson also suggests that knowledge pertaining to superhuman power was a closely guarded secret. The legend of Samson has parallels in modern-day Africa where diviners offer esoteric medicine in the form of charms, potions, codes of conduct, or dress that give strength and provide protection.[14] Such magic is thought to make an

---

12. The messenger or envoy (*mal'āk* – מלאך) who met Samson's mother in the field is called an "angel" in many translations, including the Septuagint, but both the woman and her husband Manoah regarded the individual as a human being. Although heavenly beings commonly appear in legends and myths, it is equally logical to assume the storyteller was thinking of a traveling diviner. Mieke Bal goes so far as to suggest that the storyteller regarded the exotic figure as Samson's biological father. *Death and Dissymmetry: The Politics of Coherence in the Book of Judges* (Chicago: University of Chicago Press, 1988), 104–5. As Mark S. Smith notes, ancient storytellers, who saw the world as populated with divine beings, would not have been concerned about a clear distinction between humans and gods. "Remembering God: Collective Memory in Israelite Religion," *Catholic Biblical Quarterly* 64 (2002): 631–51.
13. While נער can refer to any male youth, it can also carry the meaning of a young man on the path to becoming a warrior. In that case, it would be the equivalent to the English word "squire."
14. Readers also will see parallels with the superstitious rituals used by modern athletes.

individual immune from harm (even bullets) and invisible to enemy forces. However, as with Samson, the complicated formula for obtaining such power must be followed with absolute precision. Any lapse, however momentary or inadvertent, results in the withdrawal of the magical properties. Consequently, it is easy for a diviner to deflect blame in case of failure. As was true in the story of Samson, in Africa such medicine is the property of specialists.

The Individualistic and Idiosyncratic Nature of Knowledge

Like intellectual property in Guyer's traditional Africa, much indigenous knowledge in premonarchic Israel was highly fragmented and personalized. Held in the minds of individuals rather than in libraries, centralized political institutions, or a dominant religious organization, it was varied and idiosyncratic.[15] Although much indigenous knowledge was closely linked to religious specialists, the fact that Yhwhism did not command an intellectual consensus until after 600 BCE enabled many forms of knowledge to flourish. As Morton Smith writes, "Although the cult of Yahweh is the principal concern of the Old Testament, it may not have been the principal religious concern of the Israelites."[16] Smith notes that long after the period described in the book of Judges, the ancient Hebrews intermarried with their Canaanite neighbors, named their children after non-Yhwhist deities, frequented Canaanite fertility shrines, honored El and Baal, and constructed high places and sacred pillars symbolizing the Canaanite fertility goddess, Athirat (or Asherah). They also relied on household idols, crafted figurines of naked female deities, used snakes as cultic objects, and made personal seals

---

15. This statement is not meant to deny that stories—for example, tales of the men and women of valor themselves—might have been written down on clay tablets and eventually stored in a royal archive.
16. Smith, *Palestinian Parties and Politics*, 14.

indicating reverence for the sun. Furthermore, in times of great stress they practiced human sacrifice.[17]

Except for reformist interludes, until the time of the exile, even Jerusalem was characterized by a climate of religious toleration, if not interreligious cooperation.[18] In a gesture that was not unusual, in the year 842 BCE King Ahaziah of Judah consulted the god Baal-zebub of Ekron to obtain a prognosis regarding the illness that eventually took his life (2 Kgs. 1:2–17). Later, King Manasseh (687–642 BCE) constructed high places for Baal and Asherah, worshiped the host of heaven, relied on soothsaying and augury, dealt with mediums and wizards, and sacrificed his own son.[19] According to a detailed account by Ezekiel, formerly a temple priest, even the Jerusalem temple was the site of semisecret non-Yhwhist rituals as late as 600 BCE.[20] Smith contends that those cults could not have continued without the tacit, if not active, support of temple officials.[21]

---

17. Ibid., 2–23.
18. For a summary of reform movements, see ibid., 24–29.
19. 2 Kgs. 21:1–9. For more details about the multiplicity of religious ideas and practices in Israel, see chapter 2, "Religious Parties among the Israelites before 587," in Smith, *Palestinian Parties and Politics*, 11–42. See also Jean-Michel de Tarragon, "Witchcraft, Magic, and Divination in Canaan and Ancient Israel," in *Civilizations of the Ancient Near East*, ed. Jack M. Sasson (New York: Charles Scribner, 1995), 3:2071–81; and Bill T. Arnold, "Necromancy and Cleromancy in 1 and 2 Samuel," *Catholic Biblical Quarterly* 66 (2004): 199–213. Both de Tarragon and Arnold describe a wide variety of practices enabling people to gain access to special knowledge. Some of the evidence for such practices comes from the many detailed and specific condemnations in the Hebrew Bible; other evidence comes from nonjudgmental or favorable depictions. Casting lots, interpreting dreams, and seeking out prophecies were all regarded as acceptable, even by later editors (1 Sam. 28:6 and Num. 27:21). Although by the time Deuteronomy was compiled (ca. 640–600 BCE) astrology, soothsaying, sacrificing a child, consulting necromancers or wizards, going to a charmer or sorcerer, and augury had been condemned by people associated with the god Yhwh, the long list in Deut. 18:9–14 of such strategies for accessing knowledge suggests that they were still being practiced. For a discussion of human sacrifice, see J. Andrew Dearman, "The Tophet in Jerusalem: Archeology and Cultural Profile," *Journal of Northwest Semitic Languages* 22, no. 1 (1996): 59–71.
20. Ezekiel 18. As well as being a priest, Ezekiel was a prophet prone to ecstasy and he was famous for his dramatizations of calamitous events (he mimicked the siege of Jerusalem, the tragedy of military defeat, and the plight of going into exile). Deported to Babylon in 597, Ezekiel remained there for another 15 years.
21. Smith, *Palestinian Parties and Politics*, 20.

The fact that partisans, both in the northern and southern kingdoms, occasionally engaged in missions to cleanse the land of religious competitors is proof more of syncretism than of orthodoxy. In the very first century of the monarchy's existence, Judah's king Asa (913–873 BCE) tried to ban ritual copulation, destroy ancestral idols, and take action against his mother because of her devotion to Asherah. Asa's efforts are evidence of the vitality of non-Yhwhist institutions of knowledge about fertility and fate. Not long after, in the north, during the reign of Ahab of Israel (869–850 BCE), the competition between the prophets of Baal and of Yhwh turned violent as leaders on both sides attacked and killed large numbers of their rivals. First, Queen Jezebel murdered the prophets of Yhwh and then Elijah slew the prophets of Baal. As described in 1 Kings 18 and 19, this was a competition among purveyors of indigenous knowledge—specifically, experts in the control of rainfall and lightning. Elijah's successful purge of Baal prophets came after a lengthy drought, a calamity that would have seriously undermined the partisans of Baal, a god renowned for his power to guarantee moisture and fertility.[22]

The massacre of failed workers in magic has parallels to the waves of violent retaliation against diviners in African societies. After periods of stress—drought, disease, famine, invasion, or defeat—people have turned against spiritual leaders formerly revered for their knowledge about the weather, health, and defense. This may explain Gideon's deed of defiance in destroying his father's shrine. Such acts of revenge do not signal a rejection of the underlying philosophical principles of indigenous wisdom, only of the men and

---

22. For Baal's importance to agricultural people depending on rain, see Fred E. Woods, *Water and Storm Polemics Against Baalism in Deuteronomic History* (New York: Peter Lang, 1994), 13–14. Woods notes that one of Baal's praise names was "rider of the clouds" (ibid., 14).

women claiming to dispense the knowledge and of the ultimate origin of their information.

The book of Judges offers little information about the specific content of indigenous knowledge dispensed at the provincial level, but the book is full of references to the demand for such knowledge. While very wealthy, powerful, or desperate individuals may have traveled long distances to seek guidance, most people would have no choice but to rely on resident professionals working at hometown ancestor shrines, divining sites, and fertility temples. Because much of the demand was for locally relevant indigenous knowledge, experts offering advice about disease, conflict resolution, marital relations, fertility, personal safety, travel, commerce, and wealth would have been local as well. Such particularity would have resulted in variety, creativity, and some degree of specialization.

An important task of local diviners would have been to adjudicate charges of infidelity. Mieke Bal's *Death and Dissymmetry* is a reminder of the enormous level of gender tension described, directly and indirectly, in Judges. In Bal's view, gender-based violence was a result of the efforts of husbands, fathers, and lineages to assert control over females. At a time when women—daughters, wives, and concubines—were a major source of wealth and when a man's stature was measured by his progeny, female fidelity was an abiding economic, social, and legal concern. Therefore, ancient Israel's reservoir of indigenous knowledge offered remedies to deal with accusations of female unfaithfulness. Numbers 5:11–31 outlines one of the very early magical-judicial procedures used by experts to determine paternity. After committing a curse to writing, the ordeal's administrator washed off the words with water, which had been sprinkled with dust taken from the floor of a shrine. The woman accused of betraying her husband was then required to drink this "water of bitterness." In the case of guilt, she would later miscarry.

As Michel de Tarragon observes, the course of action blended magic, ritual, and the judicial.[23] Presumably, the water of bitterness ordeal was commonly used at the divining sites mentioned in Judges.

The desire for information in Israel would have stimulated the multiplication of people willing to pose as purveyors of knowledge. Looking at specifics in Judges, we note that many experts described in the book were tied to a local shrine in a particular geographic region. For example, Deborah offered oracular advice from her sacred oak near Bethel (House of El). Gideon, a diviner par excellence, was based at Ophrah, the site of a divining oak, perhaps in the Jezreel Valley. Elon, whose name means "Oak," may not have been remembered as an individual at all, but as a line of diviners working at a place of oracular inquiry located midway between the Sea of Chinnereth (later known as the Sea of Galilee) and the Mediterranean Sea (Judg. 12:11).[24] While local shrines would have been associated with resident spirits or ancestors, even powerful gods such as Yhwh and El were thought by some to have only parochial powers, thus exercising jurisdiction over restricted locales and phenomena. Excavations at Kuntillet 'Ajrud in the northeast Sinai Desert have uncovered early eighth-century Hebrew inscriptions to "Yahweh of Teman (Edom)" and to "Yahweh of Shomron (Samaria)."[25] During the time of King Ahab, advisors to the king of Syria assured their monarch that he would easily prevail against Israel because Yhwh was a god of the hills, not a god of the valleys (1 Kgs. 20:23, 28). Ahab's victory proved those information experts wrong. In the Song of Deborah, there is an explicit boast about Yhwh's ability to provide

---

23. De Tarragon, "Witchcraft, Magic, and Divination," 2078.
24. While Elon may have been a personal name or title, I believe it is more likely that the word referred to a divination site. From my own work in Africa I know that place names or impersonal titles often find their way into lists of rulers or diviners.
25. See Ze'ev Meshel, "Kuntillet 'Ajrud," in *Oxford Encyclopaedia of Archeology in the Near East* (New York: Oxford University Press, 1997), 3:311–12. These inscriptions also refer to Yhwh's Asherah (wife).

assistance beyond the mountainous desert region where he was thought to reside (Judg. 5:4–5, 19–21). When Gideon began his career, he sided with Yhwh, but performed a series of tests to determine whether Yhwh or Baal had the greater control over sources of water (dew, rain, and the torrents of the deep). If particular gods had more power over specific natural realities or over certain regions of the land, then it follows that their spokespeople would be regarded as having greater expertise in those domains.

Some forms of knowledge were associated with specific ethnic groups or economic enterprises. The Kenites, a tribe of metalworking specialists who traveled throughout Israel, were native to the desert region south of the Dead Sea. Midianite and Kenite caravan leaders, who may have passed through the hill country in an effort to circumvent Canaanite tax collectors, were the guardians of commercial expertise. In turn, these merchants/smugglers relied on local guides, suppliers, and guards who offered their specialized knowledge for sale.[26] Similar to the Kenites, the Levites, another desert people, itinerated around the land offering divination services to whoever would pay. Perhaps capitalizing on claims of an exotic origin, one of the leading Levitical families declared descent from Phinehas, an Egyptian name meaning "African" or "black man."[27]

The Mobilization and Monopolization of Knowledge by the Mighty Men

The personalized, idiosyncratic, and dispersed nature of knowledge—both secular and supernatural—meant that it was not easily controlled. Consequently, a big man, house, town, or

---

26. See J. David Schloen, "Caravans, Kenites and *Casus Belli*: Enmity and Alliance in the Song of Deborah," *Catholic Biblical Quarterly* 55, no. 1 (1993): 18–38.
27. The reference to Phinehas may indicate that indigenous knowledge from sub-Saharan Africa had found its way to Palestine.

institution able to capture and monopolize wealth in knowledge would have been richly rewarded. Many details in the book of Judges prove that big men were successful, not only because they themselves dispensed knowledge, but also because they mobilized subordinates with specialized knowledge or information. Some of that "intellectual wealth" was consumed directly by the big men; other knowledge was distributed, almost in an entrepreneurial manner. However, because legends and oral histories tend to present the past as a parade of archetypal individuals, the "compositional" and institutional nature of big men's and women's knowledge efforts is easily overlooked.

In Judges, Gideon is depicted as the quintessential man of knowledge. Like Deborah, the other prominent diviner in Judges, he did not rely on others for supernatural or secular information. Gideon himself was a source of indigenous knowledge, knowledge that he both consumed directly and provided to others in return for their support or payments. As a powerful diviner, Gideon claimed to have received knowledge directly from the supernatural realm. He then used that knowledge to achieve military success, to operate a celebrated site for dispensing information, and to enrich and enlarge his house. Although Gideon (a name best translated as "Hacker") earned renown for his brutality and confrontational nature, he owed his position to his abilities as a diviner. Gideon proved those powers by directly challenging the supremacy of Baalism. Not only did he destroy a Baal altar along with its Asherah pillar (both the altar and the pillar had been operated by his family), he also demonstrated his ability to conjure forth dew, a natural element regarded as under Baal's control. After showing his ability to make dew appear on a fleece while the surrounding earth remained dry, he repeated the display, except that in the second demonstration he commanded the earth to be damp and the fleece dry. Gideon was also described as skilled at interpreting dreams; supposedly even the enemy Midianites were aware of his power in that domain. In addition, Gideon used the powers of divination to select the warriors and develop the strategy for his stunning victory over the Midianites. In the final story of Gideon's life, he is portrayed as a triumphant war leader who melted down the spoils of battle to create divining implements. So successful was he that the book of Judges claimed that all Israel came to his shrine and that Gideon employed his entire family as keepers of an oracular site. In fact, Judges indicates that Gideon chose to manage his divination operation rather than pursue the position of king (Judg. 8:22–27). Gideon's legendary preference for divination over monarchy symbolizes a central theme in the book of Judges, and it supports the argument advanced by Jane Guyer. Gideon's story makes the implicit, but unmistakable, claim that the intellectual domain (represented by divination) held sway over the military or political realms. According to the Gideon saga, the knowledge available through oracular inquiry or dreams was regarded as more valuable than military strategy, brute strength, or a reputation for mercilessness.

Gideon's story suggests that powerful elements of continuity and transformation were at work shaping the profession of divination in the premonarchic period. In terms of continuity, Gideon was simply carrying on a tradition, conducting the family business. His father Joash, the head of a large and prosperous house, was the proprietor of a prominent Baal shrine and presumably was the region's foremost oracular expert. Gideon's first recorded actions—determining the legitimacy of the messenger of Yhwh, building an altar, and offering a sacrifice—indicate that he was an able practitioner of his father's craft (Judg. 6:11–27). The fact that, even at the end of his career, the main business of Gideon's own house was divination reinforces the conclusion that Gideon regarded divination as his line of work, perhaps as a profession more lucrative than warfare. Yet, even though he continued in the steps of his father, Gideon was an audacious innovator. Although he maintained the traditional techniques of the enterprise of divination—altars, sacrifices, oracles, spectacular displays of verification, and perhaps sleight of hand—he revolutionized his family's religious/business establishment by changing deities, thus transferring his loyalty from Baal to Yhwh. Presumably the decision was based on his belief that Baal had become increasingly ineffective and that Yhwh was the deity of the future. If Gideon's story is representative of a more generalized phenomenon, then the rise of Yhwhism can be attributed as much to the pragmatic calculations of wealthy strongmen operating divination establishments as to the religious sentiments of oppressed peasants seeking social justice.

The preeminence of knowledge over military or political power also is evident in the tale of Barak (Judges 4 and 5). While Gideon was a man of valor celebrated for his powers of divination, Barak was a big man who depended on the services of another, the renowned diviner Deborah. Thus, Barak is remembered as a man of valor who relied on a woman, not for her labor or sexuality, but for her knowledge.[28] The text describes in detail Deborah's function as an established knowledge expert. Not only does the story identify her as a prophetess, it also notes that "she was judging," that she was presiding (sitting), that she was stationed under a tree (probably an oak), and that Israelites "went to her for judgment" (*mišpāṭ* – משפט) in response to a particular inquiry.[29] The probability that

---

28. Robert Boling suggests that Deborah may have been Barak's wife. The marital link is posited because the name Barak means "Lightning" (suggesting his power with rain and thunder) and because Deborah is identified as the wife of Lappidoth (Torch or Flasher). *Judges: A New Translation with Introduction and Commentary*, Anchor Bible 6A (Garden City, NY: Doubleday, 1975), 95. Other scholars have not repeated this assertion. The story of Deborah and Barak is told in prose form in Judges 4 and as an epic poem in chapter 5.
29. Although the later Deuteronomistic editor claims that all the big men "judged," Deborah is the only figure identified by the epic-bardic storyteller as acting in a judicial capacity, as passing out judgments (*mišpāṭîm* – משפטים).

the prophetess's tree was the renowned Oak of Weeping, located at the gravesite of the matriarch Rebekah's nursemaid Deborah, is also significant (Gen. 35:8).[30] The term "weeping" (*bākût* – בכות) reinforces the likelihood that Deborah's primary function was divining answers to legal disputes, for "weeping" is linked to cases of legal pleading or appeal, to times of regret, and to cases where litigants express hope for reversal. The association with Rebekah would have heightened Deborah's prominence as a diviner. Deborah's name, which means "honeybee," may offer additional insight into her particular appeal. In Isa. 8:19, the prophet speaks of the whirring and chirping of diviners. The reference may be to the utterances coming out of the mouths of seers overtaken by ecstatic seizures that bridged the gap between the temporal and supernatural worlds. Perhaps the whirring and chirping of ecstatic expressions was Deborah's trademark.

Although the text offers few additional details about how Deborah functioned at her oracular site, a tale involving the seer Samuel and the young man Saul provides a more complete picture of an early divination operation. The story in 1 Samuel 9 is rich in relevant detail. Saul is introduced as the son of Kish, a mighty man of valor (גבור חיל). When Kish's herd of donkeys became lost, Saul was dispatched to find them. Unsuccessful, he was about to return home when his servant told Saul about a seer, "a man of Elohim . . . held in honor, whose sayings come to pass" (1 Sam. 9:6). Furthermore, the servant stated that he was carrying enough silver to pay the seer. Arriving at a city where the seer was practicing, Saul and the servant learned that the seer was about to bless a sacrifice the townspeople were offering on the official high place. According to the story, Yhwh had revealed to the seer that Saul would be coming

---

30. The fact that both Rebekah's nurse and the diviner described in Judges 4 were named Deborah suggests that the name was a positional title handed down from one practitioner to the next.

to consult him. When Saul approached the seer (at this point in the story identified as Samuel) the seer invited the handsome young man to accompany him to the high place where they would eat together. Without any prompting from Saul, Samuel informed him the donkeys had been found. Then Samuel brought Saul and his servant into the hall where they sat at the head of a table with thirty guests Samuel had invited. Samuel ordered the cook to bring a choice portion of meat from the sacrifice (the leg and thigh) which was set before Saul. After the meal, they returned to the city where Samuel provided lodging to Saul. The next morning, in a private ceremony, Samuel anointed Saul with oil, thus empowering him to rule over Israel.

If the example of Samuel can be used as an instructive parallel, we can assume the following about Deborah. She would have boasted divine authority, she would have been held in honor by the people, and she would have carried a title. Not only would Deborah have been the proprietor of a shrine/divining place, she would have had a separate private residence in a town, and she would have had access to a hall and a cooking staff to entertain people coming to inquire of her. Finally, she would have awed her petitioners with personal information only they knew, she would have offered specific answers to questions posed by her visitors, she would have offered sacrifices to give thanks or to determine divine approval for her pronouncements, she would have expected payment for her services, and she would have bestowed supernatural power and blessing on favored petitioners.

The knowledge Deborah offered to Barak was relevant for the battlefield. More important than the specific tactical advice about how Barak should organize his battle was Deborah's counsel regarding the celestial forces. First, Deborah told Barak that Yhwh himself had commanded him to act. Second, she assured Barak that the spiritual world was aligned in his favor. Finally, as the human voice of the divine realm, she promised to accompany Barak into battle. Barak's refusal to go to war without her is a measure of the importance people assigned to the role of a diviner. While most commentators interpret Barak's hesitancy as an example of cowardice, clearly it is evidence of prudence. The presence of a spiritual expert with the ability to interpret supernatural forces would have been considered as essential as proper weaponry or an advantageous field position. As celebrated in Deborah's song, the ancient Israelites believed a battle unfolded in the heavens as well as on earth. According to the song, Yhwh, marching from the mountains of the Sinai desert, joined the battle. The fact that the "stars in heaven fought" and that rain, clouds, and thunder took part indicates that the real contest was a struggle between the desert god Yhwh and the storm god Baal (Judg. 5:4–5, 20).[31] Given that reality, only a foolhardy commander would have ventured into a fight without an expert on the supernatural at his side.[32] Although Barak trusted Deborah, who represented the power of Yhwh, other warriors in other battles would have staked their fortunes on the powers of gods such as El, Baal, Molech, or Chemosh.[33]

---

31. Woods, *Water and Storm Polemics*, 65–66. Woods reminds us that Barak's name, Lightning, heightens the supernatural drama. Although not stated by Woods, because images of Baal always portray him holding a lightning bolt, it is very possible that Barak was originally a partisan of Baal and that his reliance on the Yhwhistic prophet Deborah represented a defection from Baal.
32. The practice of relying on diviners in battle continues today in Africa. Before embarking on a cattle raid, the Pokot people of East Africa are careful to consult prophets or seers (*werikoi*) who can foretell the fortunes of an attack. Able to mediate between humans and the gods, the *werikoi* serve as "consultants for rustlers." Without their blessing, Pokot warriors will not act. Although the *werikoi* take no part in the physical fighting, the value of their spiritual participation is recognized by the fact that they receive an equal share of the spoils. See Powon Losuran Kapello, "Conflict among the Pastoralists in Kenya's North Rift Valley," unpublished student paper (Daystar University, Nairobi, Kenya, 1998). Before Westerners dismiss Pokot customs as primitive, they should recall that Americans launched Operation Iraqi Freedom with the assurances of political theorists and religious thinkers that the elemental forces of history—justice and the yearning of every human being for freedom—were on their side.

Gideon and Barak are the best examples of how preindustrial big men in Israel turned to others as much for their knowledge as for their physical work and ability to produce children. However, every other big person depicted in Judges depended upon the composition of knowledge. These leaders acquired people of knowledge as they brokered marriage arrangements, engaged mercenaries, installed their kin as keepers of profitable shrines, hired diviners, and sought out commercial and trade experts.

The view that the big men in Judges regarded women as more than workers and child bearers is supported by the account of Othniel (Judg. 1:11–15). From the story we read that Othniel's initial rise to prominence was the result of kin linkages, military valor, and the good fortune to attract the attention of the region's dominant big man (his lineage elder, Caleb). However, the tale in Judges credits Othniel's material wealth to the shrewdness and negotiating abilities of his forceful wife, Achsah. Given by Caleb to Othniel in return for conquering Kiriath-sepher, Achsah was anything but a docile or uninformed individual useful only for her strength and sexuality. Instead, she is remembered for her skill in cajoling both Othniel and Caleb until her new husband became the owner of cultivable and well-watered land. Although socially subordinate to two men, one her father and the other her husband, she is the one credited with using her knowledge of land, the traditional legal rights accorded to a daughter, and human character to generate wealth for her husband (Judg. 1:11–15).[34]

---

33. To avert catastrophe during times of great danger, high-ranking Israelites offered human sacrifices to Molech, a Canaanite deity linked to the underworld. For the identity of Molech, see John Day, *Molech: A God of Human Sacrifice in the Old Testament* (Cambridge: Cambridge University Press, 1989). Chemosh was the god of Moab to whom victories were attributed (Judg. 11:24).
34. The story's wording in Hebrew is a bit unclear. It may be that the storyteller pictures Othniel "nagging" his wife so that she then negotiates with her father. In any case, Achsah is useful for her facility in striking a deal, not for her ability to work or bear children.

Although less permanent than alliances established through marriage, many mighty men acquired the services of knowledge experts by hiring mercenaries. The example of Eglon and Ehud is perhaps the most revealing (Judg. 3:12–30). Ehud is remembered as the man who defeated Eglon, a powerful ruler from Moab located east of the Dead Sea. The narrator introduces Ehud, a left-handed Benjaminite, as one of Eglon's top mercenary vassals. Traveling with his own company of warriors, Ehud collected taxes and maintained order in or near his home area. Thus, we can infer that Eglon engaged Ehud as much for his local political knowledge—knowledge about whom to trust, whom to fear, who had wealth, who had influence, and who might cooperate—as for his military skill.[35]

The most dramatic incident in the story of Eglon and Ehud revolved around supernaturally derived information. Traveling home with his troops after presenting his tribute to Eglon, Ehud stopped at the stone images at Gilgal where he would have had an opportunity to consult a diviner.[36] Ordering his men to remain at Gilgal, he alone returned to Eglon's palace where he gained a private audience with the Moabite big man by promising to reveal the contents of a confidential message from the supreme god, El. Once Eglon dismissed his attendants in order to receive the message in private,

---

35. Felicitas Becker provides an informative description about how early twentieth-century African big men gathered subordinates with knowledge. See Becker, "Traders, 'Big Men' and Prophets: Political Continuity and Crisis in the Maji Maji Rebellion in Southeast Tanzania," *Journal of African History* 45, no. 1 (January 2004): 1–22. Becker highlights the interplay among the forces of commerce, the powers of divination, and the dangers of political insecurity. She goes on to chronicle the efforts of big men who competed to gain control of trade, magic, and warfare in order to protect and advance their positions. The parallels between Becker's account and the story of Ehud and Eglon are striking.
36. It is also possible that, like Gideon, Ehud may have conducted divination rituals himself. The word "Gilgal" means "circle of stones." Such circles, which can still be found in eastern Palestine, were used for political, military, and religious rituals. Gilgal was an especially prominent site. Samuel went to Gilgal as part of his circuit; Saul was made king and deposed as king at Gilgal. See James Muilenburg, "Gilgal," in *The Interpreter's Dictionary of the Bible* (Nashville: Abingdon Press, 1962), 2:398–99.

Ehud drew out a double-edged sword and assassinated the excessively fat (wealthy and greedy) lord. Exiting through the vestibule, Ehud did not raise the suspicions of the king's attendants who are portrayed as somewhat dim-witted. Returning to the west side of the Jordan, Ehud again stopped at the stone images. Capitalizing on that visit, Ehud rallied the people of the hill country of Ephraim by claiming he had received the message that Yhwh would support a revolt against Moab.

A duplicitous man in the middle, Ehud relied on his military, political, and supernatural knowledge to gain power. He used his military and political knowledge to advance in the ranks of Eglon's officials. Then, employing deception, stealth, and a claim that he possessed supernatural information, he killed his suzerain and sought the favor of the Ephraimites who earlier must have regarded him as a self-serving mercenary traitor. Significantly, Ehud betrayed his Moabite master by offering access to the counsel of El while he won over the people of Ephraim by convincing them that he was privy to encouraging information from Yhwh. Although the story ends with the complete defeat of the Moabite overlords, we should not assume this freed the Ephraimites from all political obligation. Ruling as their protective big man, Ehud would have continued to collect tribute. Ehud's story shows that all players—Eglon, Eglon's attendants, Ehud, and the people of Ephraim—valued and sought information. The story also contains a warning that knowledge could be a double-edged sword. As other stories in Judges make clear (for example, the accounts of Abimelech and Samson) gaining knowledge and knowledgeable subordinates were essential for any man of valor. However, that knowledge could be employed treacherously to destroy those it had previously elevated.[37]

Near the end of the book of Judges, a story about the house of Micah offers a negative commentary on the relationship between men of valor and the practitioners of indigenous knowledge.[38] This fictive tale censures men of valor for engaging professional diviners for commercial gain and criticizes the seers as untrustworthy (Judges 17). The narrative, written by the humanist, begins with a gift of silver that the big man Micah received from his mother. Taking the metal, Micah commissioned the manufacture of teraphim (divinatory objects) and an ephod, which he placed in a shrine in his house. He then installed a junior member of the house (a "son") as the shrine priest. The fact that Micah intended the shrine as a venture for profit, not just as a convenient place for personal consultation, is made clear by what happened next. According to the story, Micah contracted the services of a young divination professional (a sojourning Levite from Judah). In return for acting as the official priest at the shrine, the Levite was to receive a salary of ten pieces of silver per year (the divining equipment had cost two hundred pieces), a suit of apparel, and room and board. At this point in the tale, Micah commented, "Now I know Yhwh will prosper me because I have a Levite as a priest" (Judg. 17: 13).

Continuing the story, the book of Judges describes how the shrine functioned as an entrepreneurial institution. Five mighty men of valor from the landless tribe of Dan stopped at the shrine to get advice about a reconnoitering expedition they were planning far north of the Sea of Chinnereth. After consulting Yhwh through divination, the Levite assured the five that Yhwh approved of their mission. "Go in victory (šālôm – שלום)," he said. Although not stated in the text, we must assume that the men paid the Levite for his services at the

---

37. In writing about Tanzanian big men, Felicitas Becker notes that they also had to contend with double-dealing on the part of the information experts with whom they had allied ("Traders, 'Big Men' and Prophets," 19–22).
38. While the story of Micah could have been an older tale retold by the humanist, the narrative's sophisticated literary structure, the cynical tone of the story, and the fact that the main protagonist is a Levite all suggest a late date for the account.

shrine. The Levite's counsel was reliable and the expedition proved a great success. Far north of the Sea of Chinnereth, the five men came upon Laish, the perfect prey. A prosperous, unwalled community, Laish had no powerful allies and no jealous imperial suzerain. The spies returned to their military encampment and invited their "brothers" to take advantage of the good fortune. In the end, a Danite force of six hundred men (i.e., a large number) set out to plunder the defenseless peasants the spies had found with the help of the Levite diviner.

The story, a striking testimonial to the value of knowledge dispensed at Micah's shrine, ended happily for the Danites. Sadly, the big man Micah was less fortunate. On their way to pillage and capture Laish, the Danite company made a second visit to Micah's shrine. Recognizing the value of the Levite and his implements, they had determined to seize the diviner and the tools of his trade. Although prepared to forcibly abduct the Levite, they were able to entice him peacefully with the offer of a more lucrative position, one that involved working for an entire tribe rather than merely one house. According to the story, the Levite went with a "glad heart" (Judg. 18:20). But Micah, who relied on the shrine as an important source of revenue, lamented his loss of income with the words, "What have I left?" (Judg. 18:24). Although the big man Micah mustered his own warriors to retrieve the Levite and the shrine objects, the overwhelming superiority of the Danites forced him to retreat, both militarily and economically.

Conclusions

The stories about the men of valor in Judges illustrate the importance of knowledge for achieving and maintaining power and wealth. Contained in the minds of living people rather than committed to writing, indigenous knowledge in premonarchic Israel was diffused and idiosyncratic. Although hard to access and difficult to control, indigenous knowledge was regarded as essential to the success of all human endeavors. Specialized knowledge, often connected to the supernatural and frequently available only at shrines, was needed for raising crops, breeding animals, conceiving children, engaging in commerce, coping with the weather, determining the fidelity of a valued spouse or daughter, warding off disease, protecting against witchcraft, and winning a battle. Men of valor sought this knowledge to guide their own actions and also to redistribute information to their clients. For them it was important to have a superior source of knowledge that they could access or even monopolize.

Gideon is one example of a mighty man of valor who derived power not just from his wealth or martial abilities, but from his claim of extraordinary access to knowledge from Yhwh. Gideon aggressively confronted the spiritual and intellectual foundations of a rival divination site dedicated to Baal and his consort. Exercising the power of divination and dramatically demonstrating that Yhwh himself supported his revolutionary claims, Gideon launched his career by successfully challenging the house of his father, the political ambitions of his brothers, and the leaders of his town. Gideon's accomplishments, both as a warrior and as an intermediary with the realm of the supernatural, enabled him to establish and prosper the house of Jerubbaal.[39] Eventually he organized a profitable divination center where he employed his kin. Gideon's story claims that the ability to dispense specialized indigenous knowledge could be a man of valor's most valuable political resource.

Other men of valor turned to established experts for knowledge. Unlike Gideon, who achieved power and fame as a spiritual medium in his own right, Barak is an example of a man of valor who made

---

39. After his battle with Baal, Gideon received the praise name, Jerubbaal, "Let Baal contend with him." See chapter 4, "Power and Honor," for further discussion of the name.

no claim to having extraordinary insights into the mind of Yhwh. Instead, he enlisted the services of a professional diviner, the renowned prophetess Deborah, who operated a divination site in the hill country of Ephraim. Deborah's ability to discern the rise and fall of celestial forces and to predict the outcome of temporal battles helped Barak in his decision about going to war. While a warrior like Barak might engage a seer to predict the future, men of valor like Abimelech and Jephthah relied on knowledge experts who specialized in legal matters such as writing contracts and conducting diplomacy. Other leaders—for example, the Moabite king Eglon—hired skilled mercenaries whose understanding of local culture and tribute collection made them valuable subordinates. The tale of Eglon and Ehud also suggests that rulers sometimes turned to their underlings for supernatural information. As can be seen in the account of Othniel and Achsah, a man of valor might obtain knowledge through a marriage relationship. In acquiring a well-informed and forceful wife, Othniel established himself on the path to material success and on the way to becoming head of a powerful house.

However, as illustrated by the stories of Eglon, Barak, Samson, and Micah, assembling people with knowledge was fraught with uncertainty. Subordinates, wives, and clients could distort, manipulate, or steal information so that it became a tool of defeat and death. For Eglon the martial acumen of a hired mercenary literally became a destructive two-edged sword. Barak learned that the information he received from a woman of knowledge was not uniformly positive and did not guarantee him honor. Samson discovered that treacherous rivals and disloyal lovers might seek privileged information in order to undermine and destroy. In fact, the legend of Samson suggests that a man of valor had to be most on guard against those who were closest to him. Stories in other books of the Hebrew Bible—for example, the accounts of Eli and Samuel— indicate that experts dispensing indigenous knowledge, even supernatural information, could not always be trusted to act with fairness and disinterest. Finally, looking back at the period described in Judges, the humanist writer reminds readers that knowledge professionals could be hard to control, worked mainly for pecuniary gain, and might easily be induced to switch loyalty.

The book of Judges demonstrates that ancient men of valor prized indigenous knowledge in spite of the hazards associated with composing that knowledge. Along with military strength and the influence derived from the distribution of wealth, big men depended on the use of temporal and supernatural information to gain and maintain power. At a time when earthly political relationships were unsettled and when people believed the forces of heaven were shifting, information from Yhwh was gaining ascendancy over indigenous knowledge associated with El or Baal. Except for Abimelech, the great heroes in Judges regarded Yhwh as the ultimate source of the most reliable and useful information. Consequently, they hired professionals, gathered associates, and assembled clients in an effort to collect, use, and dispense this information.

The fact that the heroes in Judges valued knowledge is evidence of their awareness that martial force and economic power were not their only political and social resources. Although there is no indication that they ever hesitated to use violence, their respect for indigenous knowledge indicates that they had a range of tools to exercise control over their regions, towns, and houses. The men of valor should not be remembered only as individuals who relied on brute force and the exploitation of others for their labor and ability to bear children.

3

Power and Trust

Politics is an always uncertain and often dangerous enterprise, but wielding power as a big person in a patron-client setting is especially precarious. Every step in the career of such an individual is marked with peril. Seeking, gaining, exercising, maintaining, and even relinquishing power are all fraught with risk. As noted in the previous two chapters, the use of force and the distribution of spoils are common strategies leaders turn to as they seek to enforce compliance or purchase loyalty. Not as well recognized are the less violent, less hazardous, and less costly approaches used by leaders. The present chapter explores the ways political leaders in premonarchic Israel consciously tried to encourage allegiance by cultivating a reputation for being constant and trustworthy. Their goal was to build a reputation for reliability, thus creating a predictable environment in which orders would be followed and agreements would be honored without the constant need to employ force or relinquish wealth.

Big men, whether traditional village chiefs managing a population numbered in scores or modern dictators ruling millions, face a daunting challenge. In *Strong Societies, Weak States,* political scientist Joel Migdal explains the predicament facing personalized leaders. At its core, the problem is one of loyalty and trust. Unfortunately, the subordinates most needed by a big man for his own protection and policy implementation are the very people who pose the greatest threat. For example, a head of state needs commanders to organize external and internal security. The same leader must rely on other officials to oversee the collection of revenues and supervise regional and local administrators. The risk is that when those officials have the requisite power, knowledge, and capital to be effective public servants, they also have the resources to build an independent power base and challenge their superior. In order to deal with the situation, contemporary big men and women use a combination of rewards, promises, punishments, and threats. Placing rivals in jail on trumped-up charges, neutering enemies by offering them lucrative cabinet posts in exchange for compliance, frequently shuffling high-level appointees so none has a chance to solidify a constituent base, dangling opportunities for fiscal malfeasance in front of financially burdened underlings, using spies to monitor "trusted" aides, engaging in blackmail, and resorting to extortion are some of the ways modern strongmen retain control. However, that control is tenuous. Migdal notes that even very adept and heartless leaders find it difficult to survive long-term.[1]

If wealth, force, cunning, and ruthlessness are not sufficient and are too costly to guarantee security for big men and women, those leaders must turn to other political resources. Ideally, using those resources should not deplete a leader's possessions or destroy his or

---

1. Joel Migdal, *Strong Societies, Weak States* (Princeton: Princeton University Press, 1988). In studying modern warlords, William Reno describes the ways these most rapacious of big men are threatened and/or burdened by the existence of government institutions. Therefore, warlords prefer to bypass normal institutions of government. Reno, *Warlords and African States* (Boulder, CO: Lynne Reinner, 1999).

her political capital based on friendship and pragmatic alliances. A central theme of the Hebrew Bible's book of Judges is the struggle to achieve constancy in a world of political peril. In addition to drawing on the typical set of tools available to strongmen (wealth, bravery, generosity, kin linkages, and physical strength), the powerful leaders in Judges sought to cultivate an additional political resource: a reputation for trustworthiness and reliability. Through the skillful use of contracts—formalized with bilateral agreements, blessings and curses, oaths, and rituals involving human sacrifice—they attempted to forge binding agreements and demonstrate that they could be counted on to complete their promises, no matter what the personal cost.

According to Judges, while deceit, revenge, trickery, and double-dealing were to be expected from enemies or political rivals, not even allies, friends, family, and lovers could be trusted to uphold agreements. Consequently, the quest for contractual reliability is a dominant theme in the book of Judges. Like a trompe l'oeil in an illustration, once drawn to the reader's attention, contracts dominate the tableau. The many specific phrases such as "he spoke all his words before the face of Yhwh" (*waydabbēr 'et-kol-dĕbārāyw lipnê yhwh* – וידבר את־כל־דבריו לפני יהוה) or "we will deal faithfully with you" (*wĕʿāśînû 'immĕkā ḥesed* – ועשינו עמך חסד) indicate how frequently protagonists in Judges used formal contract language as they brokered political deals. More important, accounts of the big men Abimelech and Jephthah focus almost entirely on agreements they arranged with their supporters, allies, and adversaries. Although less central, key episodes in the stories about Barak and Samson deal with contracts. In addition, Samson's story includes a discussion of riddles and wagers, recreational simulations of real-life contracts.

Broken Promises and Scheming Subordinates

Later monarchic and exilic writers who compiled the final versions of Judges begin the book with two chapters of commentary about political precariousness (Judg. 1:1–3:6). Invasions, incomplete conquests, and military defeats are the stock of a litany of setbacks at the tribal and national level. In chapter 1, the overall formulaic recitation of failure is punctuated by three brief stories the humanist editor inserted as reminders of the reversals and challenges experienced by individual political leaders, important houses, or communities.[2] According to the message of these three pericopes, a big man might be brought down by rival counterparts, by outsiders living in his territory, or by his own ambitious kin. The first tale, that of Adoni-bezek (lord of Bezek), is a commentary on the uncertain fortunes of a petty potentate typical of Syria-Palestine in the centuries immediately before 1000 BCE (Judg. 1:5–7).[3] Adoni-bezek recalls a time when he had exercised authority over a multitude of defeated kings who were forced to eat scraps from under his table and whose thumbs and great toes he had chopped off. This account of the victorious king feasting while his humiliated and disfigured underlings consume leftovers is a vivid symbolic reference to patronage, an institution often described by the cliché of eating.[4] Adoni-bezek's description of lavish consumption and stingy

---

2. While chapter 2 was compiled by the Deuteronomistic editor(s) writing after the time of King Josiah (640–609 BCE), and chapter 1 was added by an even later editor living after the fall of Jerusalem in 587, the four short tales embedded in the two chapters date from much earlier times.

3. Bezek (בזק) may be related to the Aramaic word *bzr* (scatter). The word appears in Dan. 11:24 in reference to a powerful tyrant who scatters wealth. From the text in Daniel, it is not clear if the tyrant was collecting or dispensing the spoils and plunder.

4. One of the most insightful descriptions of the politics of redistribution is that of the medieval thinker John of Salisbury, who recorded his conversation with Pope Adrian VI. According to John, the pope drew an analogy between redistributive patron-client politics and human digestion. John complained that government, like an insatiable stomach, consumed incessantly. In response, Adrian pointed out that such consumption, however much resented, was essential for the life of the larger body. John of Salisbury, *The Statesman's Book*, trans. John Dickinson

redistribution presents the patron-client system as inherently asymmetrical. For the editor, however, the most important point is that Adoni-bezek's fate is a reminder of the fragility of big-man power. By the time Adoni-bezek tells the story, he himself has been defeated, disfigured, and forced to live out the rest of his life in captivity.

The second account in Judges 1 describes how the pressures from a big man's own clients and kin could erode his wealth (Judg. 1:8–15). The big man Caleb was the leader of a prominent Judahite family, a man tradition honored as a close associate of the great conqueror Joshua. Extrapolating from history's memory of Othniel, one of Caleb's subordinates, we may presume that as a big man Caleb built a circle of ambitious and aggressive warrior underlings whom he rewarded with the opportunity to engage in battle, the prospect of marrying a female dependent, and the chance to gain access to land. This is a common pattern marking the dynamic relationship between the big men offering favors and their clients providing services.[5] As the example of Caleb suggests, this arrangement is costly for the patron. In order to win a military victory against a Canaanite stronghold, an action with the potential to bring more land and dependents, Caleb had to transfer some of his wealth in women and fields to the young men whose martial abilities were needed for success in the quest for plunder. Several details in Caleb's story demonstrate the burdensome nature of this transaction. Achsah, the "daughter" given to Othniel, must have come with a substantial dowry since she is described as riding on a donkey, a sign of wealth and status. In addition, Judges recalls that Achsah "nagged" or

---

(1927), in *Great Political Thinkers: Plato to the Present*, ed. William Ebenstein and Alan Ebenstein (New York: Harcourt, 2000), 199–217.

5. Jan Vansina and many others have observed this pattern in African societies. See Jan Vansina, *Paths in the Rainforests: Toward a History of Political Tradition in Equatorial Africa* (Madison: University of Wisconsin Press, 1999).

bargained with her father to upgrade the value of the land he gave to Othniel. While the story, perhaps an archetypal cliché about big men, does not suggest that Caleb's wealth was depleted, it serves as a reminder that a big man's hold on power was purchased at the expense of his accumulated capital.

The humanist editor's third story contains a warning about the danger of strangers and aliens. Judges has numerous references to such people living in or passing through Palestine. Itinerant iron-working Kenites, rootless Levites acting as diviners, Midianites plying their caravan trade, "worthless fellows" hired as mercenaries, and Danites grouped in military encampments are some of the most prominent.[6] Sometimes these outsiders are described as useful and cooperative, at other times they are depicted as objects of suspicion and hostility. Judges 1:22–26 is a pointed reminder of how strangers in one's midst could act treasonously. Every character in the tale is untrustworthy. The narrative begins with spies from the house of Joseph reconnoitering the prominent cultic center Bethel (House of El). As the spies approach, they encounter a man coming out of the city. That man, identified as a Hittite, betrays Bethel by telling the spies how the city's walls could be breached. The theme of treachery and double-dealing is reinforced by the editor's claims that Bethel had formerly been called Luz (Deception) and that the Hittite later relocated far to the north where he founded a second city also named Luz. The editor inserts a crucial bit of irony by reporting a conversation between the spies and the traitor. "Just show us a way into the city," they say, "and we will treat you with covenant loyalty (ḥesed – חסד)!" (Judg. 1:24).[7] This contradictory

---

6. Like the Philistines, the Danites were originally seafaring invaders. Both groups had a reputation for violence. The Levites, featured only in the humanist's tales, were displaced after the fall of the northern kingdom in 722 BCE.
7. The exclamation point is my own. The same term was used when Israelite spies made a deal with the harlot Rahab. In return for betraying her city, she and her family were provided safety

combination of fidelity and treason underscores the theme of the fragility of trust, especially when dealing with ethnic interlopers. In a book about big men who build their fortunes by attracting outside clients, the message is particularly significant. Although big men needed outsiders for their skill, knowledge, and labor, like the Hittite all outsiders were possible turncoats, people potentially willing to traffic with the big man's enemies.

In Judg. 2:1–5, the Deuteronomistic editor offers yet another tale of a broken promise. Intensely theological, the story's main figure is a messenger of Yhwh, who described a contract forged between the people and their deity. According to the messenger, Yhwh earlier had made a promise of land, a pledge sealed by an oath. Although saying that Yhwh had sworn never to break the agreement to provide land to the people, the messenger qualified that commitment by announcing that the land would be shared with Israel's enemies. The reason for the reversal was the people's own violation of the original pact. The Deuteronomistic editor concludes this short account with the report that the people cried out and wept and that they named the place Bochim (*bōkîm* – בכים) or Weepers. Elsewhere in the Hebrew Bible, the term "weeping" refers to attempts to repeal the terms of a contract or to petition to annul a decision. From a religious perspective, this vignette claims that even agreements reached with Yhwh have the potential to unravel. The unavoidable political conclusion is that earthly arrangements would be even more uncertain.

Other chapters in the book of Judges continue the saga of betrayal, double-dealing, and uncertainty. Every character in the main body of the book struggles with the issue of reliability. For leaders, whose power was rooted in their personal ties to political allies, clients,

---

(Josh. 9:12). In Judg. 8:35, the Deuteronomistic editor again used the word *ḥesed* (חסד), but condemns Israel for its lack of faithfulness.

kin, children, and wives, such insecurity posed a deep challenge to their rule. The very first account in the main body of the text—that of the Moabite big man Eglon and his Benjaminite subordinate Ehud—illustrates the depth of the problem. Paradoxically, the very assets a big man most needed in a client were identical to those that could undermine the overlord. In every respect, Ehud demonstrated all of the characteristics a big man desired in his closest associates. Among Ehud's qualities and resources were extraordinary military strength and skill, his own troop of warriors, stature and influence within a conquered ethnic community, the ability to collect tribute from that community for the benefit of the big man, and connections to reliable sources of supernatural information. Furthermore, Ehud is described as a man of great audacity, courage, cunning, and shrewdness. However, as Judges makes clear, the problem facing a big man such as Eglon was that those essential qualities could be turned against him. Remembered as a duplicitous person, Ehud not only defeated Eglon, but it appears that he used the same resources that had once made him a valuable client to establish himself as an independent big man over his own people west of the Jordan River.

According to the account in Judges 3, the Moabite Eglon gained control of Israelite territory in the vicinity of Palm City (Jericho) by recruiting allies or mercenaries from among the Ammonites and Amalekites, peoples living east of the Jordan, and from among the Israelites living west of the river. Only one of those mercenary vassals, a left-handed Benjaminite named Ehud, is described in Judges. Although many commentators have argued that left-handedness was a handicap, in fact it identifies Ehud as an exceptionally skilled warrior. The tribe of Benjamin was renowned for its specially trained fighters (mighty men or *gibbôrîm* – גבורים) who could "shoot arrows or sling stones" with either the right or left hand (1 Chron. 12:2). As a left-handed Benjaminite, Ehud would have been one of those highly competent and feared warriors. It is reasonable, therefore, to assume that he entered Eglon's services because of his martial skills. Like the Ammonites and Amalekites stationed in Israel, he may have started his service under Eglon as a mercenary in another part of the king's domain. Eventually, Ehud may have been rewarded with a position in or near his home area. Elsewhere in Judges, details from the stories about the big men Sisera and Abimelech show that some big men functioned more as bandits attacking trade caravans and pillaging villagers than as institutionalized tax collectors. This may have been the case for Ehud.

Ehud did not serve Eglon as a lone individual. As one of the big man's military agents, Ehud moved about in the company of his own troops. The fact that he led this group of warriors suggests that he was not a mere pacified puppet. For his part, Ehud could not have completely trusted the men in his employ. These individuals would have been "worthless and reckless fellows" (*'ănāšîm rêqîm ûpōḥăzîm* – אנשים ריקים ופחזים), ambitious individuals who attached themselves to any successful man of valor.[8] Rather than following Ehud out of personal devotion, they would have been motivated by the prospect of obtaining booty, access to women, land, and glory. These rootless men would have remained with a leader like Ehud only so long as he could generate rewards or inflict punishment. For his part, while Eglon depended on Ehud's warrior troops, he would have known that the warriors' loyalty was to themselves first, to Ehud second, and to Eglon not at all. Although absolutely essential to Eglon's success, this arrangement was fragile in the extreme.

---

8. Judg. 9:4, referring to the men hired by Abimelech; Judg. 11:3, men hired by Jephthah; and 2 Chron. 13:7, men hired by Jeroboam. The word רק means "empty, vain, and idle," while פחז, which appears only in Judge, suggests "wanton, reckless, boastful, haughty, and lascivious." These qualities describe the type of daring and audacious individuals ready to serve the strongman offering the richest rewards.

The conclusion of the story, which describes Ehud's ability to rally the Israelite people in the region of Mount Ephraim, suggests that Ehud had standing within his own ethnic community. Such respect, whether gained by affection or fear, was another quality that made Ehud valuable for Eglon. Whatever the source of that respect, we must assume the Israelites had very ambiguous sentiments about a man such as Ehud. As Eglon's vassal, Ehud served as the administrative link between the external ruler and the local subjects. Thus, Ehud would have been regarded by his own people as a self-serving mercenary traitor. On the other hand, as a person from the region, he may have been grudgingly respected as a local success and tolerated as an overlord preferable to an Ammonite or Amalekite.

In addition to Ehud's contributions as a military leader, ethnic liaison, and tax collector, he provided Eglon with advice and counsel. Ehud is portrayed as a man who enjoyed a high level of trust on the part of his superior. His ability to gain entrée into Eglon's inner chambers, the fact that he was left completely alone with an unguarded king, and his familiarity with the layout of the big man's house all identify Ehud as a confidant and trusted advisor with easy access to his lord. In fact, the plot of the story revolves around Ehud's role as an advisor. In order to be alone with the king, Ehud informed Eglon that he had a confidential message from the god El. Eglon then dismissed his attendants in order to hear the message in private. At that point, Ehud drew out the double-edged sword he had concealed under his clothes and plunged the weapon into Eglon, whose excessive fat covered up the sword, blade, handle, and all. Ehud then locked the door of the king's chamber and departed. By the time the king's dim-witted attendants broke down the door to the room, Ehud was long gone.

The book of Judges portrays Ehud as an untrustworthy man in the middle. An audacious and shrewd political operative, he used deception, assassination, and stealth to achieve his ends. The story of Ehud points to the fundamental instability of the political process. In order to expand their domains and to enforce their rule, big men such as Eglon needed the services of individuals such as Ehud. But the same qualities of courage, cunning, and deceit that recommended Ehud were then used to overthrow and replace the Moabite suzerain. Starting as Eglon's vassal, Ehud turned the tables and took control of the region he formerly administered (or plundered) as a subordinate. The tribute that formerly flowed across the Jordan now remained in his own coffers. Although Ehud represented everything needed in a vassal, he converted each of his essential qualities into a weapon. This process must have been repeated over and over by other big men in late second-millennium Syria-Palestine.

Besides warrior underlings, big men based much of their power on female dependents. However, the book of Judges cautions its readers that women can turn against their male superiors. One of the most gripping accounts of treachery in the book of Judges is that of Jael and Sisera (Judg. 4:17–22; 5:24–27). Although defeated by Barak, a man from Naphtali, the renowned warrior Sisera was destroyed by a double-dealing woman. Routed by Barak's army, Sisera sought refuge in the tent of an itinerant Kenite woman named Jael. Sisera had every right to expect that he would be safe with Jael. First, her husband was a member of a clan at peace with Sisera's suzerain, Jabin the king of Hazor. Second, Jael was living at Kedesh, a prominent and sacred place of refuge.[9] In the ancient Near East, even enemies

---

9. Judges 4:17 reports that Heber's clan had *shalom* with Jabin. Judges 4:11 notes that Jael's husband, Heber, had pitched his tent at the great oak in Zaanannim near Kedesh. The allusion to the tree suggests this was regarded as a holy place. Joshua 20:7 lists three cities of refuge west of the Jordan River: Kedesh in Galilee, Shechem in Ephraim, and Kiriath-arba (Hebron) in Judah. Four passages in the Hebrew Bible discuss the places of refuge: Exod. 21:12–14; Num. 35:1–34; Deut. 19:1–13; Josh. 20:1–9. The function of a place of refuge was to interrupt the cycle of revenge and ensure that disputes were resolved by recognized authorities, not by individual acts of immediate retaliation. First Kings 1:50 and 2:28 describe how both Adonijah,

and strangers could expect temporary protection at a recognized place of refuge. However, in spite of the ethnic alliance and in spite of the fact that Kedesh was a sacrosanct place of refuge, Jael murdered the man who came to her for asylum.[10]

As many commentators have noted, the tale of Jael and Sisera is filled with symbols of deception and violence.[11] According to the story, it was Jael who initiated contact by coming out to meet Sisera, freely inviting him into her tent, and voluntarily offering assurances of safety. The beleaguered big man accepted protection and sustenance from this female dependent of an allied ethnic group. After lulling him to sleep with comforting womanly gifts (milk and sex), Jael used a tent stake (another symbol of domestic security) to kill the man whom she had promised to shield. From Sisera's perspective, the narrative initially presents Jael as a perfect female subordinate. Welcoming, protective, a provider of nourishment, and sexually available, she gave Sisera everything a big man could want from his women. Sisera's deep sleep, however, symbolically reminds the reader that he was completely oblivious to Jael's true intent and her lethal powers. Never confronting him openly—the text notes that she stole back into his presence quietly—she schemed and acted with fatal stealth. For any big man the message of this story is that behind a comforting and nurturing female exterior lurks a calculating heart that cannot be trusted. Sisera's fate is a warning that female dependents can be fickle schemers and that a man must exercise uninterrupted vigilance.

Solomon's brother and rival, and Joab, Adonijah's backer, sought refuge at the horns of the altar. However, both men were killed by Solomon, who violated the laws regarding refuge.

10. For a discussion of Kedesh as a place of refuge, see Benyamin Mazar, "The Sanctuary of Arad and the Family of Hobab the Kenite," *JNES* 24 (1965): 297–303, cited in Frank Moore Cross, *Canaanite Myth and Hebrew Epic: Essays in the History of the Religion of Israel* (Cambridge: Harvard University Press, 1973), 201n28.
11. See, for example, Mieke Bal, *Death and Dissymmetry: The Politics of Coherence in the Book of Judges* (Chicago: University of Chicago Press, 1988).

The legend of Samson is another reminder of the dangers posed by untrustworthy women. Samson was twice betrayed by a wife or a lover. The first woman was identified as a Philistine woman from Timnah. Although Samson said she was "the right one in my eyes" (Judg. 14:3), it is obvious that he had misjudged her and that she could not be trusted. During the betrothal feasting, Samson made an extravagant wager based on a riddle. Unable to answer the riddle and fearing they were about to lose a costly bet, the Philistine warriors (choice young men or *baḥûrîm* – בחורים) threatened to kill the bride and her family unless she pried the answer out of her new husband. For seven days she nagged Samson until he finally confided in her. Immediately she explained the riddle's answer to her countrymen. Equating her actions with infidelity, Samson accused the Philistine men of having "plowed with his heifer" in order to solve the riddle (Judg. 14:18). The case of the Timnite woman makes it clear that, in addition to female fickleness, ethnic and clan loyalty was a potent source of danger from women. Torn between her new husband and her own ethnic group, the woman decided in favor of ethnicity. The second woman in Samson's story, the Philistine Delilah, also betrayed Samson to her own kin group. This time, instead of taking the big man's wealth, she stole the secret of his strength. As with his Timnite bride, Samson tried to resist the woman's nagging. But, in the end, her persistence and proximity led to his downfall (Judg. 16:4–22).

The stories of Jael, the Timnite woman, and Delilah suggest that people believed women could not be trusted because of their character, ethnic partiality, and allegiance to their natal household.[12]

---

12. In *Death and Dissymmetry*, Bal claims that the fundamental tension about women in the book of Judges reflects a conflict between two social systems, matrilineal and patrilineal. Bal argues that as Israelite society was undergoing a transition from matrilineal to patrilineal, older patterns of marriage and rights over females were being challenged. However, Bal's argument seems weak. First, conflict about women—most acute at marriage when rights are transferred from the woman's family of birth to the family of her husband—is common even in patrilineal societies dependent on female labor. Second, there is no archeological or textual evidence of a primitive

This was an especially urgent problem for big men, who accumulated women for their productive and reproductive abilities. Gathered from many regions and families, such women, although essential for the success of a powerful house, had the potential to undermine that establishment from the inside. The more powerful a big man and the more numerous his women, the more vulnerable he was to the lurking disloyalty of his female charges.

Besides needing to cope with disloyalty from subordinates, both male retainers and female dependents, Syro-Palestinian big men also had to contend with powerful and treacherous rivals competing for their positions. Of all the accounts in Judges of big men in premonarchic times, the story of Abimelech provides the most detail about the inner workings of politics and about peoples' perspectives regarding the nature of political leadership. The narratives about Abimelech in Judges 9 explain his rise to power in the Canaanite city-state of Shechem. The stories also describe the contractual agreements he made with the people he ruled, the religious underpinnings of those political pacts, the administrative and economic arrangements of Abimelech's regime, and the intrigues and political arguments that led to his fall. In describing the complex inner workings of politics, Abimelech's story, which must have been all too typical in late second-millennium Syria-Palestine, is one of struggle, violence, and betrayal.[13]

Although in seeking power Abimelech first turned to his maternal uncles for support, he pointedly drew on an association with his

---

matrilineal family structure in Syria-Palestine. And third, the most important evidence for Bal's assertion is the imaginary and anachronistic story of the Levite and his concubine in Judges 19. That account is almost certainly a literary fantasy created by the humanist in exilic or postexilic times. However, Bal's point that Judges gives an enormous amount of attention to gender struggles—between men and women and between men trying to exert control over women—is entirely correct.

13. The name Abimelech (אבימלך – My Father is a King) has been interpreted to mean that Abimelech was arrogantly boastful and/or that he represents a step on the road to an institutionalized monarch.

putative father, Gideon, the most dominant and ruthless big man in the book of Judges.[14] Not related to Gideon through one of his primary wives, Abimelech claimed a link as the son of one of Gideon's concubines whose kin lived in distant Shechem. By using the prestige of his Gideon connection Abimelech was able to rally his mother's brothers and larger clan family in Shechem. Abimelech's relationship with Gideon points to a number of realities. It indicates that the houses of big men became increasingly politicized as the men gained wealth, power, and stature. In part, for a big man like Gideon, wealth and political reach would have been measured by the number of wives. As agricultural workers, food preparers, and bearers of children, women were essential economic assets. As social and political liaisons with other families, towns, and regions, women served as symbols and instruments of power and standing. They also may have been employed as spies and diplomats. Furthermore, some of the women may have been used by the big man to attract young male subordinates who otherwise had little prospect of gaining dependable access to a female.[15] While large numbers of women were

---

14. While many assume Abimelech was the biological son of Gideon, there are reasons to doubt that assertion. It is possible that Abimelech simply capitalized on Gideon's fame and claimed to be the son of one of Gideon's many women. Nevertheless, the story that a pretender to office would seek support from maternal uncles is plausible. In Central Africa, the multiple patrilineal rivals for power, who all have equal claims to paternal legitimacy, turn to their maternal uncles for material and military support. See Thomas Q. Reefe, *The Rainbow and the Kings: A History of the Luba Empire to 1891* (Berkeley: University of California Press, 1981) and Jan Vansina, *The Children of Woot: A History of the Kuba Peoples* (Madison: University of Wisconsin Press, 1978). Powerful Central African chiefs with a multitude of wives often have a large entourage of youthful male subordinates allowed to establish liaisons with some of the wives. Consequently, the biological parentage of the chief's sons and daughters is never certain. In fact, among some African groups, sons known to be the biological offspring of the chief are ineligible to succeed him. Only the offspring of wives allowed to take other lovers can compete to succeed their father. See John C. Yoder, *The Kanyok of Zaire: An Institutional and Ideological History to 1895* (Cambridge: Cambridge University Press, 1992).
15. See Robert Harms, *River of Wealth, River of Sorrow: The Central Zaire Basin in the Era of the Slave and Ivory Trade, 1500–1891* (New Haven: Yale University Press, 1981). Harms describes how older, wealthy men monopolized the women. Young men had to attach themselves to the elders in order to gain a female partner.

an asset, the large numbers of sons they produced were a danger. Especially in the household of a combative and wealthy man such as Gideon, whose influence extended far beyond his hometown, one could expect the sons to be calculating, contentious, and aggressive. Such sons could pose a threat to their father, their brothers, and to the community. Abimelech's maneuverings also indicate the fluid and tenuous nature of political associations. Early in the story, the man from Shechem relied on reputed kin linkages with Gideon to advance his career; later on those linkages were recalled by rivals in order to discredit him. Such selective uses of the past must have played a constant and critical role in the formation of kin and tribal groups. While genealogies claim to provide an accurate record of descent, they actually indicate who chose or was permitted entry into a family or tribe. Such choices and permissions would have been based on calculations and perceptions of power and opportunity.

After gaining the support of his mother's kin group, Abimelech had to convince Shechem's city elders (baʿălê šĕkem – בעלי שכם), who controlled the town treasure stashed at the house of Baal of the covenant, to bankroll a campaign against his warrior "brothers." The brothers were Gideon's putative sons at Ophrah. Because Judges claims Shechem had been subordinate to Ophrah, the narrator is arguing that Abimelech could rule securely only if he succeeded in neutralizing the influence of his father's house. In hopes that Abimelech could free them from Ophrah, the leaders of Shechem gave him a great deal of silver from the town treasury. Using the money to hire "worthless and reckless fellows," Abimelech then went to Ophrah where he slaughtered all but one of his many "brothers."[16] Like the Roman myth of Romulus and Remus, the tale suggests that fratricidal treachery and violence lie at the very heart of politics.

---

16. Abimelech's "brothers" would have been fellow big men or fellow warriors, individuals of higher standing and greater wealth than the "worthless and reckless" mercenary recruits.

Once Abimelech had defeated Gideon's sons, the men of Shechem associated with the Beth-millo (the house of meeting used by town leaders) gathered at a sacred oak where they made Abimelech king.[17] The final act at the oak completed Abimelech's rise to power. The ceremony would have unfolded according to the provisions of the typical political contract described in the Hebrew Bible and in other ancient Near Eastern texts. Therefore, the agreement between Abimelech and Shechem would have contained provisions about titles, duties, compensation, and services.[18]

In addition, the covenant between Abimelech and Shechem may have spoken of justice as a guiding principle for officeholders. Evidence for that possibility comes from 2 Samuel, chapters 5 and 23. Prior to being anointed king, David made a covenant with the elders of Israel at Hebron (2 Sam. 5:3). Scott Starbuck believes that 2 Samuel 23, a poem attributed to David, contains the words used in that oath of office. Second Samuel 23 emphasizes the connection between fearing God and ruling justly.[19] The passage, commonly referred to as the "last words of David," contains the following words:

> When one rules over men in righteousness,
> When he rules in the fear of Yhwh,
> He is like the light of morning at sunrise on a cloudless morning.
> (2 Sam 23:3–4)

As will be seen below, Abimelech did not uphold that promise.

---

17. Robert Boling posits that the Beth-millo was a large earthen platform upon which the temple to Baal stood. *Judges: A New Translation with Introduction and Commentary* (Garden City, NY: Doubleday, 1975), 171.
18. In Judges 11 the covenant between Jephthah and the elders of Gilead ratified detailed and protracted negotiations about rank and title. See the discussion later in this chapter.
19. Scott R. A. Starbuck, *Court Oracles in the Psalms: The So-Called Royal Psalms in Their Ancient Near Eastern Context* (Atlanta, GA: Society of Biblical Literature, 1999), 192–95.

As part of the covenant ceremony, Abimelech and the other parties would have sworn oaths to adhere to their vows. Employing both blessings and curses, the ritual would have brought down powerful divine sanctions upon anyone who failed to uphold the bargain. Abimelech also may have received supernatural oracular approval for his new role. The solemnity and supposed contractual finality symbolized in these acts stand in sharp contrast to the deceit that followed.

The storyteller in Judges may have been aware of an ancient tradition associating Shechem not with deceit, but with contractual reliability. According to G. Ernest Wright, Shechem had long been the site of covenant ceremonies sealed by the sacrifice of an ass.[20] Ironically, Hebrew lore turned that history on its head by linking the name of Shechem to treachery, not covenant integrity. Genesis 34 contains a very old tale indicating a long history of animosity between the Israelites and the Canaanite town of Shechem. The story in Genesis says that Shechem, the son of the town's founder, Hamor (Ass), seized and raped Dinah, the daughter of Jacob's first wife, Leah. In order to set things right, the house of Hamor approached the house of Jacob with an offer of marriage and the promise of a dowry for the woman. With this proposal, Hamor hoped to enter into an arrangement with Jacob's family, thus opening the door for the exchange of women and trade goods. The house of Jacob accepted with the condition that the house of Hamor submit to the ritual of circumcision. By yielding to Jacob's request (the preconditions of the contract), Hamor's house placed itself in a position of fatal vulnerability. According to the legend, while the men were immobilized from the wounds of circumcision, Jacob's sons attacked and killed them all. This story is laden with sentiments of deep ethnic

---

20. G. Ernest Wright, *Shechem: Biography of a Biblical City* (New York: McGraw Hill, 1965), 213–18.

tension. By circumcising and killing the men of Shechem, the sons of Jacob destroyed them twice, first ethnically and then physically. The allegorical tale of Dinah's rape suggests not only that contracts will be broken, but that an ulterior purpose of a contract may be to weaken and defeat a rival. This memory of treachery was the background to the deal struck between Abimelech and Shechem.

A series of related events not long after Abimelech and Shechem reached their solemn agreement further illuminate the duplicitous inner workings of Shechemite politics. Judges 9:22–23 indicates that Abimelech was in office for only a short time before tensions arose between him and the leaders of the town. Specifically, the men of Shechem began ambushing and robbing travelers. Probably these actions were led by Gaal ben Ebed, a rival big man, who "went on the prowl together with his brothers" (mercenary or warrior retainers).[21] In any event, the action undercut Abimelech's right to control the roads and to plunder or tax for his benefit.[22] Judges 9:26 says the men of Shechem "put their confidence in Gaal," which was tradition's way of indicating that Shechem's leaders entered some type of contractual or covenant agreement with the new big man. Initially the arrangement may have been covert.

Whether the narrator was recounting actual events or offering the readers an imaginary recreation of what might have happened, the report contained in Judges represents affairs as ancient political observers expected them to unfold. By combining this tale about election and rejection with the earlier story of the way Abimelech won the favor of the city leaders, we have a window on the dynamics of how men of valor gained control of an ancient Syro-Palestinian

---

21. Boling uses the word "prowl" in his translation (*Judges*, 176–77). The name Gaal (*Ga'al* – געל) means "loathe" or "abhor." Like Charles Dickens, the storytellers and editors of Judges often named their characters according to the qualities they represented.
22. Almost certainly, Abimelech would have passed a percentage of his earnings to the town treasury and to the town leaders.

city-state or region. Besides the actual mechanics of political rise and fall, the most intriguing element in the process is the discrepancy between descriptions of duplicity and the testimonies about strategies for ensuring adherence to sworn promises. Eventually, Shechem's elite formally reneged on the solemn contract they had made with Abimelech (Judg. 9:22–29).

According to Judges, the plotting began when the town leaders gathered at the house of Baal of the covenant to deliberate about Abimelech. The meeting took place during the grape-harvest festival, thus in August or September. At this assembly, the men ate, drank, and discussed politics. In the course of their exchanges, "they reviled Abimelech" (Judg. 9:27). Then Gaal addressed the group, reminding them that Abimelech was both an outsider and a subordinate functionary in the town's employ. Gaal boasted that if he were in charge of the town he would remove Abimelech and challenge the big man to a battle. While Gaal and the leaders of Shechem violated the agreement with the city's incumbent big man, for his part Abimelech betrayed Shechem's trust. Although he had earlier assured the people of the town that he was of the same "bone and flesh" and they responded by calling him "brother" (Judg. 9:2–3), in typical big-man fashion he treated them as their predator rather than protector. For Abimelech, Shechem would have been only one city he sought to exploit. Living in a hilltop fortress nearly ten kilometers to the southeast, he ruled Shechem though an appointee Zebul, whose name was the equivalent of "Big Man."[23]

The story in Judges asserts that duplicity even infected the dealings of the conspirators deliberating to unseat Abimelech. An informant at the raucous meeting betrayed the men to Zebul, who in turn alerted Abimelech to the proposed rebellion. Together, Zebul and

---

23. The name Zebul (זְבֻל) derives from the root *zbl* (זבל), meaning (in verbal form) "to elevate, exalt, or honor."

Abimelech attacked and defeated Shechem. The book of Judges contains three separate but complementary accounts of the battle (Judg. 9:31–55). These stories assert that Abimelech and Zebul drove Gaal and his men out of the town, ambushed and slaughtered the town's defenders, burned everyone who took refuge in the town's fortress (the house of El of the covenant),[24] and razed the city and sowed it with salt. In the end, the leaders of Shechem learned that Abimelech, the big man they "hired," could not be managed, let alone dismissed. Shechem's leaders had engaged Abimelech to protect them from Gideon's powerful house, defend the town against invaders, and tax or plunder people passing on the caravan routes. The very audacity, wealth, and power that must have recommended Abimelech to them meant that he also had the tools to act as their master, not their servant. Abimelech's willingness to take harsh action against rebellious towns must have been demonstrated many times. In fact, his life ended when he was killed in a siege against Thebez. As at Shechem, he forced people to take refuge in the town's tower/fortress. Tragically for Abimelech, the people of Thebez managed to crush his head with a millstone as he was preparing to burn the tower's door.

A pessimistic tale, the account of Abimelech argues that the only thing political leaders could be trusted to do was to pursue power and self-interest. They could not be counted on to uphold their most fervent promises. An editor of Judges emphasizes this point with a fable, a bit of allegorical political philosophy grafted onto the larger narrative about Abimelech. Supposedly, the fable was spoken by Jotham, the only one of Abimelech's "brothers" (rival men of valor) who managed to escape the slaughter at Ophrah. Said to have shouted the fable from the top of a mountain, Jotham offered a biting critique

---

24. The text refers to the fortress/meeting place by both Baal of the covenant and El of the covenant. Most likely they were one and the same building.

of Abimelech in particular and of big men in general.[25] In the fable, the trees decided to anoint a king from among their ranks. The olive tree, the fig tree, and the grapevine all declined because becoming king required an unacceptable sacrifice. The olive tree would have had to give up the oil by which men and gods are honored, the fig would have had to forego sweetness, while the vine would have had to leave behind the pleasure that cheers men and gods. Thus, in their refusal statements, the three trees asserted that wielding political power results in the loss of honor, contentment, and conviviality. At this point, the other trees turned to the bramble, which consented to rule. In a parody of a formal political covenant, the bramble then pronounced a blessing and a curse—that is, he "spoke the words" of a political contract. This contract, however, foreshadowed treachery. The blessing offered by the bramble was that the other trees could find refuge in its shade. The curse was that if they were unfaithful then fire would come forth to burn the cedars of Lebanon. The blessing and curse suggest that political leaders offer very minimal benefit (the shade of a bramble) to their people. In fact, they threaten to destroy the real shade (cedars of Lebanon). Jotham's fable claims that political power is harsh, punitive, and unreliable. Regardless of what they may promise during installation ceremonies sealed by divine promises, the only certainty is that leaders will be a curse on the people and the people a curse on the leaders. In other words, the only constancy in big-man politics is deceit and predation.

Presented as a folktale more than as history, the legend of Samson grapples with the same themes of constancy and betrayal. This story is filled with duplicity. Samson's very first act, as presented by the narrator, is to defy the wishes of his mother and father. In a tribal

---

25. It is impossible to know if the fable was used during the time of the men of valor described in Judges. However, its message is an appropriate commentary on Abimelech's rule. A similar story in 2 Samuel 16 contains an account of Shimei, a man from the house of Saul, who stood on a hill shouting curses at David.

society in which conventions such as circumcision defined the parameters of a civilized community, Samson insisted on marrying a woman from an uncircumcised people, the Philistines.[26] After rebelling against his parents and against convention, Samson attempted to swindle his young Philistine counterparts at the wedding feast. Proposing a wager based on a riddle, Samson hoped to trick the Philistines into providing him with a large number of costly garments, probably the battle girdles worn by warriors. Samson engaged in a scam because his riddle was unanswerable without special information that only he possessed. Although the wager and the riddle were games, like all games they echoed and anticipated real life. In this case, what was simulated was a formal contract, a solemn promise to perform a specific act if clearly delineated conditions were met. The formula was as follows: "If you do thus and so, then I will do this or that." After enticing his rivals into a contract (the wager), Samson betrayed them by offering conditions (finding the correct answer to the riddle) that could not be met. Although the Philistines eventually discovered the riddle's secret, they did so only by resorting to deception themselves. The message of this tale is that contracts of strongmen set forth unfair stipulations, that they are infected by subterfuge, and that they rely on violence. The story alleges that the purpose of a contract may be to defraud and that contracts might be built on a ruse rather than honesty. The fact that the answer to the riddle juxtaposes the sweetness of honey and the sting of the bee (an allusion to the allure and treachery of women and sex) underscores the double-sided nature of reality and

---

26. To understand the gravity of the situation we can look to parallels in twenty-first-century Africa. Even today, many people in Africa are horrified when their children contemplate marriage across ethnic boundaries, especially when one of the ethnic markers is circumcision. Among people such as the Maasai and the Kikuyu in Kenya, the act of circumcision identifies one as a member of the ethnic community and also an individual eligible for adulthood. To marry someone from a group that does not practice circumcision is to marry a nonadult, perhaps even a nonperson.

relationships. In the end, Samson upheld his end of the bargain. But he did so by slaughtering and plundering the men in the Philistine town of Ashkelon. It was their looted garments that he gave to the guests at his wedding feast. The tale of Samson's riddle suggests that fraudulent agreements result in disaster for all.

Constructing Constancy: Contracts, Vows, and Human Sacrifice

While the three major contributors to the book of Judges accentuate the high level of insecurity and double-dealing that marked Syro-Palestinian politics, they also emphasize ways to overcome the problem. The book's protagonists sought alternatives to the typical strategies of using force or the threat of force and the distribution of material resources as ways to ensure loyalty. A central theme of Judges is that some big men in the late second millennium worked hard to establish reliable contractual arrangements that they hoped would mitigate the dangers of violence and the costs of patronage. But, as the tale of Abimelech makes abundantly clear, those efforts often failed. Cunning rivals, fickle friends, unfaithful relatives, insubordinate subjects, as well as devious women undermined supposedly sacred formal agreements. What was perhaps most distressing was that even the gods, who were parties to the agreements, proved unreliable.

While the stories about Abimelech and Samson reinforce the concept of deceit, the tales about another big man, Jephthah, celebrate constancy and reliability. Often maligned by moderns as a rash man who needlessly sacrificed his own daughter, ancient storytellers had high regard for Jephthah.[27] The Judges' account of Jephthah highlights three separate descriptions of contracts. In each

---

27. As was noted earlier, the New Testament's Letter to the Hebrews lists Jephthah as a great hero (Heb. 11:32).

case, Jephthah is absolutely scrupulous in negotiating and upholding those agreements.

The first contract was brokered between Jephthah and the elders of Gilead (Judg. 11:1–11). Besieged by raiding Ammonites, the people of Gilead living east of the Jordan River turned to Jephthah, a man whose lowly lineage gave him no traditional claim to political power. Thus, as with Abimelech, all aspects of Jephthah's leadership had to be negotiated with the group seeking his services. Emphasizing the constructed and conditional nature of the arrangement, the details recorded in Judges indicate that the bargaining was both bitter and protracted. By suggesting that no love was lost between Jephthah and Gilead's elders, the narrative underscores the point that self-interest, not affection or tradition, was the only bond between the two parties.[28] The story notes that the terms offered by the elders—that Jephthah would be a military commander (*qāṣîn* – קצין)—and the demands on the part of Jephthah—that he receive the more powerful title leader/head (*rō'š* – ראש)—were far apart. In spite of their sharp differences, the account reports that Jephthah and the elders reached an agreement, the terms of which were formalized in a contract ritual whereby Jephthah swore to uphold the bargain ("he spoke all his words"). Witnessed by the people and their god Yhwh, the ceremony took place at the cultic site of Mizpah. The contrast between the animosities separating the parties and the correctness of the covenant ceremony emphasizes the power and importance of the contract. According to Judges, even though there was great tension between Jephthah and the elders, both upheld the contract without fail. While the story of Abimelech and Shechem was a tale

---

28. Jephthah addressed the elders saying, "Did you not hate me, and drive me out of my father's house?" For their part, the elders concede that they turned to Jephthah only out of necessity (Judg. 11:7–8).

of contractual failure, the account of Jephthah and Gilead was one of contractual faithfulness.

The second contract central to Jephthah's story involved his dealings with the Ammonites, the group that had been raiding Gilead.[29] Although he had been engaged by Gilead to deal with the Ammonites, instead of launching a precipitous military attack, Jephthah dispatched messengers to negotiate with the Ammonite king (Judg. 11:12–28). These talks took the form of a contract discussion in which Jephthah argued that Ammon had acted illegally. Although Jephthah ultimately failed to reach a settlement with the Ammonites, the narrative in Judges presents him as a conscientious and honorable leader seeking to reach an agreement based on precedent and legal principles.

According to Judges, Jephthah instructed his envoys to pursue their talks in line with what modern thinkers would call just-war doctrine. Instead of issuing a threat or an accusation, Jephthah asked, "What have you against me that you have come to me to attack my land?" (Judg. 11:12). In essence, Jephthah challenged the Ammonite king to demonstrate a just cause for his attack. Drawing on the same logic, the king responded by claiming the dispute between Ammon and Gilead grew out of an illegal action on the part of Gilead's distant ancestors. The Ammonite king charged that when the Hebrews fled from Egypt they had seized the land between the Arnon and Jabbok Rivers east of the Jordan. Therefore, the land now occupied by the people of Gilead rightfully belonged to Ammon and should be restored peacefully. In responding to Ammon, Jephthah's diplomats recited a series of historical details supposedly proving that Israel, not Ammon, had a legal right to the land. Among the most important elements of their rebuttal was the assertion that three hundred years

---

29. The account in Judges confuses the Ammonites and the Amorites, a detail that is irrelevant to the message of the narrative.

previously the Ammonites had refused safe passage to the Israelites and, in fact, had attacked them without cause. The diplomats went on to argue that justice had been served because, in the long-ago battle, the Ammonites suffered defeat and lost their land. Thus Jephthah's case was based on the argument that Israel had made a reasonable request for safe passage, Ammon had launched an unprovoked attack, Israel had obtained the land through rightful conquest, and Israel had enjoyed three centuries of continuous occupancy.[30] According to Jephthah, these elements were the foundation for Israel's legal right to the land and the basis for his claim that Ammon's more recent attacks against Gilead were illegitimate. Furthermore, Jephthah argued that both Chemosh, the Ammonite god, and Yhwh had been parties to the original land partition. Thus the moral correctness of a human agreement was projected onto the realm of the divine. Jephthah concluded by asserting that he had not violated this contract ("I have not sinned against you"), and that Ammon was entirely in the wrong ("you do me wrong by making war on me"). As he rested his case, Jephthah stated that Yhwh, the ultimate judge, would decide the outcome (Judg. 11:27). Significantly, not once during this closely argued discourse did Jephthah refer to power or pragmatism. Each of his points was based on an appeal to what today we would call international law. Furthermore, instead of expecting raw power to arbitrate, he expressed confidence that the case would be decided by a just authority, Yhwh. Thus Jephthah is presented as a leader far more preoccupied with legal rectitude than with the exercise of military threat. However, after diligently trying to deal with the Ammonites through diplomatic negotiations, Jephthah concluded that he had no

---

30. The right of safe passage was the collective equivalent to an individual's right to hospitality. In order to conduct commerce, pursue a livelihood (for example, herding, divining, or metalworking), and enter into marriage relations, it was essential for individuals and groups to move about. Therefore, safe passage and hospitality, which made such travel possible, were regarded as basic rights throughout Syria-Palestine.

alternative but to engage the Ammonites in battle. Again, invoking Yhwh's name, he said that Yhwh would determine the outcome of the conflict. The narrator then states that "the Spirit of Yhwh came upon Jephthah" and he stalked his foes (Judg. 11:29). In the end, Jephthah won a great victory, slaughtering many Ammonites and subduing twenty of their cities.

The third contract in the Jephthah cycle of stories involved a vow between the mighty man of valor and Yhwh (Judg. 11:30–40). The account of this contract emphasizes the nature and power of the oath as the supernatural glue guaranteeing compliance and constancy. Starting with the story of his installation, the tale of Jephthah makes it abundantly clear that an oath sworn before Yhwh was an unbending and unfailingly powerful covenant. The climax of Jephthah's story comes with a personal vow he made to Yhwh. The harrowing consequences of that vow underscore Jephthah's great personal integrity and illustrate ancient perceptions about the power of an oath before Yhwh. Before he engaged the Ammonites in battle, Jephthah promised that if Yhwh gave them into his hand, he would offer a burnt offering to Yhwh when he returned home victorious ("in *shalom*" – בשלום). Specifically, he vowed to sacrifice the first person from his household who came out to praise and greet him. Presumably Jephthah expected a servant or even a wife to lead the procession hailing his triumphant homecoming.[31] To his utter horror, the first person he encountered was his only child, a beloved young and innocent virgin. Jephthah now confronted the same choice that tradition recalls Abraham faced.

While modern readers are confused and embarrassed by Jephthah's story, people who first told the tale had nothing but respect and

---

31. First Samuel 18:7–8 describes the common practice of joyful women coming out of towns to dance and sing the praises of returning warriors. Deborah's song in Judges 5 is probably the oldest version of such a song.

admiration for the man of valor. No matter how high the cost, no matter how strong his desire to escape his obligation, no matter how much he lamented what he had promised, Jephthah stood true to his oath, the contract he had made with Yhwh. The most powerful words in the account are spoken by his condemned daughter when she says, "My father, you have opened your mouth to Yhwh. Do to me just what came forth from your mouth." The daughter goes on to remind her father that Yhwh had upheld his end of the oath in bringing vengeance upon Jephthah's enemies, the sons of Ammon (Judg. 11:36). The daughter's affirmation of the vow is reemphasized by the poignant claim that all she asked was to delay the sacrifice for two months so that she could go with her friends to the mountains, where they could mourn the fact that she would never bear children. At the end of two months, in a final act of fidelity, the daughter voluntarily returned to her father who carried out his tragic obligation to Yhwh.

The central message of Jephthah's story is that a big man making an oath before Yhwh could be trusted. Jephthah's tale illustrated that an oath to Yhwh took precedence over familial love and the possibility of having descendants. By explicitly noting that Jephthah had only one child and that the girl was still a virgin, the narrative depicts Jephthah as a hero who placed fidelity to an oath to Yhwh over personal happiness and the continuation of his own lineage. While we can never know if a big man named Jephthah actually sacrificed his only daughter, we can be certain that such a story circulated as a testimonial to the trustworthiness of men of valor who certified their words with an oath to Yhwh sealed by the sacrifice of a precious family member.[32]

---

32. Human sacrifice certainly existed in Palestine during the time of the judges and it continued to a limited extent during the monarchy. In times of profound crisis or in response to a great event of deliverance, powerful people offered a sacrifice of great cost. Although condemning human sacrifice, Ezekiel 20 acknowledges that it once existed and that it was regarded as having been

More troubled by moral ambiguity than either the epic-bardic storyteller or the Deuteronomistic editor, the humanist writer concluded the book of Judges by weighing the social and political costs of holding firmly to a promise. The final story in Judges, the sequel to the account of a Levite and his concubine, struggles with the negative consequences of a just, but ill-advised, contract. As a punishment for the house of Benjamin, which had broken the implicit cultural contract of hospitality, the rest of Israel bound itself to an explicit formal contract prohibiting anyone from offering a daughter as a wife to a Benjaminite. Solemnized at Mizpah, the contract was sealed with a "great oath" (Judg. 21:5).[33] Immediately, the people of Israel regretted their action because its result would have been to extinguish the tribe of Benjamin. Using the cliché

---

commanded by Yhwh. Second Kings 16:3 reports that King Ahab sacrificed his own son as a burnt offering. Alice Logan describes how Israelite kings, like their counterparts in neighboring countries, engaged in human sacrifice in times of great crisis. Logan, "Rehabilitating Jephthah," *Journal of Biblical Literature* 143, no. 4 (2009): 665–85. By giving a very precious gift (their own child) to God, the kings hoped for supernatural intervention in return. Logan argues that sacrificing a child was regarded as a royal duty, almost an expression of noblesse oblige in which a member of the elite pays a great price on behalf of the people. This sacrificial act exalted the king as the people's supreme patron. For Jephthah, the motivation was somewhat different. Living in turbulent times, his goal was to demonstrate his trustworthiness, not his selfless generosity. In light of Jephthah's story, it is possible that during early times the great patriarch Abraham would have been lauded for having engaged in human sacrifice. The account about substituting a ram for the son may have been a change required by later sensibilities. In discussing the *tophet*, a place in the Hinnom Valley near Jerusalem where child sacrifice was practiced, J. Andrew Dearman says it is impossible to determine if children were actually slaughtered for sacrifice, or if the bodies of children who had died accidentally or of natural causes were sacrificed. Dearman links the Jerusalem *tophet* with similar sites in Carthage and Tyre. Those sites were associated with Baal. Dearman, "The Tophet in Jerusalem: Archeology and Cultural Profile," *Journal of Northwest Semitic Languages* 22, no. 1 (1996): 59–71. The fact that it would have been unethical to offer the body of a dead animal for sacrifice suggests that humans offered for sacrifice would have been alive and healthy prior to the ritual. This conclusion is consistent with the Abraham story. In a study of teeth and bones at an infant burial site in Carthage, Patricia Smith discovered that a much higher percentage of the burials were of children under the age of three months than one would expect from ancient child mortality data. Smith concludes that the higher rates (67 percent rather than the normal 55 percent) are evidence that living infants were sacrificed. Smith, "Infants Sacrificed? The Tale Teeth Tell," *Biblical Archeology Review* 40, no. 4 (July/August 2014): 54–56, 68.

33. The term "great oath" suggests the oath may have involved human sacrifice.

of weeping, the narrative suggests that the Israelites appealed, and thus sought to reverse, the contract. Like the story of Jephthah, the tale about the agreement at Mizpah emphasizes the inviolability of a contract backed by an oath to Yhwh. Nevertheless, the account about obtaining wives for Benjamin describes a clever tactic used to circumvent the deal. Recalling that the family of Jabesh-gilead had not responded to the call to come to Mizpah and that any tribe not at Mizpah had been condemned to death, the people of Israel concluded that it would be legitimate to slaughter all of Jabesh-gilead's men, children, and married women. The surviving virgins, four hundred in all, could then be given to Benjamin. As if to emphasize the strategy of getting around a contract and oath by means of a technicality, the story presents an additional subterfuge. Recalling that the oath bound Israel not to offer wives to Benjamin, the people of Israel suggested that Benjamin might seize females participating in a ritual dance for nubile girls. The logic of this scheme was that since the women had been taken by force, their fathers and brothers could not be accused of violating their oath.

The meaning of the account in Judges 21 is ambiguous. Is the story an affirmation of holding fast to the terms of a contract, or does the story celebrate a lawyerly scheme for getting around those terms? We cannot be sure of the answer. What is clear, however, is that like the stories of Abimelech and Jephthah, people in premonarchic Israel struggled with issues related to reliability and holding fast to legal promises. While the tales of Abimelech and Jephthah affirm the importance of adhering to a contract sealed by an oath, the account of Benjamin's wives suggests uncertainty. If following a contract comes in conflict with important elements of kinship and marriage—keys to human survival— then some way must be found to circumvent the contract's consequences. Nevertheless, even this story reinforces the notion that contracts could not simply be ignored or undone. Thus even the breach of the contract in Judges 21 affirmed its legitimacy.

Conclusions

The lack of fidelity and trustworthiness was a central problem during the time represented by the big men chronicled in Judges. Making sure that another party would uphold political agreements was nearly impossible. From Ehud, who assassinated his overlord, to Samson who was betrayed by his women, the book of Judges is replete with accounts of treachery and faithlessness. That fact is especially evident in the tale of Abimelech. Early in his career, Abimelech turned against the warrior brothers of his father's house. At his installation as town leader he took a solemn oath to work in the interests of Shechem, but in the end he attacked and destroyed the people he had promised to protect. For their part, the people of Shechem were even less reliable than Abimelech. This scheming, double-dealing, and blatant disregard for political agreements characterized the general instability of the times. While towns sought out or submitted to big men in the hopes of gaining protection and revenue, the story of Abimelech makes it clear that such agreements offered little comfort to either the town or the big man.

In Syria-Palestine, as in many traditional societies throughout the world, taking oaths and pronouncing blessings and curses were important enforcement tools. Such verbal acts invoked the power of the supernatural. Thus, even if one party in the agreement was unable to compel compliance, unseen and ever-present divine forces would punish unfaithfulness with sickness, defeat in battle, crop failure, infertility, economic reversal, or social shame. Such divine action was essential because, in the uncertainty of premonarchic times, both the men of valor and community leaders often lacked the ability to monitor or enforce the deals struck at political gatherings or the promises and pacts made among friends.

However, as can be seen in the story of Abimelech, conventional Canaanite supernatural sanctions were inadequate to guarantee the relationship between town elders and aggressive big men. Even swearing an oath in the house of Baal (or El) of the covenant was not enough to prevent powerful people from reneging on their vows. Thus towns could not trust the warriors they engaged to protect them, and the warriors could not be sure that the towns would honor the agreements into which they had entered. In an age plagued by insecurity, this lack of confidence in the power of traditional oath taking and of blessings and curses was a dangerous and costly problem. Finding a way to enforce political contracts would have improved security, decreased cost, and lowered risk for town leaders, big men, and ordinary citizens.[34]

The account about Jephthah proposes a robust solution to that quest. Jephthah's story suggests that the growing adherence to Yhwh may have been linked to the conviction that people who swore by Yhwh were more trustworthy. For men of valor, the perception of reliability would have complemented the belief that Yhwh's spirit was a powerful ally in battle and a dependable voice in divination. As other accounts indicate (for example, the stories of Barak and Gideon), Yhwh's trustworthiness was a critical concern of the storytellers reciting or writing the tales in Judges. For Barak, the issue was steadfastness in warfare. For Gideon, the concern was reliability in the process of divination. But for Jephthah, the challenge was dependability in contractual agreements.

---

34. Modern politico-economic theory emphasizes the importance of contract reliability. Reliability lowers transaction costs for both political and economic dealings. In the absence of reliability, parties are reluctant to enter agreements and they must bear the costs of added enforcement tools once they enter agreements.

With the story of Jephthah, the book of Judges argues that more than being rapacious and rich, a successful (or good) leader needed to be trustworthy. In contrast to Abimelech, the least reliable leader, Jephthah is offered as a man who kept his word at all costs. Remembered for his constancy rather than for his brutality or generosity, Jephthah represents an alternative to raw force or giving away wealth as a means of maintaining political control. His story, which emphasizes contractual reliability as an essential ingredient for successful rule, may also reflect a growing regard for trustworthiness as a critical component of the Yhwhistic faith.

Although celebrating trustworthiness, in the stories discussing punishment for those who abused the Levite and his concubine, the humanist editor acknowledges the paradox that insisting on justice and contractual reliability can lead to disaster. From the prophets of the Hebrew Bible and Jesus to modern thinkers such as Hannah Arendt, Donald Shriver, and Miroslav Volf, religious and secular sages have struggled to balance the desire for justice, consistency, and retribution with the need to accept the inevitable reality of human failure.[35] Arendt, Shriver, and Volf argue that for human society to survive, people must find approaches to dealing with injustice that do not destroy community. The common path, punishment for the misdeeds of others, is problematic. Not only is keeping punishment in bounds by limiting vengeance to an eye for an eye difficult, but also many injustices are too egregious or too tragic to be set right. Shriver and Volf remind us that the attempt to achieve justice can easily degenerate into a cycle of revenge. What is justice for one appears to be injustice for another. Arendt says that human society faces two challenges. The one is ensuring justice and contractual

---

35. Miroslav Volf, *Exclusion and Embrace: A Theological Exploration of Identity, Otherness, and Reconciliation* (Nashville: Abingdon Press, 1996); Donald W. Shriver Jr., *An Ethic for Enemies: Forgiveness for Enemies* (New York: Oxford University Press, 1995); Hannah Arendt, *The Human Condition* (Chicago: University of Chicago Press, 1958).

reliability so that life is orderly and predictable. The second, which Arendt believes is generally overlooked, is finding ways to offer clemency so that people are not destroyed or immobilized by the inevitable grievances of the past. Sensitive to moral ambiguity, the humanist's story of conflict between Benjamin and the other tribes of Israel concedes that a rigid adherence to a principle, in this case the principle of justice, can destroy the fabric of society. With the story of Israel's militant response to the outrageous injustice against the Levite and his concubine, the humanist confronts the tension between fairness and forgiveness. In considering this matter, the humanist's concern is warranted, but the humanist's answer is imperfect. The Hebrew prophets, Jesus, Arendt, Shriver, and Volf advocate forgiveness; the humanist suggests a resort to trickery and casuistry. Although less satisfying, the humanist's response was a tentative step in the direction of social concord.

4

Power and Honor

Notions of Honor

Anticipating a central theme in the book of Judges, the humanist editor explicitly references honor in the first chapter. Attributing the source of honor to the supernatural, the editor elevates the tribes of Judah and Simeon over all the others.

> And the sons of Israel asked Yhwh, "Who will be the first to go up for us against the Canaanites to wage war against them?" And Yhwh said, "Judah will go up. Behold I give the land into his hand." Then Judah said to Simeon his brother, "Go up with me to my allotment and we will fight the Canaanites." (Judg. 1:1)

The editor's second reference to honor is contained in the description of Judah and Simeon's first conquest.

> In Bezek they smote ten thousand men.¹ And in Bezek they found the Adon (Lord) of Bezek and they fought against him . . . And the Adon of Bezek fled. Then they pursued him and captured him. They cut off his big toes and thumbs. Then the Adon of Bezek said, "Seventy kings with their big toes and thumbs cut off scavenged under my regal table. Just as I did, thus *shalom* to me did Elohim." Then they (Judah and Simeon) brought him to Jerusalem and he died there. (Judg. 1:4–7)

According to the logic of these two stories, honor is based on rank (Judah is first among all the tribes), depends on the grace or opinion of others (the deity recognizing Judah and then Simeon being selected by Judah), can be linked to kinship (Simeon gains honor as Judah's junior family member), and may be related to victory in battle (Judah's defeat of the Canaanites and of the Lord of Bezek). Honor can easily be lost and give way to shame (the Adon of Bezek fleeing and being disfigured, seventy former kings forced to scavenge like dogs at the feet of the royal table, and the Adon of Bezek's displacement and death in exile). Finally, honor can sometimes be a zero-sum game (the Adon of Bezek's honor coming at the expense of the defeated and humiliated kings, and Bezek's using the verb form of the word "shalom" as a term suggesting equity and reciprocity to describe the cause of his own disgrace).²

A third vignette featuring the woman Achsah is also important for understanding the humanist writer's perspective about honor. The story begins with Caleb, a strongman from the southern part of Judah, making plans to capture Kiriath-sepher (Document Town),

---

1. Normally the word '*ălāpîm* (אלפים) is translated as "thousands," thus reflecting story-telling hyperbole. Noting that the word is derived from '*ālep* (the letter *A*) and also the word for "cattle," Robert Boling links it to fighting units and male allotments from rural clans. Thus Boling suggests the term refers to a more prosaic number, perhaps ten to fifteen men, not one thousand. *Judges: A New Translation with Introduction and Commentary*, Anchor Bible 6A (Garden City, NY: Doubleday, 1975), 17, 54–55.
2. In the Hebrew of this passage (Judg. 1:7), the root letters of "shalom" (*šlm*) are written as a *piel* perfect verb, a grammatical construction that sometimes is used to transform a noun into a verb. A very awkward and ungrammatical way of translating Bezek's utterance would be to say, "Just as I did (to my enemies), so Elohim shalomed me."

a Canaanite political center.³ Caleb offers his daughter Achsah as a prize to the warrior who can defeat Kiriath-sepher. Caleb's nephew, Othniel, rose to the challenge and as payment received Achsah as his wife. From this point on, Achsah becomes the story's leading actor.

> And when she came, she implored him (Othniel) to ask her father for land. She slammed down from her donkey. Then Caleb said to her, "What is with you!" Then she said, "Give me a blessing for you have given me the Negeb land. Now give to me pools of water!" Then Caleb gave her upper and lower pools of water. (Judg. 1:14–15)

Although this tale reaffirms important traditional ideas regarding women as custodians of domestic wealth (the name Achsah means "Bangles") and as valuable commodities to be traded among men, the language and the plot of the story challenge conventional notions about female honor. Achsah's honor is not dependent on her fertility or her obedience. Her sitting on a donkey,⁴ her aggressive entry,⁵ the pressure she exerts on her new husband, her demand for a blessing, and the fact that Caleb takes her seriously all point to a woman who expected and received the honor one might suppose would be reserved for men. Significantly, Achsah is only one of many dynamic female characters in the book of Judges whose stories defy gendered stereotypes of honor.

As foreshadowed by the humanist editor, honor is a prominent and reoccurring concept in almost every part of Judges. Deborah

---

3. English speakers will recognize the word "cipher" in the town's name. Presumably, Kiriath-sepher was a center for drawing up, ratifying, and storing important written documents such as treaties or contracts.
4. As seen elsewhere in Judges, riding on a donkey was a sign of wealth and status (Judg. 5:10; 12:13).
5. There is an urgency to the words translated as "implore" and "slam." The term *swt* (סות), rendered here as "implore," means "to incite, allure, instigate, or make a request." The word *ṣnḥ* (צנח) means "slam, pound, or drive down." The dramatic meaning of "slam" or "pound" is derived from the context of the word, which is used only two times in the Hebrew Bible. The other example is when Jael drove the tent stake through the head of Sisera. Many translations use the less dynamic word "descend" or "alight" to describe how Achsah dismounted.

tells Barak that although he will be successful in battle, in the end a woman will receive the honor. Barak's opponent, the cowardly Sisera, is dishonored when he flees the battlefield and seeks the protection of an iron-willed seductress. Two elite men of valor captured by Gideon beg to be executed by Gideon, their social equal, rather than suffer disgrace from being killed by Gideon's frightened young son, their inferior. Similarly, as he lies dying after being struck on the head by a millstone dropped by a woman, Abimelech commands his male servant to kill him in order to avoid the humiliation of perishing at the hand of a woman. Samson, mutilated and taunted by the Philistines, regains his honor by pulling down the temple upon himself and his foes. From these examples, it is obvious that for many of the characters, honor was more important than life itself. In addition to stories featuring honor, throughout the book honorific terms, praise names, titles, and conventions of greeting reflect a preoccupation with honor.

Although honor is universally cherished, it is a concept that resists easy classification. One of the most frequently cited descriptions of honor is that of Julian Pitt-Rivers, who explains honor as a sentiment (people think of themselves as honorable or virtuous), as conduct (honorable individuals pattern their lives according to established ideals), and as reputation (a person is honorable only when others acknowledge that quality). According to Pitt-Rivers, honor is both subjective (a person's own sense of honor) and objective (behavior is honorable when it is consistent with social conventions and when it receives public recognition). Pitt-Rivers also notes that honor can further be understood by considering shame, disgrace, humiliation, and disrespect, the subjective and objective elements of dishonor.[6] Along with J.G. Peristiany, Pitt-Rivers also argues that grace is an

---

6. Julian Pitt-Rivers, "Honor," in *International Encyclopedia of the Social Sciences*, ed. David L. Sills (New York: MacMillan Company, 1968), 6:503–11.

essential component of honor. Without the assent (gift) of another, whether a mortal or a deity, an individual's claims to honor are hollow. Both pretentious and foolish, such claims are cause for scorn.[7]

Honor (Pitt-Rivers)

Type	Measure of Honor	Standard of Validation
As Sentiment	Consistent with Personal Values	Self-Assessment–Subjective
As Conduct	Consistent with Social Norms	Actual Behavior–Objective
As Reputation	Appears Consistent with Social Norms	Public Opinion–Subjective

Building on Pitt-Rivers, Frank Stewart, who conducted anthropological field research among modern Bedouin groups in the Sinai, argues that honor is best understood as "the right to be treated as having a certain worth." Like all rights, this implies obligation. On the one hand, the bearer of honor has a right to be respected because of some personal quality, either ascribed or achieved. On the other hand, the one who extends honor has a "duty to treat the bearer with respect."[8] This respect may be the respect between equals (horizontal honor) or that of a subordinate to a superior (vertical honor). For Stewart, the right to respect goes beyond the realm of attitudes to include the right that something will be done by another. That might be extending the right to testify or render judgment in a legal dispute, to serve in the councils of government, to act as head of the family or household, to offer protection as a patron, or to collect a ransom or blood money.[9] Expanding on the idea of

---

7. J. G. Peristiany and Julian Pitt-Rivers, eds. *Honor and Grace in Anthropology* (Cambridge: Cambridge University Press, 1992).
8. Frank Stewart, *Honor* (Chicago: University of Chicago Press, 1994), 21.
9. Ibid., 38.

honor as a right, Stewart notes that honor is often contested. Rivals or discontented subordinates may attempt to diminish or destroy an individual's honor. Sometimes those attacks claim the individual has failed to uphold a commonly agreed upon code of honor, at other times the attacks may challenge the validity of the code itself.[10]

Both Pitt-Rivers, who focuses on the Mediterranean region, and Stewart, who compares honor in a wider variety of cultures, agree that strength, courage, generosity, hospitality, and wealth are the attributes most frequently considered honorable. It is always more honorable to be a giver than a recipient, a protector rather than one seeking refuge, and bold rather than timid. Other elements of honor are more situational. While honesty toward one's ally is honorable, outwitting an adversary through duplicity can be equally honorable. Also, as Stewart notes, the measures of what is honorable may differ from one social group or society to another.[11] Referencing Stewart, John Iliffe, who studied honor in Africa, looks at how specific notions of honor vary from place to place, from time to time, from class to class, and from one gender to another. Iliffe is especially interested in how honor can be dependent upon age—for example, the honor of an impetuous young warrior differing from the honor of an elder responsible to manage a house and mediate conflict.[12] Looking at competing criteria, biblical scholar Zeba Crook argues that even within a given culture people challenge the standards of honor. As evidence, Crook offers many examples of women receiving honor for "manly" deeds, of social inferiors impugning the honor of their social betters, and of public opinion reshaping the limits of honor and dishonor.[13]

---

10. Ibid., 37. As will be discussed later in this chapter, one might ask if the level of irony in the tale of Samson is intended as a challenge to the primary code of honor apparent in the surface meaning of the story.
11. Ibid., chapter 12.
12. John Iliffe, *Honour in African History* (Cambridge: Cambridge University Press, 2005).

Although there are differences from one culture or subculture to the next and the nature of honor may be contested within a given society, virtually all people agree that a challenge to honor must be met with a response. In the absence of a response, the person—or even deity—who has been challenged forfeits their honor. The proper way to respond to a challenge is prescribed by a "code of honor," which might be contained in unwritten assumptions or might be codified in explicit rules protected by laws making it possible for someone to seek recourse in court for the loss of honor.[14]

At this point, it is important to consider the function of honor, asking what its utility is. Honor's first useful quality is in the realm of sentiment. Even Westerners, who are tempted to reduce everything to economics, must concede that honor produces an intensely satisfying emotion. Although contemporary Westerners tend to think of "honor cultures" as archaic, from birth to burial their own lives are marked by a quest for honor. Sitting at the head of a banquet table, standing first in an academic procession, having one's children accepted into a prestigious university (or even preschool), living in the most affluent zip code area, buying coffee at the trendiest bistro, wearing impressive military medals, winning a glamorous trophy wife, or boasting of the largest number of attendees at a retirement dinner or funeral are all symbols of honor valued by people in modern societies. Not all elements of honor are so superficial. A long life of unblemished integrity and service, a willingness to sacrifice individual comfort for the common good, successful parenting, or faithfulness in marriage are also recognized as noble achievements that bring honor. In considering the emotional

---

13. Zeba Crook, "Honor, Shame, and Social Status Revisited," *Journal of Biblical Literature* 128, no. 3 (2009): 591–611.
14. See Stewart, *Honor*, chapter 5.

value of honor, the point is that honor can be regarded as a good in itself, not a mere servant of another value such as wealth or power.[15]

While honor is a primary emotional value that can stand on its own, honor also has social, political, and military utility. From a social perspective, the concept of honor strengthens community norms and encourages behavior considered desirable. Shared norms of honor contribute to stability and predictability. A code of honor offers guidelines for how the elite should act among themselves and toward their inferiors and the concept of honorableness encourages appropriate deference on the part of subordinate classes. The idea of honor also provides clear rules for how members of each gender should behave. For women, premarital chastity, faithfulness in marriage, and fertility are common marks of honor. For men, sexual prowess and the obligation to protect the honor of the women in their charge are common, but potentially contradictory, values.

From a military perspective, the qualities many consider honorable for males are useful for defending territorial boundaries. In his study of Homeric Greece, Moses Finley claims that for the youthful warrior, "everything pivoted on a single element of honor and virtue: strength, bravery, physical courage, prowess. Conversely, there was no weakness, no unheroic trait, but one, and that was cowardice and the consequent failure to pursue heroic goals."[16] According to Iliffe, in Africa as in ancient Greece, these aggressive qualities gain special prominence when security is uncertain. Iliffe notes that African pastoral societies, where water rights and grazing territory must be defended and where raiding is an ever-present reality, have a heightened sense of warrior honor.[17]

---

15. In his classic study, *Politics: Who Gets What, When, How* (1935; repr., Cleveland: Meridian Press, 1958), Harold Laswell lists respect, the equivalent of honor, as one of the eight basic values that people seek through the political process. Thus, in Laswell's mind, honor is not a subordinate or dependent value, but a value in its own right.
16. Moses Finley, *The World of Odysseus* (New York: Viking, 1977), 28.

Standards of Honor

For Young Men	For Male Heads of Households	For Women
Strength	Good Judgment	Premarital Chastity
Sexual Prowess	Sexual Prowess	Fertility
Physical Courage	Ability to Protect Household	Marital Faithfulness
Bravery	Ability to Protect Female Honor	Beauty
Willingness to Take Risks	Management and Mediation Skills	Good Household Management

It should not be thought that the exercise of martial honor necessarily results in physical violence. In many societies boasting, shouting insults (often vulgar), sporting menacing attire or hairstyles, throwing stones or weapons from relatively safe distances, or engaging in wrestling matches serve as less dangerous proxies for actual combat. Excelling in the recitation of heroic poetry, outwitting an opponent through riddles, or prevailing in gambling are other common substitutes for bodily battle. Even the hyperbole of war stories, which claim that hundreds or even thousands were killed, can be seen as a strategy to reduce violence. Slaughtering people on the battlefield of boasting can be an honorable nonlethal replacement for actual bloodshed.

Honor's political utility derives from the fact that at its most elemental level honor is the right to be taken seriously, to be considered consequential. Herein lies the connection between honor and power because political leadership is about getting others to do what they would not have done otherwise. Emphasizing the links between honor and qualities such as power, wealth, social

---

17. Iliffe, *Honour in African History*, chapter 7, "Honour without the State."

stratification, and control, Pitt-Rivers argues that honor is a key ingredient in politics, especially in patron-client relationships.[18] While one might get people to follow by exercising material generosity or by employing brutality and terror, the costs and risks of those strategies can be unbearably high. So high are those costs that gaining the voluntary compliance of subordinates is essential for any political system. To a large extent, giving honor is the equivalent of offering obedience. Honor is politically expedient because it disguises the rough edges of power, reduces the costs of ruling, and softens the pain of subordination. Systems or individual leaders considered honorable have the right never to be disobeyed or even insulted. Because it facilitates the maintenance of social hierarchies and privilege and cements the bonds among social equals, honor is essential for political order and harmony.[19]

In addition to acting as a servant of power, honor also provides a path to conflict resolution. In Europe and preindustrial America, for members of the elite the ultimate end of that path was the duel. To some extent, the duel was an affirmation of social standing. To offer or accept the challenge of a duel was to acknowledge the adversary as a social equal. By rejecting the challenge, a man signaled either that he was a coward or that the challenger was not an equal and therefore was unworthy. From a practical perspective, as Stewart explains, the duel can be an efficient way to end a dispute. Avoiding time-consuming and costly litigation, contending parties can settle a difference by a simple duel.[20] For the elite, another advantage of

---

18. Pitt-Rivers, "Honor," 507.
19. See Saul M. Olyan, "Honor, Shame, and Covenant Relations in Ancient Israel and Its Environment," *Journal of Biblical Literature* 115, no. 2 (1996): 201–18.
20. It should be noted that duels were not generally fatal. Frequently, after a few blows were struck or a few shots fired from relatively safe distances, a winner was declared, the matter was deemed resolved, and honor was preserved. While the celebrated competition between David and Goliath ended in death, the duel between the two men served as a substitute for a war involving large numbers of combatants.

dueling is that it does not entrust disputes to a higher authority or third party. Thus the duel affirms the courage of members of the elite and it prevents outsiders from interfering in their affairs. While the duel has been prominent in the West, other societies use different strategies to settle conflicts regarding honor. For example, the Bedouin group studied by Stewart assigns honor disputes to a council of elders.[21]

In thinking about honor, it is important to recognize that modern conventions of morality may not be consistent with honor in ancient societies. Lying to an enemy, flying into a rage and slaughtering dozens or hundreds of innocents, killing or mutilating a close family member who has been sexually contaminated, keeping a mistress, sleeping with the king's concubines, or even seducing the wife of a friend are not always regarded as dishonorable acts. With the development of state-centric legal codes in Europe, the logic of honor and the morality of the law often came into conflict. Dueling, an honorable way for equals to settle disputes, was forbidden by law. Paying a gambling debt, required by honor, might not be enforced by the state. Such tensions between honor and legality reflect shifting standards of propriety, the fact that social classes hold different notions of right and wrong, and the efforts of a centralizing political elite to monopolize dispute resolution.[22]

The Language of Honor and Shame in Judges

The language used in the book of Judges is consistent with modern studies that consider the essential nature of honor and that examine honor as sentiment, conduct, and reputation. Every category and concept explored by scholars such as Pitt-Rivers, Peristiany, and

---

21. Stewart, *Honor*, 82.
22. Ibid., chapter 7. Stewart points out that by moving dispute resolution to the courts, the monetary gain to the state and the financial and time cost to individuals rose substantially.

Stewart is named by one or more terms used in Judges. The rich honor-related vocabulary in Judges is proof that people were intensely conscious of honor and that honor was an explicit part of social and political discourse. People's sentiments of honor were expressed in what they saw as the foundational nature of honor, the ways they spoke and acted to confer honor on others, and in what they regarded as honorable behavior. The following paragraphs will survey positive and negative Hebrew word pairs used in Judges. These terms describe honor's essence, ways to bestow or withdraw honor, and external attributes of honor.[23]

The Essence of Honor

The closest Hebrew equivalent to the term "honor" is the word *kābôd* (כבוד). When the root *kbd* and its derivatives are used in relation to Yhwh or prominent people, the words are rendered in English as "honored" or "glorified." However, the underlying meaning of *kbd* is "heaviness" and the word should be understood as "significance." In a positive context, the adjective *kābēd* might refer to an abundance (heaviness) of wealth, a great herd of cattle, a considerable number of people, or plentiful fountains of water. When used negatively, the word can mean "burdensome" or "oppressive." Thus, *kābēd* is

---

23. The discussion of honor-related words draws heavily on the entries in Francis Brown, S. R. Driver, and Charles A. Briggs, *A Hebrew and English Lexicon of the Old Testament* (1907; repr., Oxford: Oxford University Press, 1955). Completed more than one hundred years ago, the work remains useful because all forms of a root are grouped together. Other lexical resources used for this word study were G. Johannes Botterweck and Helmer Ringgren, eds., *Theological Dictionary of the Old Testament*, 11 vols. (Grand Rapids, MI: Eerdmans, 1974); and Ludwig Koehler and Walter Baumgartner, *The Hebrew and Aramaic Lexicon of the Old Testament*, 2 vols. (Leiden: E. J. Brill 2002). The discussion of honor also parallels Saul Olyan's work on Israel's early monarchy and expands the conversation to include the time of the judges. Drawing on Pitt-Rivers and Peristiany, Olyan notes that honor and shame were key political ingredients in ancient Israel, but that biblical scholarship has given too little attention to either the language or stories related to those notions. In particular, Olyan examines the way that honor and shame reinforced hierarchy and affected the stability of covenant relationships ("Honor, Shame, and Covenant Relations").

used to describe the heaviness of sin and transgressions, the weight of battle, the affliction of infirmity and age, the bulk of corpulence, the unyielding heart of a stubborn ruler, an uncountable swarm of locusts, the crush of warriors in an opposing army, the depth of calamity, and the direness of famine. What is common to all of these usages is the idea of being weighty or consequential. To have *kābôd* is to be taken seriously or, to combine terms from sociology and physics, to have social mass. For a human or a deity this means, in the words of Frank Stewart, that honor is "the right to be treated as having a certain worth."[24]

When used in Judges, *kbd* refers to all three elements: abundance, oppression, and the social weight of honor. Recalling the conflict between the Sons of Israel and the Canaanites, the humanist writer said, "The hand of the house of Joseph rested *heavily* on the Amorites and they became subject to forced labor" (Judg. 1:35). Toward the end of the book the same writer described an intertribal battle as *heavy* (Judg. 20:34). The humanist writer also equated *kbd* with the abundance of wealth. As the people of Dan traveled, they grouped their things of consequence, their little ones, their cattle, and their *kbd* (wealth) (Judg. 18:21). In the epic-bardic section of Judges the root *kbd* is used explicitly to describe social or political honor. In Jotham's fable the olive tree says, "Why should I be stopped from producing the luxuriant oil that *honors* gods and humans (makes gods and humans heavy)" (Judg. 9:9).[25] In another story, Samson's father Manoah says to the messenger of Yhwh, "Tell us your name so that when your words come true we may *honor* you (make you heavy)" (Judg. 13:17). The *piel* verbal form used in both cases reinforces the

---

24. Stewart, *Honor*, 21.
25. Oil (דשן), a symbol of extravagance and luxury, can be the fat (the richest and most flavorsome part) of the gift of sacrifice or the lavish substance used to anoint an honored individual.

idea that honor is conferred on someone by the declaration or action of another.²⁶

The negative counterpart of *kbd* is expressed by the roots *knʿ* (כנע), *ʿnh* (ענה), and *nbl* (נבל), in words suggesting weakness and a lack of consequence, import, definition, or social weight. The first root, *knʿ* (כנע), meaning "to be humble" or "be subdued," is used frequently by the book of Judges' Deuteronomistic editor to refer to the impotence and dishonor of military defeat (Judg. 3:30; 4:23; 8:28; 11:33). When linked to an action, the second root, *ʿnh* (ענה), means "bowing down" and "submitting." When describing a state of being the root can mean "affliction, subservience, weakness, having been brought low, or humbled." In all cases the range of meanings for *ʿnh* (ענה) stands in sharp contrast to the weight, power, and prestige of honor. In fact, in the book of Jeremiah the term is intentionally juxtaposed with *kbd* (Jer. 14:21). The root *ʿnh* (ענה) is also used in the tale of Delilah's undoing of Samson and is explicitly coupled with the turning away of his strength.²⁷ In Judg. 19:23, *ʿnh* (ענה) refers to the extreme helplessness and dishonor of suffering sexual assault. The humanist writer also suggests that *ʿnh* (ענה) is the equivalent of the third root, *nbl* (נבל), which means "to be completely senseless or foolish." After offering his own daughters to the unruly townspeople threatening to sodomize his Levite guest, the householder trying to protect the Levite begs the men "not to do this thing of senselessness/disgracefulness" (Judg. 19:23). The word *nābāl* (נבל) is used to describe David's son Amnon who is called a wicked

---

26. For a discussion of the *piel* verb form see C. L. Seow, *A Grammar for Biblical Hebrew* (Nashville: Abingdon, 1995), 173–74.
27. Delilah's name, derived from *dll* (דלל), also suggests dishonor. In verb form, *dll* (דלל) can mean "hang down, be brought low, or languish." As an adjective, the word suggests thinness, weakness, poverty, helplessness, or sexual availability (compliant, unable to defend oneself). When approached by the messenger of Yhwh, Gideon feigns humility, saying he was the youngest of the lowest (*dl* – דל) family (Judg. 6:15).

fool for scandalously violating social conventions by raping his sister Tamar (2 Sam. 13:13). Elsewhere in the Hebrew Bible, *nbl* (נבל) is linked to foolish prophets who pander to their own spirits, people and nations who are foolish because they do not follow Yhwh, or a man who is foolish because he is an unreliable scoundrel.

Bestowing Honor

Although honor is based on an inner quality—one's social, political, or economic weight and consequence—honor can also be granted by others. In ancient Israel, blessings and curses invoked by third-party forces or actors were seen as potent sources of grace or disgrace (disgrace). Honor was given or withheld when a deity or human spoke or acted to increase the significance or weightiness of an individual, family, community, or kingdom. These words or deeds affecting honor could not be controlled by the object of the blessing or curse.

Ultimately, the power ensuring the good fortune of a blessing (*bĕrākâ* – ברכה) derives from the supernatural, either an impersonal magical force or a deity. In addition to the idea of blessing as bestowing good fortune—usually wealth, a long life, or many children—the concept also implies respect and recognition of relative social worth. Not a zero-sum game, the act of offering a blessing can enhance the standing of the giver as well as the receiver because extending a blessing marks the benefactor as a person of stature. Related to the verb "to kneel" (*brk* – ברך), the act of blessing can also involve a physical gesture indicating either deference or importuning. In all cases, the one pronouncing the blessing is giving honor or weight to the object of the blessing. W. J. Harrelson suggests that in its primitive form the phrase "Blessed be Yhwh" actually was spoken to increase the power or stature of the deity.[28] When the object of a blessing is a human, that person also gains respect, strength, or wealth. Emphasizing the relationship between blessing and the increased strength of a man, the tale of Samson announces that as the lad grew Yhwh blessed him and that after blessing Samson the Spirit of Yhwh began to energize (*p'm* – פעם) him (Judg. 13:24–25).[29]

The concept of honor can also be understood by considering the nature of curse, blessings' negative counterpart. In Judges, two roots with different meanings are used for the English term "curse." The first, *'rr* (ארר), is connected to the invocation of supernatural misfortune, either through the instrument of impersonal magic or through the direct action of a deity. The person voicing the curse is calling on the supernatural to cause harm, such as sickness, bad luck, defeat in battle, infertility, poverty, or even death.[30] The second term for curse, *qll* (קלל), is more closely related to the concept of weightiness or consequence because it refers to an attempt to undermine an individual's substance. In Gen. 8:8, 11 the verbal form of *qll* (קלל) is used to describe the waters of Noah's flood *abating*, thus being reduced or becoming slight. Based on the logic of diminution, instead of being recognized as substantial, which is the essence of honor, someone who is cursed risks becoming an insignificant nonentity. In Judges, when the lords of Shechem berate Abimelech as

---

28. W. J. Harrelson, "Blessings and Curses," in *The Interpreter's Dictionary of the Bible* (Nashville: Abingdon, 1962), 1: 446.
29. The root *p'm* (פעם), which in its verbal form literally means "to impel, thrust, hit, or strike," can also suggest a wild and disruptive burst of auditory energy. The word *pa'am* (פעם) can also describe a sharp intrusion such as the clattering of horses' hooves or the clanging of a hammer on an anvil. When referring to time, *pa'am* (פעם) can signify a propitious or noteworthy moment which must be seized urgently before it passes. Delilah tells Samson's Philistine enemies to seize this *favorable time* (*pa'am* – פעם) to subdue Samson because he has told her his whole heart. Similarly, when attacked Samson proclaims that he will escape as at the *other time* when he was able to elude the Philistines (Judg. 16:18, 20). Gideon as well uses the word to indicate a significant moment when he asks Yhwh to permit him to test the fleece just *one more time* (Judg. 6:39).
30. The word *'rr* (ארר) is used in the Song of Deborah (Judg. 5:22) to berate Meroz and in Judg. 21:18 to condemn any tribe giving a wife to Benjamin.

unworthy of obedience and then proceed to unseat him from power, the narrator uses the root *qll* (קלל) (Judg. 9:27). The root is repeated in noun form when the storyteller claims the death of Abimelech confirms the curse (*qllt* – קללת) of Jotham (Judg. 9:57). As seen in the tale of Micah, a blessing can undo the annihilating action of a curse, thus restoring the stature of the accursed. After cursing (making insignificant) the unknown person who had stolen her silver, Micah's mother reverses her action with a blessing (making consequential) when she discovers that she had unwittingly diminished her own son (Judg. 17:2).

Recognizing Honor

Blessings and curses, which invoke third-party forces or actors, are seen as the source of either good or ill. Thus blessings and curses point to grace or dis-grace and indicate that honor is bestowed or withheld when a deity or humans speak or act to increase or decrease the significance or weightiness of an individual, family, community, or kingdom. Other expressions such as "praise," "beautify," or "taunt" suggest perception and recognition rather than agency or causation. The root *hll* (הלל – "shine, praise"), which appears frequently in Psalms and which underlies "hallelujah," was used in ceremonies of thanksgiving to the deity during the time period depicted in Judges. When used in a self-referential manner, the word also implied boasting. The Philistines chanted *halal* (הלל) when praising their god Dagon in his temple (Judg. 16:24), while a noun form of the word is used to describe the annual harvest festival in which the men of Shechem celebrated their god Baal in his holy place (Judg. 9:26). Evidence that the honorific term הלל was linked to the Hebrew men of valor in Judges comes from the list of so-called minor judges. The father of the minor judge Abdon was named Hillel, or "He praised"

(Judg. 12:13). The words *tip'ārâ* and *tip'eret* (תפארה and תפארת), meaning "beauty" or "glory," point to the outward accouterments of honor. The noun form derived from the root *p'r* – פאר can mean a headdress, turban, fine garments, or jewels worn by a person of honor, the rod or scepter of a ruler, or even the boasting of an individual warrior. While the use of *tip'ārâ* (תפארה) may suggest justified admiration, it also can imply conceit if the persons claiming honor draw attention to themselves through unmerited and extravagant attire or words of self-importance. Thus, terms honoring warriors and rulers may cross the line separating praise from pretention and respect from ridicule. The story about Gideon selecting his warriors expresses concern that elite warriors fighting for glory will vaunt themselves instead of giving honor to Yhwh (Judg. 7:2). Barak, a warrior who sought honor in battle, is remembered as the grandson of Noam (*n'm* – נעם), a name suggesting "beautiful, pleasant, delightful, and lovely" (4:12). While the praise name of Barak's ancestor may be entirely positive, there could be a hint of affectation.

Like the word "beautify," the negative term *ḥrp* (חרף), meaning "taunt, mock, or scorn," makes an assertion or judgment, but does not actually add to or diminish the honor/weightiness of the person, place, or people being described. While a curse is an instrument to reduce worth, a taunt is simply an allegation. Related to the verb "to sharpen," *ḥrp* (חרף) implies saying sharp things that reproach or contradict. In the Song of Deborah, the fact that Zebulon lives contradicts death (Judg. 5:18). Elsewhere in Judges and the Hebrew Bible, the act of mocking questions people's honor as they are taunted or scorned for sexual misdeeds, wounds or disfigurement, barrenness, widowhood, poverty, political impotence, sin, or not being circumcised. While by itself a taunt does not take away honor, unanswered mockery can. Unless a taunt is so obviously false that it does not merit a response, the failure to react reveals weakness and results in dishonor.

Tales of Honor and Dishonor in Judges

A lexical study is informative, especially about sentiments of honor, but a literary analysis of the stories in Judges leads to a richer understanding of honor as conduct and reputation. The tales illustrate the elements of honorable behavior (code of honor) and the stories themselves are examples of the way an honorable reputation was crystallized and transmitted. To have one's story celebrated in oral poetic form or written on a clay tablet made one's reputation fixed and possibly permanent. Thus, the reputation of honorable behavior could persist beyond the life of an individual warrior, poet, or bard. The greatest honor in the book of Judges was reserved for the *gibbôrîm*, the mighty warriors praised by the bardic storyteller, the Deuteronomistic editor, and the humanist writer.[31] As noted in chapter 1, the term *gibbôr* is sometimes complemented by the word *ḥayil* (חיל), meaning "strength, prosperity, wealth." In ancient Israel, men of *ḥayil* (חיל) were rewarded with women's laud and praise. For example, the word *mĕḥôlâ* (מחולה), a noun form of *ḥyl*, refers to a celebratory dance that honors a strong individual or action. In Judg. 11:34 Jephthah's daughter danced in honor of her father's victory and in Judg. 21:21 the nubile daughters of Shiloh danced before their male suitors.

The literary record of reputation suggests that the authors and hearers of the accounts in Judges were well aware that mighty men of valor attempted to follow a code of honor. Although every account

---

31. The word *gibbôr* (*gbr* – גבר), meaning "to be strong or mighty," is best translated as "strong warrior." The great force of the term *gbr* is evident in the very last line of the Song of Deborah which projects the concept onto the celestial realm by announcing that those who love Yhwh are "Like the going forth to battle of the Sun in his strength (*gĕbûrâ* – גברה)" (Judg. 5:31).

in the book of Judges dramatizes one or more aspects of honor, when considering the honor of the male warrior, none is more direct than the tale of Gideon. Not only does Gideon's story illustrate various components of honor such as courage in battle, taking revenge, and the importance of defending honor, the narrative gives great attention to the concept of weightiness as a foundational characteristic of honor. To emphasize this quality the storyteller begins the account with references to honor's negative counterpart, lowliness or inconsequence. According to the tale, unable to defend themselves, the Israelites cowered in caves and rocky dens. Bemoaning Israel's plight at the hands of Midian, the text says, "And made low (*dll* – דלל) was Israel before Midian" (Judg. 6:6).

Turning from the general situation to the plight of an individual Israelite, the story introduces Gideon as fearful (he furtively grinds wheat in a winepress to avoid detection by the Midianites and he is afraid of the members of his own household) and as the youngest and least important member of his family. Very soon it becomes apparent that the initial references to weakness and fear are a literary foil for the honor soon to be accorded to Gideon's brashness and strength. Although somewhat hesitant (he acts at night to avoid detection and confrontation), Gideon brazenly dismantles Baal's altar, cuts down Asherah's sacred grove, constructs a new altar on the local fortress, and on that very spot honors a competing deity (Yhwh) with a burnt offering (an honorific spiritual feast) consumed by igniting the wood cut from the sacred grove. While Gideon's actions honor Yhwh, the emphasis of the story is on the dishonor inflicted on Baal. When the townsfolk discover that it is Gideon who defied Baal, they demand that Gideon's father, Joash, the head of a prominent household, hand over the son so that the townspeople can execute him. Using the terminology of a lawsuit or perhaps a battle between champions, Joash responds by saying,

"Will you contend (*ryb* – ריב) for Baal? Will you deliver him? ...
If he is a god, he will contend for himself because someone broke down his altar."
Then they called him (Gideon) Jerubbaal (*yĕrubbaʻal* – ירבעל)[32] That is to say, "Let Baal contend with him,"
Because he broke down his altar. (Judg. 6:31–32)

"Contend" (*ryb* – ריב), the key word in this passage, has a very public connotation for it can also mean "to strive or quarrel noisily."[33] By his audacious act, Gideon issued a dramatic challenge to the honor of his brothers, his father's house, the men of the town, and most of all to Baal.

Gideon's efforts to defy Baal's supernatural honor and power were part of a strategy to dishonor and disempower temporal rivals. At a time when the Midianite threat had undermined the people's confidence in the ability of an elite loyal to Baal to protect them, an intrepid young warrior stepped forward to undercut Baal, the established elite, and leaders of the house of Joash. Gideon's rebuke to the honor of the supposedly all-powerful Baal was a challenge to all those who identified with Baal. As the head of an influential house, Joash found his honor (consequentialness) called into question for not being able to control his son or defend the deity of his divination site. By their association with a seemingly weak father and because of their inability to stand up against their junior "sibling," the brothers' honor was tarnished as well. And, when the townsmen failed to follow through on their threat to kill Gideon, their consequentialness was undermined.

Apparently Joash regarded an attack from the townspeople as a greater threat than the defiance of his son. In an attempt to neutralize the danger to his son and his house, Joash turned the threat against

---

32. Meaning, "let Baal contend" (for himself).
33. The word *rîb* (ריב) is a technical term for a lawsuit.

Gideon into a direct challenge to the townsfolk and to Baal. Now the townsfolk were trapped in an impossible dilemma. If indeed Baal was a deity of honor or consequence, he had no need of the town contending for him by killing Gideon. Paradoxically, if the men of the town defended Baal by taking matters into their own hands and gaining revenge, they would dishonor Baal by revealing his weakness. Just as in a duel, where the two parties maintain their honor only if they act without assistance, Baal could escape disgrace only if he did not have to rely on the succor of mere mortals. As the god of storm and lightning, Baal should have had ample power to defend his honor by striking down Gideon and the house of Joash. His inability to do so was clear evidence of impotence. In the end, Gideon and his god Yhwh gained honor at the expense of every other actor in the story. Gideon's new praise name, "Let Baal contend (if he can)," was a sharp affront to the deposed deity who lost honor by being unable to defend himself.[34]

The struggle for honor in the story of Gideon was in fact a contest for power. Although readers often take Gideon's self-effacing statements about his junior status in a lowly family at face value, Gideon was an aggressive and ambitious warrior carrying out a palace coup. The fact that Gideon is described as a *gibbôr ḥayil* (strong warrior of valor), that he came from a prominent and exceptionally wealthy house (few families would have had the means to make the extravagant sacrifice of a bull, that Gideon himself had more than ten servants), that his father was the proprietor of an important divination site, that Gideon could muster a large band of warriors, and that at the end of his life Gideon had acquired enough wives to father seventy sons all point to Gideon as an aristocratic warrior of uncommon

---

34. The words in parentheses are my addition. The message of Gideon's actions parallels linguistic affronts to Baal when the term "Baal" was replaced by the somewhat similar sounding word for "shame," בשת.

wealth and status. That conclusion is confirmed by the statement of two defeated enemies who identified Gideon as having the form of the son of a king (Judg. 8:18).

The account in Judges suggests that Gideon's coup was not a creation of his own calculations. If the tale of the messenger of Yhwh is more than a literary device fashioned by the storyteller, Gideon was encouraged by an itinerant outside agitator who represented an upstart deity.[35] In a context of political, social, and economic crisis, the wandering stranger approached Gideon, a junior member of a prominent house associated with Baal. Encouraging revolt against the young warrior's house, town, and shrine, the stranger promised supernatural support.

While Gideon's challenge to the honor and power of established leaders was indirect (ostensibly he was targeting a deity), other examples from Judges show that people attacked the honor of their human rivals more openly through taunting. In fact Gideon himself was the target of a taunt after he asked the elders of Succoth to provide food for his exhausted warriors (Judg. 8:6). The most extensive accounts of taunting in the main body of Judges are contained in the stories of Abimelech and Samson. Like another character Jephthah, Abimelech is introduced to listeners with the announcement that his ancestry was less than honorable. As the son of a concubine, Abimelech would have been less worthy or consequential than his putative brothers whose mothers had higher status as wives. Although like Jephthah, Abimelech advanced to gain political control by virtue of his military skill, his rule over Shechem was never uncontested. At a harvest feast, which Abimelech did not attend, some of the town leaders cursed him. After the curse, a rival then mocked or taunted Abimelech by reminding the men of

---

35. See the discussion of the messenger of Yhwh in chapter 1. As noted there, the word *mal'āk* (מלאך), meaning "messenger," can refer either to a human or to an angel.

Shechem that Abimelech was a mere servant, not a legitimate leader. The rival Gaal raised the issue by saying,

> "Who is Abimelech and who is Shechem? Why should we serve him? Did not the son of Jerubbaal[36] and Zebul his deputy serve the men of Hamor (Donkey), father of Shechem? Then why should we serve him?" (Judg. 9:28)

Putting Abimelech in his place by telling the town leaders to remember who was who, Gaal recalled that Abimelech and his deputy had once served in an "inferior vassal-type relationship to the rulers of Shechem."[37] Thus Gaal's first step toward unseating Abimelech was to dishonor him through a taunt. Left unanswered, such a taunt would have diminished (made less weighty) Abimelech.

Although Gaal managed to gain the support of Shechem's elders, Abimelech responded by attacking and defeating the town. As his forces were advancing against the town temporarily under Gaal's leadership, Abimelech's lieutenant then said, "Where now is your mouth which said, 'Who is Abimelech that we should serve him?' Is not this (the group of advancing warriors) the people which you rejected as worthless?" (Judg. 9:38).[38] With these words of derision, Zebul now taunted Gaal, who would soon die at the hands of the supposedly "worthless" Abimelech.

The story of Samson is also filled with the language and imagery of honor and dishonor, especially as expressed through feats of strength, acts of taunting, and deeds of vengeance. Composed as a legendary account, the tale of the animal-like hero opens with the shame of his mother, a barren woman. The barrenness was cured by a roving

---

36. In other words, Abimelech, Gideon's putative son.
37. Susan Niditch, *Judges: A Commentary* (Louisville: Westminster, 2008), 117.
38. The root of the word translated as "worthless" is *m's* (מאס), which as a verb means "reject, devalue, disobey, refuse to follow," and as a noun means "worthless." This is consistent with the idea that to lack honor is to lack consequence.

messenger of Yhwh who embodied honor in his name (*pl'* – פלא), meaning "extraordinary" or "incomparable." Seeking to recognize the messenger's honor (weightiness, heaviness), the woman's husband, Manoah, offered to prepare a lavish meal which the messenger rejected in favor of a sacrifice—spiritual feast—to honor Yhwh. As the flames and smoke of the sacrifice rose toward heaven, indicating that Yhwh accepted the honor, the man and his wife gestured their deference by falling on the ground. The contrast between the flames ascending to the deity and the mortals lying prostrate dramatized the honor of the divine being and the humbleness of the humans (Judg. 13:17–23). Once the messenger's promise had come true, Yhwh blessed and thus elevated Samson, whose honor was manifest in his uncommon strength (Judg. 13:24–25).

After he grew up, Samson's Philistine adversaries repeatedly tried to weaken, humble, or dishonor him. The lords of the Philistines bound him with cords to bring him low (*'nh* – ענה) (Judg. 16:5) or weaken and sicken him (*ḥlh* – חלה) (Judg. 16:7, 11, and 17). Overcome by the wiles of his woman and the persistence of the Philistine lords, Samson eventually was subdued and horribly disfigured. Samson's dishonor inspired the Philistines to shout triumphant acclamations of praise and honor to their god Dagon, who had delivered Samson to them (Judg. 16:24).[39] At his nadir, the disgraced Samson was shackled, forced to grind grain like a slave or animal, and mocked by his Philistine captors. However, Samson's story ended with his restoration to honor or consequentialness. Successfully imploring Yhwh to restore his strength, Samson regained his honor by taking vengeance (*nqm* – נקם) in the act of pulling down Dagon's temple on scores of assembled Philistines.

---

39. As noted earlier, the word *hll* (הלל), used to describe the taunts against Samson, is retained in English as "hallelujah" (praise Yhwh)

Honoring him in death, Samson's family retrieved his body and gave it a dignified burial.[40]

While the tale of Samson chronicled his life from birth to death, Samson is never pictured as anything but an intemperate youthful warrior. His prodigious feats of strength are paralleled by his unlimited sexual appetite, his propensity to violence and revenge, his disrespect for cultural mores, his unwillingness to take parental advice, and his delight in drinking, gambling, and riddling. Lacking judgment and balance, Samson is easily tricked by a coquettish female and has no ability to put off immediate pleasure for personal safety or long-term satisfaction. Similar to a perpetually out-of-control adolescent, Samson inhabits the world between barbarism and civilization.[41] Living like a beast, he is seen as both a menace and a savior. Like a wild animal he possesses enormous strength; rips apart his prey; seeks only to satisfy his primal needs for food, water, sex, and sleep; terrorizes local villagers; takes refuge in the crags of the rocks; and is pursued, captured, and bound. Samson is celebrated as a man of honor, but his honor is not that of a mature and responsible adult. Although Samson is characterized in idealized, larger-than-life terms, he is never described as a person with any administrative duties or organizational concerns. He never leads a military contingent or engages in diplomacy. He does not participate in political bargaining with city elders, enter a covenant agreement with a community, rule a town, or manage an oracle site. Nor does he ever parent a child or head a household, aspects of domestic responsibility and honor. Never taking part in organized combat, even his great warrior

---

40. The importance of offering honor in death, even to an adversary, has been noted by ancient Greek and Roman political philosophers. Even Machiavelli acknowledges the importance of an honorable funeral.
41. A number of scholars have linked the violence and tumultuousness of premodern societies to short life expectancy, which meant that a very high percentage of the population consisted of teenagers and that inexperienced people with high levels of hormonal activity were in positions of power and authority.

feats are all described as acts of personal revenge, not community protection. However large Samson looms in legend, the fact remains that he is consistently remembered as a young and unsocialized man of valor, the kind of person who would have been recruited by the more politically ambitious or strategically cognizant men such as Ehud, Gideon, Abimelech, or Barak. Samson is a warrior, not a leader. His role is to go wholeheartedly and unthinkingly into battle. Samson embodies the combative values Moses Finley observes in Homeric Greece where "strength, bravery, physical courage, (and) prowess" were the singular attributes of youthful honor.[42]

Although he was no more real than Paul Bunyan, Samson's story would have been prized by young Israelite men who hoped to emulate his strength and bravado. A youthful adventurer, Samson is the archetype of one of the "turbulent and aimless men" (ănāšîm rêqîm ûpōḥăzîm – אנשים ריקים ופחזים) who hired themselves to a more established warrior.[43] The word rēq (רק), which means "empty, foolish, vain, and idle," suggests someone without direction or enduring loyalty to anyone but himself, someone susceptible to or needing the guidance and direction of another.[44] While pḥz (פחז) is generally translated as "worthless," the root form means "boiling" or "turbulent" and suggests undirected and explosive power. Other connotations of the word—"wanton, rash, boastful, haughty, and lascivious"—are reminders that left on its own the turbulence could become turmoil. These qualities of recklessness and aimlessness describe the type of daring and audacious individuals ready to serve any strongman offering to reward them. Like the hero Othniel, these young men would have been attracted by the prospect of booty,

---

42. Finley, *World of Odysseus*, 28.
43. Judg. 9:4, referring to the men hired by Abimelech; Judg. 11:3, men hired by Jephthah; and 2 Chron. 13:7, men hired by Jeroboam.
44. Plato and Aristotle described young warriors as all courage and no wisdom. Although essential for the defense of the community, they needed the guiding hand of wise and mature elders.

access to women, land, and glory. Although some would have been bound to their headman by ties of kinship, others were unattached (rootless or empty) and would have remained with their leader only so long as he was successful. As the stories of the big men Gideon and Abimelech demonstrate, loyalty endured only if subordinates could count on the power of a man of valor to punish or reward.[45]

Samson's animal power and temperament were symbolized by his uncut hair, a key mark of honor and identity for a charismatic warrior group known as Nazirites.[46] Growing rapidly, hair is regarded as a symbol of life and energy in many preindustrial cultures.[47] Called by and dedicated to the deity, long-haired Nazirite warriors represented "the natural end of a nature/culture continuum."[48] Left uncut, the hair of the Nazirites suggested primal power and untamed vitality. Susan Niditch draws a parallel between Samson and the call to war in the Song of Deborah. While some English versions translate the words *biprōaʿ pĕrāʿôt* (בפרע פרעות; Judg. 5:2) as "leaders leading," Niditch renders בפרע פרעות as "flow did the flowing locks."[49] Thus Niditch reads,

> When flow did the flowing locks in Israel,
>   When freely offered themselves [for battle] did the people.[50]

---

45. Gideon savagely punished disloyal towns (Judg. 8:13–17) and Abimelech's entire group of mercenary followers fled when he was killed and could no longer benefit them (Judg. 9:55).
46. See Niditch, *Judges*, 171, from which much of the following discussion of hair is drawn.
47. In many African societies, fingernails, toenails, and the placenta fall into the same category. Because they are thought to contain so much life force, they are regarded as potent sources of magical power. Thus, the hair, fingernails, and toenails of a chief are carefully guarded to make sure they do not fall into the hands of an adversary or malevolent magic worker.
48. Niditch, *Judges*, 171.
49. The word *prʿ* (פרע) can mean either "to lead" or "to sprout/grow." The RSV reads "leading" while Niditch chose the second meaning. Elsewhere in the Hebrew Bible the term clearly refers to long uncut hair (Num. 6:5; Deut. 32:42; Ezek. 44:20). In my view, Niditch's translation is preferable.
50. Niditch, *Judges*, 225 (brackets my insertion).

Niditch captures the image of wild-looking warriors rising to the defense of the people. Samson, the Nazirite, fits that category.

From both the Song of Deborah and the story of Samson, it is evident that ideally the turbulent energy of young warriors was to be channeled into the service of society. As Niditch notes, although Samson's hair was uncut, it was not uncoiffed. Braided into plaits, the hair on Samson's head suggested some level of cultural conformity and pointed to Samson's social usefulness. However, when Samson's hair was woven by Delilah, conformity was replaced by control. A modern counterpart to Samson would be the young Masaai *moran* living in Kenya and Tanzania. After being circumcised in mid to late adolescence, Masaai males ascend to the status of warrior, whose task is to protect the settlement and its cattle from dangerous animals or raiding rivals. Although not permitted to marry, the *moran* are afforded great sexual liberty with young girls and even with the wives of the elders. Not responsible for making community decisions, they have a reputation of spending their time fighting, hunting, exchanging insults, telling tall tales, eating large quantities of meat, drinking, and womanizing. Like the Masaai *moran*, Samson's behavior was honorable for a particular stage in life.

The legend of Samson is not an unequivocal endorsement of youthful warriors. The obvious use of irony is evidence that the bardic storyteller was reminding listeners that the explosive energy of young men needed to be contained.[51] While the accounts praised Samson, and by extension other young warriors, the narrative also contained admonitions. The tale's many ironic couplets would have been intended as warnings to chide and educate spirited young males.

---

51. Based on the Greek word εἰρωνεία (*eirōneia*), irony suggests a literary device using double meaning. With irony one party—more naïve—hears one meaning while a more sophisticated party recognizes the critical message underlying the narrative. Certainly the use of irony was not foreign to biblical writers. See Carolyn J. Sharp, *Irony and Meaning in the Hebrew Bible* (Bloomington: Indiana University Press, 2009).

Born with high expectations and favored by Yhwh, the intemperate Samson repeatedly fails to reach his potential. A prodigiously powerful man, Samson is rendered defenseless by an unarmed woman. Although clever enough to devise an unsolvable riddle, Samson foolishly betrays his own secret. A great warrior, capable of pursuing enemies, he spends much of his time chasing women. Repeatedly, he naively extends trust to the untrustworthy. Although he inflicts devastation on the Philistines—burning their shocks, standing grain, and olive groves as well as killing great numbers of their people—his boundless vengeance endangers his own people who themselves bind him and turn him over to the Philistines.[52] These and other ironies contained in the Samson story would have reminded daring young men that their potential could be squandered, that their passion needed to be moderated, that lust could lead to downfall, that cleverness could be misspent, and that excessive violence against an enemy could jeopardize one's own community.

Because the ironies in the story of Samson are so obvious and so numerous, one must ask if they were intended as more than

---

52. For these and other examples, see Lillian Klein, *The Triumph of Irony in the Book of Judges* (Sheffield: Almond, 1988), 109–39. While Klein's book contains many useful insights, her overall analysis is strained. In large part, this weakness results from the fact that she works only from the final redacted version of Judges. Klein gives little attention to the fact that the book of Judges was compiled over many centuries. Thus, she interprets the stories, phrases, and even turn of words in the epic-bardic account according to the theological and moral expectations of the much later Deuteronomistic writer. Granted, irony depends on the existence of two perspectives. But Klein juxtaposes perspectives so distant in time and worldview that neither the original storytellers, nor the first listeners, nor the protagonists could have been aware of both views. Klein may regard it as ironic that while Samson's birth was heralded by a messenger of Yhwh, Samson's behavior resembled that of an amoral untamed animal. But for people first hearing Samson's tale there would have been no dichotomy and therefore no irony. Those people would have only admired Samson's divinely endowed strength and virility. Furthermore, Klein does not hesitate to reshape the Hebrew language to fit her goals. At one point she says the word "Samson" means "sun " (*šemeš* – שמש), the interpretation all scholars accept, while later she says it might mean "name " (*šēm* – שם), a very idiosyncratic reading. Each meaning is used by Klein to support a literary interpretation. Similarly, she sees a connection between the word "Deborah" (bee) and the word "Delilah" (night) based merely on the fact that both names begin with the Hebrew letter ד (*dālet*) and end with the feminine suffix ה (*hê*). See *Triumph of Irony*, 109–39.

humorous tools to warn young men of the dangers of arrogance, reckless combativeness, the wiles of women, disrespect for community, and disregard for parental guidance. Were the stories told as high-spirited tales to celebrate and also educate youthful warriors or were they meant as serious criticisms of conventional martial values? To answer the question, one must distinguish between the irony of hyperbole, which can affirm cultural values, and the irony of disruption, which challenges cultural norms. Describing how the two are used in the Hebrew Bible, Carolyn Sharp emphasizes the fact that the more skeptical form of irony is culturally disruptive because it invites the reader or listener into a conversation about the actual validity of the values presented in the surface message.[53] The milder and more positive form of irony, which Sharp labels "hyperbole," may gently criticize or poke fun at a character or value, but does not pose a real threat. Unlike disruptive irony, hyperbole does not seek to undermine fundamental cultural assumptions. Irony may be rooted in caricature, but for exaggeration to become confrontational irony it must evoke a strong element of doubt. With deep irony, a sophisticated, skeptical, or cynical listener recognizes that the story's author is actually rejecting the values represented by the surface meaning of the account. Such skepticism and cynicism are evidence of serious uncertainty about the social, spiritual, political, or moral values endorsed by the ostensible message of the text.

Were the stories of Samson told to malign the qualities he exhibits even as the storyteller seemingly praised the youthful warrior? If meant only as friendly hyperbole, then the Samson stories affirmed

---

53. In her first chapter, "Interpreting Irony: Rhetorical, Hermeneutical, and Theological Possibilities," Sharp explains the different levels of irony. She labels the milder form "hyperbole" and reserves the word "irony" for the more caustic or skeptical form. Irony, Sharp says, is aporetic, culturally disruptive, and invitational. Thus, it is inclined to doubt, it challenges conventional cultural values, and it calls people to posit new norms (*Irony and Meaning*, 24).

the values at the same time as they offered a mild rebuke of the fictional personification of those values. But, if intended as deep, negative irony, then the values of warrior honor so evident on the surface of the Samson saga were being challenged in a fundamental way. While an author's intent can be difficult to determine, most likely the guiding literary principle in stories about Samson was sympathetic exaggeration rather than denigrating criticism. Almost certainly the tellers and hearers of Samson's deeds were well aware that the sagas were over-the-top caricatures, but did not consider them fundamental indictments of a robust warrior culture. To read the story of Samson as a piece of negative irony would mean that the heroic code of aggressive and courageous warrior honor exhibited by Samson was being questioned at the time when the story was first told, a time when martial values were highly regarded. Furthermore, the fact that both conclusions of Samson's tale (Judges 15 and 16) portray him as victorious suggests that the narrator was not issuing a veiled ironic indictment of the story's hero.[54]

Of all the storytellers in Judges—bardic, Deuteronomistic, or humanist—the unvarnished bard was the least likely to have used irony as a weapon against the deepest values of his or her own society. Both the narrator and hearers of Samson's story would have recognized the obvious overstatements and they would have been critical of Samson's personal shortcomings. However, they would not have had misgivings about the boastful and bellicose qualities writ large in this fictional character. Similarly, the accounts of Achsah, Deborah, Jael, and Abimelech may have mocked male ineptitude or pretention, but they did not actually challenge the underlying masculine values of the time. Bardic irony in Judges is a mild, even

---

54. At the end of Judges 15 Samson is described as exhausted after slaughtering one thousand men; at the end of chapter 16 he is remembered as a tragic hero who brings death on a multitude of Philistines. While there is irony in both accounts, the irony is not directed against Samson. Instead, his deeds are regarded as completely heroic.

humorous irony that affirms rather than undermines conventional values.

In response to those who might disagree and interpret the story of Samson as harshly ironic, the mere presence of the story is proof that the values evident in the surface reading were embraced by many, if not most, Israelites. Because the only purpose of a powerful and negative irony is to criticize conventional values, even the modern reader who sees unfriendly irony in the story of Samson must acknowledge that such values were once present in and presumably dominated premonarchic Hebrew society. However, as in the age of Homer, the level of cultural skepticism required for deep irony seems uncharacteristic of the Early Iron Age period in Israel.

Most of the stories in Judges, especially those in the oldest corpus making up Judges 3–16 emphasize the military and political qualities of honor such as strength, valor, courage, vengeance, daring, and constancy. For the bardic-epic narrator, concepts of honor and dishonor were related to the warrior (Barak, Gideon, Samson) or the political leader (Abimelech and Jephthah). The honor of the warrior and political leader was particularly useful in times of turmoil brought about by the decline of Egyptian and Canaanite power and by the conflict with Philistine interlopers. Stories of military and political honor would also have been of great interest during the rise of the monarchy, thus providing a strong incentive to preserve them.

Unlike the bardic tales, accounts presented by the humanist editor express misgivings about the prevailing code of honor. However, the doubt of the humanist is directed to nonwarriorly expressions of honor. Composing his or her work in the absence of a functioning kingdom, the much later and more cosmopolitan humanist writer had a different set of concerns. The humanist writer shared the epic-bardic storyteller's interest in honor as worth and worthlessness, honor as grace and disgrace, honor as behavior and reputation, collective honor, and the need to avenge challenges to honor. However, the humanist was more attentive to the honor of the householder, the honor of a community or tribe, and the type of honor that affected the unity of the Hebrew peoples who had experienced the loss of their state. Reflecting the emphasis on the collective rather than the lone individual and in contrast to the epic tales of heroes such as Ehud or Gideon, the humanist assigned a name to only one person—Micah—and otherwise referred to people by their position, profession, or tribe.

The story of the Levite and his concubine emphasizes key aspects of householder and community honor (Judges 19). The account makes it clear that the honor of the head of a house is expressed through generosity and hospitality and depends on the willingness and ability to afford protection. In the first part of the tale the Levite's father-in-law demonstrated honor by acting with extravagant generosity toward a hapless man who was his social, economic, and ethnic inferior. As a Levite, the young man had no claim to land and perhaps had no fixed home. In Bethlehem, the town of his father-in-law, the Levite had no local kin support. Furthermore, he may have been without means to pay the dowry for a wife—the woman is described as a concubine—and he certainly was unable to keep the loyalty and affection of the woman who abandoned him by returning to her father's house. Although the Levite sojourner was inferior to his father-in-law, the older man spoke kindly to the Levite, expressed delight in seeing the man his daughter had rejected, and for five days lavished food and shelter upon the less fortunate visitor. Even when the Levite finally departed, the father-in-law was urging him to spend another night and to let his "heart be happy" (Judg. 19:9).

The honor and hospitality of the father-in-law are contrasted with the dishonor and inhospitality of the people of Gibeah. Every detail of the story is designed to intensify this difference. Avoiding the city of Jebus (an older name for Jerusalem), a city of "strangers," where he might expect rejection, the Levite pushed on to the Benjaminite town of Gibeah (Ramah), where he had a right to be welcomed. However, even though he sat conspicuously in the town square and even though he had his own provisions—bread and wine for himself and even straw and grain for his donkey—not one local person offered him hospitality. Finally, as the day was dying, a resident alien in the town, an old man from the hill country of Ephraim, offered to shelter him. The words of the man were "Be at ease, your needs are my responsibility" (Judg. 19:20). The old man then demonstrated his honor and hospitality by taking the Levite to his house, foddering the donkey, washing the man's feet, and plying him with food and drink. According to the words of the story, the hearts of the Levite and host were made happy.

In sharp contrast, in a final act of egregious inhospitality, the townsfolk interrupted the conviviality and demanded that the host allow them to assault the Levite sexually. As a literary cliché, the threat of sodomy (treating a man as a woman) against a guest is an intense accusation of dishonorable behavior and extreme inhospitality. The story of Lot uses the cliché to disgrace the men of Sodom and Gomorrah. Calling the men of Gibeah "sons of Belial," the tale of the Levite and his concubine accuses them of being reprobate, dissolute, and uncouth, the complete opposite of honorable.[55]

While the story about the Levite and his concubine was composed to reflect on honor in general, the narrative may also have had a more pointed and specific intent. Marc Brettler argues that the book of Judges has an anti-Saul and therefore anti-Benjaminite bias.[56]

---

55. The phrase *bĕnê bĕlīyaʿal* (בני בליעל) can mean either "sons of worthlessness" (worthless, useless) or "sons of Belial." The latter meaning is stronger for it evokes the base quality of the Canaanite netherworld. See 2 Sam. 22:5–6 and Ps. 18:4–5 for the more cosmic allusion.

While the favorable account of Ehud—an ambidextrous man of Benjamin—tempers Brettler's blanket statement, the stories at the end of Judges do suggest antipathy to the tribe of Benjamin. In addition, the tale of the Levite may imply a criticism intended to dishonor the powerful and wealthy houses and towns that managed to retain control of land during the exilic period. The real hero of the story is the alien householder from Ephraim. Through his generosity and his efforts to protect his guest, he is the most honorable individual in the cycle of stories. Although not honoring the Levite, the storyteller does argue that Levites should be treated charitably and that they deserve protection. While it is difficult to associate an anti-Benjamin, anti-Saul sentiment with any single time period in Israel's history, except of course during the time of Saul and David, the argument for sympathy toward Levites would have been most alive after the fall of the northern kingdom when displaced Levite priests sought refuge in the south.

Claiming that people refused to offer hospitality, that they treated men like women, or even that they killed or raped visitors, appears to have been a common cliché used to bring disrepute upon a house, town, or tribe. The inflammatory and polemical nature of such stories suggests that people in ancient Israel regarded the loss of honor as the loss of a prized asset. Thus storytellers could be just as dangerous to big men, towns, and tribes as powerful enemy warriors. To be defeated after putting up a valiant fight gave hope and pride; to suffer disgrace could ruin any prospect of future power and restoration. That was true for an individual and for any group or cause linked to that individual. Presumably, there was a constant struggle to enhance one's own honor and the honor of one's associates and ancestors. At

---

56. Marc Brettler, "The Book of Judges: Literature as Politics," *Journal of Biblical Literature* 108, no. 3 (1989): 395–418.

the same time, there would have been an effort to heap shame on opponents and their forbearers.

While allegations about the despicable conduct on the part of the men of Gibeah continue the theme of hospitality as a key ingredient of honor, the aggressive actions of the townspeople were used by the storyteller to introduce a second honor-related theme, the obligation to protect those in one's charge. As Frank Stewart observed when studying a Bedouin group in the Sinai, the ability to protect people within a house can be a primary element of honorable behavior. Again, the Ephraimite householder behaved with utmost honor. Forced to make a choice about whom to protect, the householder safeguarded his guest. Hoping to appease the members of a disorderly mob, the householder offered them his own virgin daughters and the Levite's concubine if only they would stop threatening his guest. Thus, the householder placed his obligation to protect a guest above his obligation to safeguard the sexual honor of the females in his house. In the end, the mob was assuaged when given the Levite's concubine, who was ravished and left to die. With this story, the humanist writer not only explains a key element of honor—the obligation to offer protection—but also indicates there are deep ambiguities and tensions within the code of honor. When faced with the unhappy dilemma of choosing whom to protect, the humanist writer argues that male guests come first, women of the household second, and that concubines, even if guests, come last. Like Jephthah, who had to decide between protecting his own daughter, thereby ensuring the future of his own lineage, and upholding his covenant oath, the householder faced excruciatingly painful options.

The next episode in the saga of the Levite deals with the honor of revenge and the importance of tribal solidarity. Continuing the examination of moral ambiguities, the humanist writer explores the destructive implications of protecting honor through seeking retribution. The humanist sets the stage by making it clear that there was no uncertainty about the horrific nature of the offense. After gang-raping the concubine, the dishonorable men of Gibeah discarded her. She then managed to make her way to the doorstep of the Ephraimite's house where she expired. Although expressing no affection for the concubine, once he discovered that she had died the Levite rightly determined that the affront must be avenged. Chopping the body into twelve sections, the Levite sent a piece to each of the twelve tribes of Israel. By this action, the Levite announced that all the tribes had suffered insult and that all must respond. Reflecting a segmentary lineage arrangement where an offense against one was an offense against all, the story makes it clear that the Levite's action obligated all Israel to assist him. Emphasizing the legitimacy of the Levite's position, the humanist writer stated that everyone who learned of the rape and murder was horrified. All agreed that nothing so egregious had ever been done since the Israelites had come from Egypt. Once they learned of the evil, the men of Israel were honor bound to respond. The same logic obligated the tribe of Benjamin to come to the defense of their Gibeah kin. Thus when the other tribes of Israel asked the tribe of Benjamin to hand over the dishonorable/worthless men of Gibeah so that they could be executed, Benjamin refused.[57] Indeed, now that their honor was also at stake, the men of Benjamin rallied around their kin, the men of Gibeah, and went forth to war against the rest of Israel. The result was a protracted and destructive series of battles that led to the deaths of tens of thousands of mighty men, the slaughter of entire populations of people and animals, and the burning of all the towns of Benjamin. In addition to suffering complete ruin, the tribe of Benjamin faced the threat of future extinction. For not only had the

---

57. The writer again uses the phrase *běnê běliya'al* (בני בליעל).

tribes of Israel pledged to wage war against the Benjaminites, they had also taken an oath not to give their daughters in marriage to any man of Benjamin.

With this tale, the humanist writer reflects on the dilemma caused by this exercise of righteous revenge. Although the honor of the Levite and all Israel was now restored, the result was the potential annihilation of Benjamin as a tribe. Allowed to run its course, the quest for honor would be unacceptably destructive. In the end, the sons of Israel fashioned a strategy to solve the dilemma. Unlike Jephthah, who had to live with the dire consequences of his pledge, Israel resorted to an artifice that enabled Benjamin to obtain wives and thus ensure its future. First, after determining that the men of one community, Jabesh-gilead, had not mustered for the battle against Benjamin, Israel attacked Jabesh-gilead, killing all the men and married women. Four hundred virgins were spared and given to Benjamin as wives. Second, because four hundred was not enough, Benjamin was instructed to lie in wait at the annual festival to Yhwh at Shiloh where young girls would be dancing a whirling dance. Each man of Benjamin could seize a woman and the people of Shiloh would not incur guilt from breaking the oath prohibiting them from voluntarily exchanging wives with Benjamin. This tale, clearly a literary creation, is used by the humanist writer to express doubts about the utility and morality of protecting honor through revenge. As we have seen earlier, Frank Stewart extols the positive social and political functions of defending honor. Taking a more pessimistic view, the humanist, writing 2,500 years ago, calls attention to the destructive consequences of turning the defense of honor into the pursuit of revenge. The result could be the extinction of a house, tribe, or even nation.

In addition to describing the honor associated with hospitality and revenge, Judges considers female honor. When compared to the humanist, the epic-bardic tales are less nuanced, but the earliest accounts in Judges provide evidence that premonarchic peoples questioned stereotypical notions of female honor. Nowhere is this more evident than in the Song of Deborah. The song robustly challenges conventional ideas about female honor. In many respects, the book of Judges reinforces standard norms about women's honor. The legend of Samson reaffirms the belief that a woman's honor was linked to fertility and that infertility was a great source of anxiety and dishonor. Samson's story also presents women as deferential (even though the messenger of Yhwh appeared to the wife, the husband took charge of the sacrificial feast), as coquettes (Delilah), as whores (the prostitute in Gaza), as untrustworthy (the wife in Timnah), or as the interchangeable and disposable property of men (the wife and her sister). Jephthah's tragic saga emphasizes the concept that the proper role of women is to praise the warriorly accomplishments of men (lauding military triumph with singing and dancing), complete obedience (the daughter encourages her father to keep his word), and virginity and fertility (the daughter's only request is to have time to mourn the fact that she will never marry). By their near-exclusive focus on male actors, the stories about Gideon marginalize women and give scant consideration to female honor. The only females mentioned in the entire cycle of stories are the goddess Asherah, a discredited symbol of fertility (Judg. 6:26–30), and Gideon's many wives who serve only as passive vessels for bearing the great man's offspring (Judg. 8:30). The stories of Abimelech and Jephthah and the tale of the Levite and his concubine indicate that the status of a subordinate concubine or secondary wife was less honorable than that of a primary wife for whom the full dowry had been paid. While Judges notes that it was a woman who killed Abimelech, even that woman is dismissed with faint praise. Presented as a mere woman, the female is implicitly contrasted with a strong and honorable warrior, and her instrument of battle is not a manly sword but a humble domestic tool, the small upper millstone. Micah's mother is portrayed as the head of the house, or at least the manager of household wealth, but she is easily manipulated by her conniving son. In the story of the Levite's concubine, even the honorable householder regards women as objects to be controlled and bargained away. The Levite himself treats his concubine with absolute indifference except when her disgrace undermines his own honor. The final episodes in Judges, describing the anguish over the loss of wives for Benjamin, present women as passive players whose only role is to bear children and ensure the continuity of the people. The description of the calculated attack on Jabesh-gilead (21:9–12) argues that women are legitimate and valuable prizes to be taken in war. The subsequent tale of ambushing the dancing virgins of Shiloh suggests that even the institution of marriage is based on men seizing defenseless women. The ritualized capture of women has long been a feature of marriage ceremonies in many cultures. Among many ethnic groups in East Africa, the male relatives of the bride and groom engage in a stylized battle whose goal is to remove the female from the home of her father and transfer her to the home of her new husband. While, as an African friend told me, the point of the skirmish is to demonstrate "this is a woman worth fighting for," the ritual relegates women to a passive role. The woman "worth fighting for" is a compliant nubile virgin and the men demonstrate their honor through physical combat.[58]

The Song of Deborah (Judges 5) presents an entirely different understanding of female honor. Perhaps the most ancient piece of literature in the Hebrew Bible, this is likely an example of a song performed by the women who danced and chanted praises to honor

---

58. Personal communication from James Karanga, a leader in the community of Molo, Kenya. Karanga reports, however, that in mock battles the action sometimes results in physical injury.

the return of victorious warriors.[59] There also is a suggestion that the song, accompanied by tambourines, was heard at watering holes where pastoralists gathered to refresh their herds (Judg. 5:11).[60] The song begins with dramatic allusions to honor. First, it celebrates the young long-haired male warriors who earned honor through their martial abilities. Next, the song honors the people volunteering willingly for battle. The term "freely offer" (*ndb* – נדב), used in Judg. 5:2 and 5:9, means "to be generous, willing, and noble" and also "to incite or energize." Across cultures, individuals considered noble or honorable have been expected to throw themselves unreservedly into battle and to be extravagantly generous with their material wealth. Next, the song honors Yhwh by pronouncing a blessing (an act of empowering) and by evoking strong supernatural martial imagery. Yhwh's entrance unleashes forces of primal cosmic dimensions. As the most masculine warrior of all, the mighty deity Yhwh goes forth to battle in the open country of Edom, causing the earth to shake, the skies and the clouds to spout water, and the mountains to quake.

In spite of these references to male honor, both versions of Deborah's story (the song in Judges 5 and the prose rendition in Judges 4) explicitly announce that women, not men, would receive the honor and that men would be humbled. Not only did Deborah take the initiative to call Barak, the strongman honored Deborah (recognized her as consequential) by insisting that she accompany him into battle against the Canaanite commander Sisera. It is then that she tells Barak that he would not reap the acclaim (*tip'ārâ* – תפארה), but that Sisera would be defeated by a woman (Judg. 4:9).

59. Niditch, *Judges*, 76 and 78. Niditch also notes that even though the song is attributed to both Deborah and Barak, the verb "sang" (ותשר) in Judg. 5:1 is in the feminine form. As a typical victory song, the Song of Deborah would have been similar to the type of song that greeted Jephthah and David when they came home from battle.
60. In East Africa, when pastoralists come together at watering holes during the dry season, they spend much of their time recounting heroic tales of conquest and courage. Not only are norms of honor reinforced, the stories are transmitted to multiple clan groups.

By using the word *tip'ārâ* (תפארה), a term that suggests external appearance and boasting, rather than the word *kābôd*, which indicates weight or consequence, the storyteller may be subtly diminishing Barak and describing him as seeking superficial glory. While Deborah's pronouncement threatened to diminish Barak's reputation, it was devastating for Sisera's name. By falling at the hand of a woman, Sisera would forever be dishonored. Although death in battle was regarded as a tragedy, an honorable death brought fame that could last for generations. Such fame could strengthen a house, city, or tribe. But to be killed by a woman meant that one would be humiliated and scorned for all time.

According to tradition, all of Deborah's predictions came true. Barak's modestly equipped forces defeated Sisera's chariots.[61] After his army had been routed, Sisera abandoned his men and fled toward the northeast. Compounding his cowardly deed, he hid in the tent of a woman, a Kenite named Jael. Sisera believed he would be safe with Jael because the itinerant Kenite metalworkers were at peace with the Canaanites. Secreted under a skin, he huddled in the tent while shamefully relying on a female to stand guard and protect him against his enemies. In an ironic twist that explicitly denied him masculine honor, he instructed Jael to answer in the negative should his pursuers ask, "Is there a man here?" Sisera badly misjudged the woman, for while the fainthearted commander was incapacitated by sleep, the fearless and strong Jael drove a tent stake through his neck. A dramatic detail that must have delighted every Israelite storyteller and listener recalled that Sisera twitched convulsively before he died. In every respect, the tale disgraced a man and assigned martial honor to a female.

---

61. Judges indicates that the chariots were washed away or became hopelessly mired in the mud after a miraculous flash flood. Such a statement may be a literary cliché about the defeat of a powerful and heavily armed foe. Pharaoh's forces were said to have suffered a similar fate.

More important than assailing the honor of Barak and Sisera, the Song of Deborah contested the conventions of female honor. Neither Deborah nor Jael were honored for their domesticity, fertility, or beauty. As a professional diviner, Deborah offered advice to people coming to her from an extensive geographical area; she was the one who summoned Barak; and the strongman regarded her as essential for the operation's success. For her part, Jael was recognized as blessed, played the role of victorious warrior, and presented herself both as generous host and household protector. Furthermore, she deceived and outwitted the Canaanite commander Sisera. Such trickery to get the better of an adversary, considered honorable behavior for men, is here successfully exercised by a woman. Certainly it is significant that the oldest piece of literature in the Hebrew Bible honors women as powerful, dynamic, and shrewd. A woman of valor, Jael is not alone in the book of Judges. Although not a warrior, Achsah also was honored as an assertive and cunning woman.

Conclusions

The book of Judges displays a preoccupation with honor. The full range of honor concepts and behaviors described by modern anthropologists and historians is evident in the stories. People in Israel thought of an honorable individual as a person of consequence, worth, and weight. This perspective is consistent with how scholars like Pitt-Rivers and Stewart define honor. To be honored is to be recognized as a person of consequence; to be dishonored, disgraced, or humbled is to be diminished in stature and power. Honor was a conscious and conspicuous part of intellectual, social, and political life in the era of the premonarchic epic-bardic storyteller, in the seventh or sixth century when the Deuteronomistic writer offered a theological commentary, and during the exilic or postexilic period when the humanist writer-editor compiled the book's final edition. Codes of honor guided life as depicted in the book's accounts; the language of the stories is full of honor terms, and the central themes of the tales deal with honor. Without question, the material in Judges emerged from an honor society. The richness of this material allows us to draw a number of conclusions about honor in Syria-Palestine in the late second millennium.

First, it is not possible to align many of the specific ideas of honor in ancient Israel with modern Western standards of honor and morality. Although Stewart argues that honor is a universal notion, he also recognizes that views of what marks an honorable individual or what constitutes honorable behavior are situational. Therefore, to be respected as consequential and virtuous in one setting does not mean that one would be considered a worthy or upright person in another cultural context. Many of the "honorable" individuals portrayed in Judges lived in ways that would be legally, morally, and socially reprehensible in today's world. Although their behavior was considered laudable in the time their stories were told, today's readers would not regard them as moral templates for the twenty-first century.

Second, not only did Israelite codes of honor differ from the norms of our day, but the codes themselves also took a variety of forms even in ancient times according to age, gender, social position, or political role. While to be honored was to be consequential, that weightiness was not the same for each individual. As is true in many societies, an important form of honor was linked to militant warrior behavior. This is to be expected in a context of uncertainty where defense against intruders (Gideon), competition with rival states (Jephthah), antipathy to oppressive overlords (Ehud, Deborah, and Barak), prospects for conquest (Caleb), or opportunities for "protection" and plunder (Gideon and Abimelech) were constant concerns. Generally, norms of behavior in Judges honored those who offered themselves freely, those who gave themselves without restraint to martial causes. To be sufficiently strong, courageous, or wealthy to give oneself or one's possessions without holding back elevated an individual, community, or tribe.

For the youthful warrior, the honorable behavior of offering oneself bordered on the wild and savage actions of an uninhibited beast. Other situations required different expressions of honorable behavior. For example, the story of Jephthah considered the honor of a ruler. Faced with a cruel option (the same decision Antigone encountered), Jephthah had to choose between family and community. Jephthah's response was different from that of Antigone; he gave priority to his obligation to the polity and its deity above his devotion to family. Focusing on a different level of political life, the book of Judges frequently refers to the obligation of an individual tribe to respond to the common defense. Not to respond resulted in disgrace, scorn, or even the dishonor of a curse. On the other hand, to respond first was a mark of honor. In a segmentary lineage structure, where the security of each unit depended on a collective response from the other tribes, honor was an important tool of military defense.

Other examples in Judges consider domestic and social honor. The daughter's story in the account of Jephthah honors a woman for accepting the headship of father and house. In the social sphere, the story of the Levite's concubine describes the honor of a householder. A householder's honor was linked to his ability to protect daughters, guests, and inhabitants of the house, and to his willingness to extend generosity. The story of Samson's aborted wedding indicates that an honorable household head also was expected to uphold marriage agreements.

Judges provides evidence that honor was not monopolized by men nor was the honor of women a homogeneous concept dependent on domesticity. Women in Judges are remarkably strong, even dominant and aggressive. Achsah was a forceful economic bargainer, Deborah a powerful diviner, and Jael a celebrated "warrior." Even Delilah might have been seen by the Philistines as an honorable figure. Remember, it was only the Hebrew storyteller who dishonored her by claims that, unlike Jael, she worked for pay.[62]

Third, because it is so closely connected to power, honor in the book of Judges must be seen as a political expression. The fact that honor is intrinsically linked to consequentialness underscores the connection between honor and power. Disputes involving honor act as substitutes or proxies for physical engagement. Honor conflicts, therefore, can be studied to uncover fissures in society. An examination of honor reveals that younger household members sought to displace senior "brothers" or "fathers" (Gideon and Samson), that women competed with men for recognition (Deborah's song), and that tribes and ethnic groups were rivals (Judah going first, Benjamin being dishonored, Israel being honored above the Philistines). Descriptions about honor point to possible conflicts within houses or ethnic groups (Gideon challenging his own house, Jael going against the alliances of her husband's house) and to the fact that town and countryside came into conflict (Israelites against their Canaanite overlords). Because the quest for honor was a function of the pursuit for power, the protagonists attempted to mobilize outsiders and bystanders to their cause.[63] Consequently, honor

---

62. See Niditch, *Judges*, 169. Niditch notes that Delilah was portrayed as less heroic because she acted for money while Jael had no selfish motives. It is important to keep in mind that both Delilah's and Jael's stories were told from an Israelite perspective.

63. In his *The Semi-Sovereign People: A Realist's View of Democracy in America* (New York: Holt, Rinehart and Winston, 1960), E. E. Schattschneider famously compared politics to a boxing match in which the contestants invited the onlookers into the ring in order to expand their base of support.

conflicts might be projected onto the supernatural realm, the dwelling of the most powerful potential ally. As seen in the story of Gideon, the battle between Yhwh and Baal masked temporal struggles within Gideon's house and town.

In the late second-millennium setting of uncertainty and conflict, ambitious diviners, upwardly mobile houses, aggressive warriors, or aspiring rulers, in their quest for power, aligned themselves with an upstart deity, Yhwh. Seeking to exploit the opportunities created by the erosion of old social and political arrangements, they turned their backs on traditional Canaanite gods, now associated with a system under stress. Efforts to honor Yhwh and disgrace Baal suggested waning confidence in the Canaanite pantheon and/or a desire to find an alternative source of power and legitimacy to challenge the status quo. Marxist-leaning scholars have claimed that premonarchic Israel experienced a social revolution led by the downtrodden peasant class. However, the evidence from Judges suggests that the "revolution" against Canaanite centers of power was carried out by ambitious elite rivals, not oppressed rustics. The promise of support from a new deity was offered by wandering messengers and itinerant Levites, whose ideas and claims mobilized power-seeking men such as Ehud, Barak, Gideon, Jephthah, and Samson. The message of a Yhwh "revolution" was also promoted by local diviners like Deborah who operated from established sites. Perhaps it is significant that Abimelech, the only major character in the epic-bardic section presented as a complete failure, was also the only person without an explicit tie of loyalty to Yhwh.

While the association of political power and honor is obvious in every cultural setting, the link is especially important in societies that are less structured institutionally. Prior to the establishment of the Israelite monarchy, honor served as a substitute for fixed institutions used for defense, tax collecting, law enforcement, and contract enforcement.[64] For big men, whose position was constantly in peril, maintaining honor was of primary importance. The loss of honor for a big man was a sign of weakness that opened the door to defection on the part of his supporters and subjects. Such loss also made him vulnerable to attack from his enemies. Not only individuals, but also houses and entire tribes needed to defend their honor if they were to protect their power.

It is possible to argue that the emphasis on honor reduced the amount of violence needed to achieve and maintain political power. While an honorable warrior or ruler was regarded as a person willing and able to exercise violence, even brutally, that honorable reputation spared the man or woman in power from the need to actually employ violence. Subordinates remained loyal, peers did not attempt to unseat one another, and enemies feared attacking. Honorable men and women maintained order and control through the habits, gestures, and stories of honor, not only through actually unsheathing the sword. Conversely, by voicing a curse, offering a taunt, or circulating a tale diminishing an enemy, one could weaken or defeat an opponent without actually resorting to bloodshed.

Fourth, a study of honor demonstrates that the ancient Hebrews were well aware of moral dilemmas, the need to set ethical priorities, and the tragedy of being forced to choose between two distasteful options. Most of the stories give attention to this matter; some of the tales made it their central concern. In the Song of Deborah, Jael gives up her chastity in order to defeat an enemy. Jephthah, perhaps regarded as the most ethical individual in the entire book, sacrifices his own daughter in order to uphold his reputation for unfaltering reliability. In so doing, he allows his obligation to the polity and his deity to supersede his duty to protect and prolong his family. The householder puts the security of his Levite guest above his obligations

---

64. See chapter 3, "Power and Trust," for a discussion of honoring contracts/covenants.

of honor to defend the virginity of his female wards. Throughout history, in every type of society, the dilemma of being loyal to self, family, the larger polity, or to spiritual values has been a critical issue.[65] The characters in Judges were well aware of those quandaries.

It is ironic that the Deuteronomistic editor, the writer most closely associated with the great moralists of the Hebrew Bible, was least able to deal with the moral ambiguities. For the Deuteronomistic writer all was starkly black or white, there were no shades of moral gray. Unfaithfulness resulted in punishment, cries of regret brought deliverance. Even though they were more similar to modern warlords, the protagonists in Judges were presented by the Deuteronomistic narrator as upright actors. Writing after the time of the Deuteronomic awakening, the writer could only preface and end the stories in Judges with simplistic moral pronouncements that had little connection to the message and tone of the original accounts. Both the epic-bardic storyteller and the cosmopolitan humanist were far better equipped to capture the moral anguish and ambiguities of the premonarchic era of honor.

---

65. For some, the politics of patronage, which results in favoritism to friends and family, is regarded as immoral and corrupt. For others, patronage is an appropriate way to allocate resources at one's disposal.

5

Power and Wealth

Men of Valor as Men of Wealth

When the messenger of Yhwh first encountered Gideon, he addressed him saying, "Yhwh is with you, mighty and prosperous warrior" (Judg. 6:12).[1] Besides exercising great power, Gideon and the other central characters in the book of Judges accumulated and managed substantial wealth. As heads or members of prominent houses they owned fields and herds, administered revenue-generating shrines, were proprietors of threshing floors, retained servants and slaves, possessed many wives, had numerous sons and daughters, engaged the services of professional diviners, hired mercenaries, gained access to town treasuries, redistributed the spoils of battle, rode on donkeys instead of walked, and were buried with honor in family tombs.[2] The following chapter examines how they generated, used, and protected their material assets. Although the

---

1. As with all references from Judges, this is my own translation. As noted in chapter 1, the word *ḥayil* (חיל) can mean "wealth" or "prosperity." While *ḥayil* is generally translated as "valor," the semantic field could also refer to affluence.

strongmen in Judges were wealthy, they did not make their fortunes through impersonal market strategies. The Book of Judges describes a preindustrial and precapitalist society where plunder, tribute, and gifting, not markets, dominated the exchange of material goods. While some of the stories in Judges depicted individuals who were aware of market forces, the tales did not make a sharp distinction between economics and military, political, or social dealings. In Judges, the exchange of wealth was intended to advance nonmaterial values such as social standing, ethnic unity, and especially political power.

In ancient Israel, the economic realities of the temporal world intersected with the imagined economics of the heavenly domain. Sacrifice, divine generosity, supernatural contract enforcement, and celestial retribution were regarded by the men and women in Judges and by the book's authors as having a powerful influence on earthly fortunes. Consequently, the ability to access spiritual forces was a prized worldly resource that could be seized, bought and sold, and

---

2. The Song of Deborah suggests that individuals riding on donkeys were people of wealth, the same ones who sat on rich carpets or in judgment seats (Judg. 5:10). Boling identifies the riders as caravan owners. Robert G. Boling, *Judges: A New Translation with Introduction and Commentary*, Anchor Bible 6A (Garden City, NY: Doubleday, 1975), 102, 110. The RSV and NRSV render the passage as follows. RSV: "Tell of it, you who ride on tawny asses, you who sit on rich carpets." NRSV: "Tell of it, you who ride on white donkeys, you who sit on rich carpets." Later in Judges, the list of so-called minor judges notes that Abdon, who ruled for eight years, had forty sons and thirty grandsons. All rode on donkeys (Judg. 12:13–14). Evidence that men of valor were members of families owning tombs comes from the story of Samson (Judg. 16:31). Because wealth is always relative, the material stores of the characters in Judges should not be judged by modern standards. Several hundred goats and a few dozen cattle may have constituted uncommon wealth. To illustrate the point about relative wealth, one might consider East African pastoralists. Today, many Maasai herders think of themselves as very wealthy. An American rancher or dairy farmer would regard their herds as meager in numbers and the animals pathetically small in size. A story about one of the world's wealthiest individuals makes the same point about relative wealth. Several years ago Bill Gates visited a Maasai settlement near the Kenya-Tanzania border. When the Maasai were told that Gates was the richest man in the world they immediately asked how many cattle he owned. Learning that he owned none, they scoffed and dismissed him as a poor man. The observation that he probably owned a cat or dog did little to restore Gates in their opinion.

gifted. The men of valor, who monopolized this access, used it to their material, social, and political advantage.

The Social and Economic Aspects of Material Exchanges

Temporal Exchange

Using value-laden terms such as archaic, primitive, or premodern, economists and anthropologists often regard ancient economic arrangements as fundamentally different from modern, market-driven capitalism. While ancient economic systems provided for the exchange and redistribution of goods, thus functioning as markets, they also served to maintain peace, solidify friendship, confirm status, express social rivalry, ratify marriage alliances, and appease the gods. As tools of material exchange, ancient economies were sensitive to price and the laws of supply and demand, but as expressions of social and political relationships they operated according to a different calculus.[3] Although the distinction between modern and premodern economies can be drawn too sharply, the men and women described by the book of Judges regarded economic exchanges as more than pure material transactions.

One might think of nonmarket economic exchanges in terms of three overarching categories: confiscation, tribute, and gifting. Moving along a continuum from confiscation to tribute to gifting, social relationships become denser and more entangled. With confiscation or plunder, there is no mutual relationship, no equality, no affection, no trust, and little etiquette. An individual or group with superior power simply seizes what is desired and departs. The economist Mancur Olson called this actor a "roving bandit" while the anthropologist Marshall Sahlins described the process as "negative

---

3. For a concise summary of the literature on precapitalist economics, see Natalie Zemon Davis, *The Gift in Sixteenth-Century France* (Madison: University of Wisconsin Press, 2000), 3–10.

reciprocity."[4] Such a relationship ends as soon as the weaker party is able to escape.

Like confiscation, tribute takes place in an environment of inequality. Olson, who used the term "stationary bandit" to describe the dominant actor, said society has now been transformed from anarchy to tyranny. With tribute, the superior party has progressed beyond raw predation to providing (or imposing) basic levels of protection against competing roving bandits. Now regular and fixed payments have replaced unpredictable attacks that seize everything that can be consumed or carried away. However, the relationship remains one of inequality, a relationship the subordinate actor accepts reluctantly as the lesser of two evils. Taking a somewhat more positive view of the process, economist Karl Polanyi argued that tribute often tilts more in the direction of redistribution than mere plunder. In addition to extracting wealth, the central figure—a tribal leader, chief, or king—redirects a portion of tribute back to the members of society in a way that partially resembles a market and in a manner that allows the leader to claim the role of beneficent provider.[5] Thus, a tribute system may be camouflaged with a veneer of affection and reciprocity as well as characterized by a degree of trust and mutual attachment.[6] Employed both in ancient and modern

---

4. Mancur Olson, *Power and Prosperity: Outgrowing Communist and Capitalist Dictatorships* (New York: Basic Books, 2000); Marshall Sahlins, *Stone Age Economies* (Chicago: Aldine Publishing, 1972).
5. Karl Polanyi, *The Great Transformation: The Political and Economic Origins of Our Time* (Boston: Beacon Press, 2010). As can be seen from its title, Polanyi's work, first published in 1944, took an evolutionary perspective that drew a sharp distinction between premodern and modern economies. The former, he argued, relied on gift giving and reciprocity; the latter was entirely driven by impersonal, self-regulating market forces.
6. In social science literature, the types of leaders described in Judges have been called big men, strongmen, and patrons. Much of the literature on big-man politics reflects the work of anthropologists and political scientists analyzing recent societies. Building on works such as Marshall Sahlins's classic study of big-man politics in the South Pacific, scholars have identified the ability to generate and then shrewdly redistribute wealth as a key to gaining and holding power. See Sahlins, "Poor Man, Rich Man, Big-Man, Chief: Political Types in Melanesia and Polynesia," *Comparative Studies in Social History* 5 (1963): 285–303. Sahlins was not the first

times, a political system based on redistribution, whether used by big men in the Pacific islands or political operatives in large industrial states, is difficult to manage. In any patronage/redistribution system, the constant challenge is finding enough wealth to satisfy the cravings of clients. Leaders who use patronage over an extended period of time risk bankrupting themselves and their polity. Although redistribution is equated with corruption by moderns, it was considered normal and honorable in traditional societies.[7]

Closely associated with tribute, gift giving appears to be more benign because by definition it is voluntary. However, as sociologist Marcel Mauss and historian Natalie Davis explain, gifting is not without entangling complications.[8] Mauss wrote that gifts are "in theory voluntary, in reality given and returned obligatorily." Regarded as "free and gratuitous" they are actually "constrained and self-interested."[9] Because of this tension between freedom and

---

to consider the importance of redistribution. In describing patriarchalism and patrimonialism, Max Weber discussed the importance of redistributing economic goods. See Weber, *Economy and Society: An Outline of Interpretive Sociology*, ed. Guenther Roth and Claus Wittich (Berkeley: University of California Press, 1979), 2:1006–69. Although he does not refer specifically to Sahlins, Goran Hyden pursues a line of thinking similar to Sahlins's economic analysis. Looking at modern-day Africa's "economy of affection," Hyden makes a convincing case that the glue holding most societies together is the exchange of material wealth, especially among kin. See Hyden, *Beyond Ujamaa in Tanzania: Underdevelopment and an Uncaptured Peasantry* (Berkeley: University of California Press, 1980). Hyden's works since 1980 continue the theme of "economy of affection."

7. Political scientists regard redistribution as an essential part of patron-client systems that persist even in the modern bureaucratic state. While big men in Melanesia slaughtered pigs in order to offer a village feast, the leaders of modern nation-states engage in pork-barrel politics by distributing lucrative rewards through entitlements, subsidies, tax breaks, government contracts, and exemptions from costly regulations. Patronage systems are expensive to operate. In chronicling the career of Mobutu Sese Seko of Zaire, Michela Wrong discovered that the constant outflow of wealth required to purchase the loyalty of his myriad clients left Mobutu with a fortune that was surprisingly small when compared to the billions he had diverted from the national treasury. Wrong's description of Mobutu, one of modern history's most cunning and successful big men, underscores the fact that redistribution alone is an uncertain survival strategy. Michela Wrong, *In the Footsteps of Mr. Kurtz: Living on the Brink of Disaster in the Congo* (London: Harper Collins, 1990).

8. Marcel Mauss, *The Gift: The Form and Reason for Exchange in Archaic Societies*, trans. W. D. Hall, forward by Mary Douglas (New York: W. W. Norton, 1990), 3; Davis, *The Gift in Sixteenth-Century France*.

constraint, gift giving involves complex social negotiations. In offering a gift, the giver and the recipient affirm social and economic status, express respect or condescension, make statements about relative power, and enter into a relationship that can ensnare and burden one or both parties indefinitely. While gifts among associates and equals can be free expressions of affection, mutual respect, or even friendly rivalry, gifts between superior and subordinate can serve as instruments to dominate and obligate.

Confiscation, tribute, and gifting, associated with preindustrial societies, are often regarded as qualitatively different from the transactions in modern capitalist economies where prices are set by impersonal market forces, namely the law of supply and demand. In its ideal form, parties in the marketplace meet as equals, voluntarily, and with multiple options. Also in its ideal form, and unlike either confiscation or tribute, there are no predatory free riders. Theoretically, the result of a market relationship is mutual benefit, with all sides gaining from the principles of competition and comparative advantage. Although trade is dependent on trust, that trust generally relies on some type of enforcement mechanism—temporal or supernatural—and the relationship endures only so long as the exchange is valued by both sides. Once a transaction is done, and each party has gained what it sought, the relationship is over until the next deal is struck. However, unlike confiscation or tribute, there is generally no animosity and both sides often look forward positively to future exchanges. Although Polanyi believed that a market-based economy is a modern phenomenon that replaced earlier more personal arrangements, the more recent consensus is that market forces and economic calculations based on

---

9. Mauss, *The Gift*, 3.

personal relationships continue to coexist. The two are not mutually exclusive.[10]

Celestial Exchange

Because many people, both ancient and modern, regard the realm of the divine as the simulacrum of the temporal world, heavenly and earthly economics intersect.[11] People in a predatory system may think of their gods as supernatural plunderers or as defenders against plunder; people living in a tribute-based economic system are likely to picture their deity as the ultimate redistributor; people in a market-oriented society may regard their supernatural sovereign as a merchant who maintains a ledger of good and evil. Understanding how people conceptualize transactions in the spiritual world can be instructive when attempting to appreciate the nature of exchanges on earth.

Not only did they see similarities between divine and human economies, people in the preindustrial world also believed that success in human society, whether in the social or economic realm, depended on divine actions. In ancient lore, a capricious or angry god might give or even sell an individual, city, or region into the hands of another god or human enemy.[12] Consequently, the gods needed to be consulted, pleased, and appeased. In addition, they needed to be recruited as participants in human affairs. Before entering into a business venture, marrying, or going to war, prudent persons would

---

10. In a convincing study of precolonial economic systems in Central Africa, Achim von Oppen offers many concrete examples of how people along the Kasai-Zambezi watershed used the idioms of moral economics such as friendship, hospitality, and pawnship while at the same time behaving in ways consistent with the values of market capitalism. Achim von Oppen, *Terms of Trade and Terms of Trust: The History and Contexts of Pre-Colonial Market Production around the Upper Zambezi and Kasai*, Studien zur afrikanischen Geschichte 6 (Münster: LIT Verlag, 1998).
11. For a discussion of this intersection, see Davis, *The Gift in Sixteenth-Century France*, chapter 7, "Gifts and the Gods."
12. Mediterranean stories, Greek, Roman, and Syro-Palestinian, contain numerous accounts of divinities choosing to punish or protect through this tactic.

consult their deities in order to determine the likelihood of success or failure. Beyond giving advice and interjecting themselves into temporal affairs, deities also witnessed and enforced agreements regarding inheritance, land transfers, business transactions, and promises to perform services. Giving gifts to the gods followed an etiquette established for human interaction. Bowing low to the ground, voicing gratitude, expressing humility, vowing to hold nothing back, and claiming unworthiness were seen as appropriate actions when offering a gift to a divine being or emissary.

The Exchange of Wealth in Judges

Many of the struggles described in Judges were elite disputes about the control of property and people. The men of valor engaged in wars of plunder, tribute collection, gift giving, feasting, gambling, and bargaining, activities that could either destroy or solidify social relationships, generate profits, or result in loss. Because both relationships and profits were important considerations, social tension and conflict colored economic exchanges, and economic transactions were heavy with social meaning. Finally, religious sacrifice was integral to the entire economic system and the sacrifices of the men of valor often were lavish and spectacular. The following discussion will examine the involvement of the premonarchic heroes of Judges in plunder, tribute, gift giving, market-driven bargaining, and sacrifice to the gods. Less frequent will be detailed descriptions of the wealth exchanged between patrons and clients in a peaceful, routine, and reoccurring manner. As Niels Peter Lemche notes, people in patron-client settings are reluctant to describe these transactions, which are somewhat "clandestine" and not conducted in the open.[13] The book of Judges offers many accounts of plunder, the distribution of booty,

---

13. Niels Peter Lemche, "Kings and Clients: On Loyalty between the Ruler and the Ruled in Ancient Israel," *Semeia* 66 (1994): 124. My own findings in Africa are consistent with Lemche's

and gifts to Yhwh. But there are fewer explicit references to the routine flow of tribute that marked life in premonarchic Israel.

Plunder

Each section of the book of Judges—the postexilic speculations of the humanist, the theological explanations of the sixth-century Deuteronomist, and the heroic accolades of the bardic storytellers—regards plunder as a common form of acquisition. Writing at a time when the very existence of the nation and its people was in doubt, the humanist suggested that plunder in the long distant past had been the primary means of acquiring territory and even of resolving conflict among the tribes. In the book's first chapter, describing how the sons of Israel had obtained their land, the humanist used words and phrases such as "wage war," "seize," "pursue and capture," "subject to forced labor," "defeat," and "possess." Employing the terminology of holy war, the humanist imagined the tribal warriors as completely destroying cities, striking them down with the mouth of the sword, and then devoting them as a sacrifice to Yhwh. As one example, in Judg. 1:17 we read, "And Judah went with his brother Simeon and they struck down the Canaanites living in Zepath. And they devoted it to destruction and they called the name of the city Devoted to Destruction."[14] Ideally, the result for the sons of Israel was the undisputed possession of the land, a land whose previous owners had been completely eliminated (Judges 1).[15]

---

claim. While chiefs may be happy to describe their own generosity, they are much less willing to give an account of the tribute that flows into their courts.

14. The term *ḥormâ* (חרמה), "Devoted to Destruction," is the technical term often associated with "holy war" which is the meaning of the noun form *ḥērem* (חרם).

15. The frequently used term *yrš* (ירש), "to take possession," suggests complete alienation or disinheritance which erased any previous rights of ownership. Thus the humanist seems to focus more on the legal and relational results of plundering rather than on the violence of the activity, a key theme of the Deuteronomistic writer. The bardic storyteller gives more attention to the material rewards of plunder.

Realistically, the humanist writer recognized that the predatory engagements were not always successful. Even when listing the victims of Israel's plunder, the humanist acknowledged that many of Israel's tribes failed to dislodge foes who continued to live in the land. However, echoing the perspective of the book of Joshua, from which many of his or her stories came, the humanist noted that the Canaanites and other victims became forced labor. Later in the book of Judges, the humanist described the plundering activities of the tribe of Dan, which attacked, destroyed, and displaced a defenseless and peaceful community (Judges 18). All these stories were reported in a relatively dispassionate manner. Except to say the victories were a gift from Yhwh, that Yhwh was with the Israelite plunderers, and that the targets of plunder were worthy sacrificial offerings, there was no attempt to offer a deep theological analysis of the victories. Significantly, the failures were simply noted, never explained. Plunder and conquest were regarded by the humanist as a normal part of the ebb and flow of human affairs. Lands, cities, and slaves were routinely acquired or lost through the predatory actions of warriors. The humanist did not attribute success to human faithfulness nor defeat to apostasy.

Describing a long-ago time when Israel had no king, the humanist author claimed that it had been plunder that safeguarded tribal unity and ensured the existence of the nation. In chapter 1, by naming most of Israel's tribes and identifying the areas they took by conquest, the humanist signaled a concern for tribal unity.[16] And, in the final chapters of Judges, the humanist made the explicit and powerful claim that plunder actually preserved tribal integrity and saved the

---

16. In chapter 1, the humanist lists ten tribes. Judah and Simeon (associated with David) are clearly the most important. However, Benjamin, Joseph, Zebulon, Asher, Naphtali, and Dan are mentioned. In addition, the two sons of Joseph, Manasseh and Ephraim, are counted among the tribes. At the end of Judges, the humanist refers only to Judah and Benjamin by name. Nevertheless, the writer frequently speaks of "all the tribes of Israel."

tribe of Benjamin from extinction. After punishing Benjamin for the atrocities the inhabitants of Gibeah had inflicted on the Levite's concubine, the tribes of Israel vowed never to give their daughters in marriage to the men of Benjamin. The vow, however, threatened to extinguish Benjamin and thereby cause a "breach in the tribes of Israel ... blotting out one tribe" (Judg. 21:15, 17). According to the humanist, the problem was resolved by two acts of naked aggression. The first, pillaging women from the Benjaminite subtribe of Jabesh-gilead; the second, kidnapping the daughters of Shiloh who came to dance at an annual feast to Yhwh. As when describing the capture of Canaanite territories as a means for Israel to acquire an inheritance, the humanist writer expressed no moral reservations about these acts of plundering women to achieve tribal harmony.

Writing somewhat earlier than the humanist, the Deuteronomistic writer analyzed the success or failure of plunder in theological and moral terms. It may be significant that of the various Hebrew words for "plunder," the Deuteronomistic editor used terms based on the root šss (שסס), a term emphasizing the ferocious and destructive nature of plundering. In the Hebrew Bible, the root šss (שסס) is almost always used in conjunction with other terms emphasizing violent action. Various forms of the root are found in passages that explicitly describe war, death, devouring, smiting, or rapaciousness. In contrast to the word šll (שלל), which places more emphasis on the goods taken in battle, the word šss (שסס) gives more attention to the vicious deed.[17] This word choice may have reflected the Deuteronomistic writer's moralistic interest in retribution and punishment rather than in the material rewards of taking spoil. In

---

17. For examples of the use of šss (שסס), see 1 Sam. 14:48; 17:53; 23:1; Isa. 13:16; 17:14; 42:24; Jer. 30:16; Hosea 13:15; Zech. 14:2; Hab. 2:8; Zeph. 1:13; and Pss. 44:10; 89:41. While forms of the root šll (שלל) certainly connote violence, its probable root meaning—"flocks" of sheep or goats—underscores the aspect of wealth rather than the action of seizure.

Judges 2, the Deuteronomistic author/editor attributed Israel's lack of success in plundering the inhabitants of the land to apostasy. Disobeying Yhwh's commands, not breaking down pagan altars, serving the Baals and Ashtaroth, entering into covenants with the local peoples, and forgetting who had brought Israel out of Egypt all kindled Yhwh's anger. As a result, not only did Israel fail in its efforts to plunder, Yhwh sold Israel to plunderers (*šōsîm* – שסים). Thus, Israel became the object of plunder. Eventually taking pity on his hapless people, Yhwh raised up deliverers (*šōpĕtîm* – שפטים) who saved Israel from the power of the aggressors. Not only was this litany of apostasy, calamity, and deliverance the dominant theme of chapter 2 in Judges, it also was used to introduce and conclude the Deuteronomistic writer's description of every leader from Othniel to Samson. Thus, in contrast to the humanist, the Deuteronomistic commentator pictured the Israelite men of valor not so much as pivotal figures in the quest for plunder, but as key actors in the effort to escape being victimized by the plunderers sent by Yhwh as punishment for sin.[18]

Composed far nearer to the time period they claim to represent, the bardic tales of individual heroes contained in chapters 3–16 offer a more detailed and less formulaic description of how the leaders memorialized in Judges were involved in the practice of plunder. In contrast to the perspective of the Deuteronomistic editor, these heroic stories gave more attention to the material rewards of plunder. In both the Song of Deborah and in the account of Gideon, the storytellers used the word *šālāl* (שלל), which placed a bit more emphasis on the profits of plunder rather than just focusing on the violent actions leading up to the seizure of wealth.[19] The account of

---

18. Nevertheless, the humanist did view strongmen as defenders and deliverers. In describing the defenseless Laish, the humanist noted that the community was vulnerable because it had no deliverer (*maṣṣîl* – מציל) (Judg. 18:28).

Barak and Deborah depicted a time when caravan traffic on the main routes was suspended, when travelers took circuitous back roads, and when life in unwalled towns (*pĕrāzôn* – פרזון) was unbearable because of attacks launched by heavily armed Canaanite chiefs based in walled and gated cities.[20] In recounting the story from the perspective of a Canaanite war captain's wife, the book of Judges identified richly dyed cloth, embroidered textiles, and women as the most valuable spoils sought by rapacious armies. The fact that the spoils included lavish textiles is consistent with the likelihood that Barak and Sisera fought over control of long-distance caravan traffic. On the other hand, female captives probably would have been taken from weakly defended local communities rather than from passing companies of merchants.

Other heroic stories in Judges also emphasized plunder. Gideon, the Hacker, was not only a successful defender against plunder but also a vicious pillager himself. His story opened with a vivid description of the sons of Israel taking refuge in caves to escape nomadic Midianite raiders. These marauders descended like locust upon the land, destroying crops and seizing oxen, sheep, and donkeys. Gideon's story closes with him collecting the booty gathered from the defeated Midianites. Other tales featuring Gideon describe the anger of allied tribes who were not invited to participate in Gideon's rapacious forays. Gideon was not the only man of valor remembered as a plunderer. Abimelech engaged in systematic and organized marauding while Jephthah gathered a group of ruffians (worthless fellows) to go raiding from his base in the land of Tov

---

19. In Judg. 5:30 the mother of Sisera details the spoils the warriors should have captured. In Judg. 8:24–25 the storyteller lists the spoils Gideon seized from the Midianites. Both tales use the word *šālāl* (שלל).
20. There are various translations for the word *pĕrāzôn* (פרזון) in Judg. 5:7. Citing parallels in Ezek. 38:11 and Zech. 2:8, Susan Niditch suggests an "unwalled hamlet." Niditch, *Judges* (Louisville: Westminster, 2008), 71–72. All translators agree that the Song of Deborah describes an extremely unsettled time when marauders brought normal life to a halt.

(good). Based on his reputation as an effective raider and on the expectation that he would be able to defend against Ammonite raiders, the leaders of Gilead recruited Jephthah as their ruler. Like Gideon, Jephthah had to contend with angry tribesmen who had not been asked to share in the spoils of battle (Judg. 12:1).

In sharp contrast to the Deuteronomistic interpreter, the storytellers recounting the plundering exploits of Barak, Gideon, Abimelech, or Jephthah gave scant attention to the moral demands of religious faithfulness. Yhwh was thought of as an essential supernatural martial ally, an entity to be consulted and honored, but not as a moral guide as understood by later legal or religious thinkers. The bardic storytellers, who devote most of their narrative to the actions of human warriors, gave absolutely no attention to ethics or orthodoxy. As plunderers and guardians against plunder, the men of valor/deliverers were never presented as champions of morality nor as defenders of any law, whether religious, criminal, or civil.

Tribute

Although the main distinction between plunder and tribute is that one is seized by roving bandits while the other is harvested by stationary bandits, there is no sharp line between the two. In the Hebrew Bible, the root *lḥṣ* (לחץ) can refer either to plunder or tribute.[21] The term, which can be translated as "squeezing," "pressing," or "insufficient," may refer to the sudden acts of plunder, but also to the continuous action of privation, pressure, or oppression. As described in many biblical texts, both plunder and tribute were collected by a state or political leader. Just as tribute and plunder

---

21. Many biblical passages using this term refer to the long oppression in Egypt—for example, Exod. 3:9; Deut. 26:7; Judg. 6:9; 1 Sam. 10:18; 2 Kgs. 13:4; Isa. 19:20. Other passages clearly refer to an ongoing tribute relationship—for example, 2 Kgs. 13:4, 22; Jer. 30:20. Judges 10:12 most likely refers to regular tribute, not occasional plunder.

cannot always be distinguished, neither can one easily separate tribute from gift giving. In fact the Hebrew word *minḥâ* (מנחה) can mean either "tribute" or "gift." Among the many post-Judges instances where the word *minḥâ* (מנחה) was used to describe tribute are the following: when both the Moabites and Syrians carried tribute to King David, their conqueror; the time Solomon sent tribute to Hiram, king of Tyre; and when Hosea, king of Samaria, delivered tribute to Assyria. In addition the term was used when the people of Judah brought tribute to their ruler Jehoshaphat and when the Ammonites paid tribute to the powerful king Uzziah.[22]

The book of Judges contains some direct and much indirect evidence of tribute. In chapter 1, the humanist referred to Canaanite walled cities and their unwalled surrounding regions. The fortified cities and the unwalled dependent communities would have related to each other in a feudal manner whereby the powerful center provided protection and demanded regular tribute from the periphery. Repeating verbatim the account in Joshua, the humanist also told the tale of Caleb and Othniel.[23] In the story, Caleb promised his own daughter to the man who captured Debir. Caleb's nephew Othniel was the victorious hero, who took the city and claimed the daughter. In addition, Othniel received a substantial dowry of land. In this narrative, attention is given to the reciprocal nature of a tribute system lubricated by ties of kinship and fueled by the exchange of military service for women and land. The account also suggests that the pressure to compensate clients through redistribution was costly and could diminish the patron's wealth.

The most detailed examples of tribute in Judges are the stories of Ehud and Abimelech. In neither case was there any mention of redistribution to subordinates. While silence is not proof that

---

22. 2 Sam. 8:2, 6; 1 Kgs. 5:1; 2 Kgs. 17:3; 2 Chron. 17:5; 26:8.
23. Josh. 15:15–19 and Judg. 1:11–15.

redistribution did not take place, even if there was some reciprocation, the main benefit to the tribute giver would have been that capricious acts of plunder were now replaced with predictable annual or seasonal payments delivered by the tribute bearer instead of being seized by a ravenous band of warriors. The arrangement would have been less risky and less expensive for the tribute monger as well.

With Ehud, described in Judg. 3:12–30, we see the role of a vassal responsible for tribute collection. Traveling with his own company of warriors, Ehud, a Benjaminite, gathered tribute in the region of Ephraim and delivered it to Eglon, the Moabite overlord east of the Jordan. As one of Eglon's tribute collectors, Ehud relied on the assistance of warrior enforcers. Presumably, the men who followed him were the same as those elsewhere described as "worthless and reckless fellows" (*ănāšîm rêqîm ûpōḥăzîm* – אנשים ריקים ופחזים), individuals who hired themselves to a renowned warrior.[24] Like the hero Othniel, they would have been attracted by the prospect of booty, women, land, and glory. Although some would have been linked to Ehud by ties of kinship, others were rootless and would have remained with their leader only so long as he was successful.

Ehud's military strength and skill, his ability to attract and compensate a troop of warriors, his familiarity with the culture of the conquered ethnic community all made him useful to the Moabite king. However, he was also a dangerous subordinate. While it would have been difficult for a big man like Eglon to monitor the fidelity of someone like Ehud, he had no choice but to depend on such underlings to maintain the flow of tribute into his palace. Even though there may have been a great deal of leakage, the Moabite king apparently had enough tribute collectors to have generated an abundant flow of revenue. References to Eglon as an enormously fat

---

24. See chapter 3, page 87 n. 8.

man were symbolic allusions to his wealth and to the success of his tribute system.[25] For his part, Ehud's reward would have been a share of the tribute. Presumably, a substantial portion of the material goods he collected went to compensate his entourage.

The unstable and antagonistic nature of the tribute relationship was dramatically illustrated by the fact that Ehud, a highly trusted underling, carefully planned and carried out a plot to assassinate his suzerain and take Eglon's place as the recipient of Ephraimite tribute. Having killed Eglon, Ehud established himself as an independent big man who could now keep for himself the tribute he had previously collected west of the Jordan River. Gaining the loyalty of the Ephraimites may not have been easy, for they likely continued to regard Ehud as a self-serving mercenary traitor.

While Ehud was a high-level tribute gatherer, with Abimelech we see the tribute system from the perspective of a powerful tribute receiver. Gaining the support of his matrilineal kin, Abimelech took the money they gave him to hire mercenaries, which he then used to challenge and displace his putative paternal siblings. Once in power, Abimelech established himself as head of an extensive regional tribute system. Not just the leader of one walled city that extracted tribute from the adjacent hamlets, Abimelech dominated a collection of fortified towns that he controlled though a coterie of subofficials. He also provided protection over caravan routes whose travelers paid tribute for the privilege of protected passage. As seen with the description of Zebul, Abimelech's representative in Shechem, the task of a subordinate official was to enforce the regular flow

---

25. Describing someone as fat can be a reference to the wealth they acquired through tribute or plunder. Occasionally in the Hebrew Bible, soldiers are said to be fat or plump. For example, in Judges 3:29 the Hebrew word שמן-smn describes mighty warriors as "men all fat and men all strong." Clearly the intent is to depict the men as robust, not as overweight. In African oral histories and in modern-day parlance, powerful and wealthy political figures are said to have "eaten" and they are called "fat."

of tribute, to make sure the cities did not start competing tribute networks, to warn Abimelech of potential defections, and to suppress revolts.[26] In the case of Shechem, after Abimelech had ruled for a number of years, the lords or baals (*bĕʿālîm* – בעלים) of the town became disgruntled with the arrangement and began plundering passing caravans. Along with his kin, the strongman Gaal moved into Shechem in an abortive effort to displace Abimelech. However, as master over multiple towns, Abimelech could mobilize more martial forces than were available to the rebel leaders of a single city. Consequently, he was able to crush Gaal and continue his regime of tribute collection.

The story of Jephthah provides less detail about the inner workings of the tribute system, but it does show that the relationship between a strongman and a city was reciprocal (Judges 11). Although Jephthah drove a hard bargain with Gilead, he was not able to impose his will unilaterally. The examples of Abimelech and Jephthah illustrate a key difference between plunder and tribute. In both cases, the lords of the towns Abimelech and Jephthah ruled were actively involved in the maneuvering and negotiations that led to the strongmen's installation. The fact that both men entered into formal contracts ratified by a supernatural witness is additional evidence that the relationship between the strongman and the town had a degree of reciprocity and mutual benefit. Furthermore, the stories indicate that Gilead and Shechem believed that when they initially engaged Abimelech and Jephthah they had alternatives to the two strongmen. An object of plunder has no negotiating leverage, no contractual agreement, and no options regarding the overlord.

---

26. Zebul's relationship to Abimelech was the same as Ehud's to the Moabite king Eglon.

Gift Giving

The most socially complex and entangling form of economic exchange is gift giving. Gifts are not always offered freely in a spirit of disinterested generosity nor are they always received with a sense of unencumbered gratitude. The reason is that giving and accepting gifts send clear signals about power, social status, and economic security. While gift giving strengthens the social standing and economic reputation of the giver, the action diminishes the donor's material wealth. And while the recipient realizes a material benefit, accepting a gift often implies inferiority and commits the receiver to ill-defined and poorly limited future obligations. Because giving can obligate the recipient, a poor or socially inferior individual may seek to entangle a wealthy and powerful patron by giving a gift. As a result of the social and political pitfalls surrounding gift giving, the act is often highly ritualized. The rituals of gifting conceal a complicated and anxiety-laden competition regarding social standing and political power.[27]

Stories from other books of the Hebrew Bible suggest that gift giving often took place within a context of tension and fear. Genesis 32 and 33 describe Jacob's encounter with Esau, his long-estranged sibling. In returning home to meet the brother he had deceived years earlier, Jacob presented Esau with a gift of goats, sheep, milk camels, and donkeys. Jacob's cowardly tactic of taking refuge behind the herds of animals he positioned between himself and his brother suggested an atmosphere of anxiety and danger. Underscoring the tension, the story said Jacob bowed deferentially seven times when he finally met Esau face to face and announced that he offered the gifts in order "to find favor in the sight of his lord" (Gen. 33:8). Esau

---

27. For a fuller discussion of the complications associated with gift giving, see Mauss, *The Gift*; and Davis, *The Gift in Sixteenth-Century France*.

accepted the gifts reluctantly, but not because he refused to reconcile. In fact, the story emphasized Esau's attitude of joy and forgiveness. The reason Esau resisted the gifts was because he wanted to avoid the entangling complications of receiving, and he did not wish to give the slightest indication that he lacked anything. Telling Jacob, "I have enough," Esau asserted his self-sufficiency and wealth (Gen. 33:9). For his part, Jacob rebuffed Esau's offer of protection and went on his way. Instead of receiving a gift of land from Esau, and thus living under his control, Jacob continued on to Shechem where he bought land from the sons of Hamor (Gen. 33:16–20). By purchasing land, Jacob avoided any future responsibility toward the land's prior owner. From this story, it is clear that both Jacob and Esau were keenly aware that in accepting a substantial gift they would also be acquiescing to a considerable obligation.

Genesis 43, which tells the story of Jacob's sons in Egypt, contains similar themes of fear and tension. Bringing gifts of honey, gum, myrrh, pistachio nuts, and almonds, the men anxiously approached their brother Joseph, an individual they knew only as a powerful Egyptian lord, hoping to deflect his wrath. As when their father Jacob had encountered his own brother, Esau, they signaled their deference by bowing and making obeisance (Gen. 43:28). By this act, they acknowledged their inferiority, weakness, and vulnerability. At that point, they were entirely at the mercy of an official whose intentions and identity were completely unknown. Not an expression of friendship or gratitude, their gift was offered as an anxious gesture of self-defense.

Even hospitality, one of the most important forms of gift giving in ancient Israel, could be fraught with tension. Tales in Judges, whether those of the bardic storyteller or the humanist author, illustrate the entangling complications of hospitality. All the stories make it clear that the gift of hospitality involved far more than material exchanges. The legend of Samson's parents, who encountered the messenger of Yhwh, refers to the importance of extending hospitality to traveling strangers. Accounts in Judges describe an intricate web of expectation, obligation, and responsibility characterizing relationships of hospitality or inhospitality. The accounts also suggest that the recipient of hospitality needed to be wary. Jael's seductive offer of hospitality to Sisera resulted in the warrior's ignoble death. To withhold hospitality was also dangerous. The bardic story of Gideon explains how the town of Succoth's refusal to give food to Gideon's men led to brutal reprisals. The much later humanist tale of the Levite and his concubine offers a detailed description of the complicated set of relationships embedded in any act of hospitality (Judges 19). In the story of the Levite, the humanist provided three examples of hospitality: first, the lavish hospitality of the Levite's father-in-law; second, the unselfish hospitality of the old man in Gibeah; and third, the cruel and dishonorable inhospitality of the men of Gibeah.

In the case of the Levite, the father-in-law's unconstrained hospitality obligated the recipient to remain under the roof of the benefactor. Through being showered with gifts of food, drink, shelter, and companionship, the Levite was symbolically tied to the house of the patron. Even if the father-in-law's extravagant hospitality is interpreted only as a gesture of openhandedness toward a friend, the anticipation of reciprocity and deference would certainly have been an underlying expectation. For the patron as well, the act of hospitality was both a benefit and a burden. On the one hand, extending hospitality not only placed the Levite in a position of subordination and dependency, it also enhanced the patron's reputation for liberality and wealth. But on the other hand, the expenses of such boundless generosity would have diminished the giver's wealth.

The second act of hospitality in the story of the Levite occurred during his overnight stay in Gibeah. The account of this incident emphasizes the extraordinary social burdens that accompanied the extension of hospitality. After the Levite had been ignored by the townspeople, an old man, himself an outsider from the hill country of Ephraim, offered shelter to the Levite, his servant, his concubine, and his animals. Like the father-in-law, the old man was lavish in his material generosity. But while extravagant hospitality brought with it a material burden, the far greater cost to the host was social. It is clear from the story that once the Levite stepped through the door of the old man's house, the old man was obligated to protect his guest from any danger. In this case, the danger came from the egregious inhospitality of the townspeople, who threatened to gang-rape the Levite.[28] Modern anthropological work in the Middle East, which points to the high social cost of offering hospitality, may help us understand the degree of obligation one assumes when accepting a guest. Studying Bedouin communities in the central Sinai, Frank Stewart observed that once someone has entered the confines of another's house, the head of that house is honor bound to afford protection. This responsibility includes the obligation to pay compensation even should the guest be assaulted by a completely unexpected and unwelcome outsider.[29] In the case of the Levite guest in Judges, the honorable host was willing to trade the safety and purity of his own virgin daughter in exchange for the well-being of a traveler who had been a total stranger only hours before.

---

28. The reference to rape is not a comment on sexuality. The humanist used the image of rape, whether heterosexual or homosexual, as a symbol of extreme inhospitality, a most egregious violation of a guest. The rape of a man was especially humiliating because the act treated a man like a woman. While the men of Gibeah intended to shame the Levite, they themselves were completely humiliated by the telling of the story.

29. Frank Henderson Stewart, *Honor* (Chicago: University of Chicago Press, 1994), 86–98.

While extending hospitality involved accepting heavy obligations, refusing hospitality also carried serious consequences. The stark negative comparison of the inhospitality of the worthless men of Gibeah with the boundless generosity of the old man brought dishonor to the entire town. But, in addition to the loss of reputation, which in an honor-based society can be supremely damaging, to withhold hospitality can risk violence. Like the people of Succoth, who suffered the wrath of Gideon, the inhabitants of Gibeah were punished because of their extreme inhospitality. In Judges 20 and 21, the humanist author describes a devastating battle that not only destroyed Gibeah, but also shattered the entire tribe of Benjamin. In addition, because Benjamin defended the inhospitable actions of Gibeah, the other Israelite tribes refused to enter into the gifting of women. One message of the story is that inhospitality threatens the very pillars of society. Gibeah's inhospitality resulted not just in a military reprisal, but in an act of social vengeance that denied the entire tribe of Benjamin the women essential for the continuation of the tribe as an entity. The hyperbole of the account suggests that egregious inhospitality can lead to social and ethnic extinction. From all the tales of hospitality and inhospitality, it is clear that the gifting of hospitality carried enormous consequences extending far beyond material loss or gain. Those consequences had a direct bearing on the power of both the host and the guest.

In the public sphere, feasts and festivals, other occasions for gift giving, are important venues for the redistribution of wealth and for the demonstration of political power and largesse. Although at first blush the lavish supply of food and drink makes feasts and festivals times of unreserved celebration and merriment, tales from Judges suggest there could be a very different atmosphere at these events. Because of their economic, social, and political import, feasts and festivals often are treacherous affairs marked by rivalry, tension, and conflict. This tension is evident in the book of Judges, which contains descriptions of three feasts important in the life of every strongman. The first is Samson's wedding banquet, the second a political feast at Shechem where townsmen conspired to oust a dominant strongman, and the third a meal at the kingly table of the Adon (lord) of Bezek.

As important rites of passage, wedding feasts marked not only adjustments to social status but also the transfer of considerable wealth. The bride herself was an important economic asset whose value was reassigned from the house of her father to the house of her new husband. The woman's economic worth was based on the fact that she was both a producer, who worked to grow, process, and prepare food, and a reproducer, who bore children. As can be seen in the account of Othniel and Achsah, the bride might bring a substantial dowry into the marriage (Judg. 1:14–15). Also, the example of Achsah suggests that a clever woman could play a key role in managing and multiplying the wealth of a house. In addition to their immediate economic import for the two families, weddings feasts were opportunities for prominent members of society to exhibit their social standing, wealth, and cunning. Involving far more than the bride and groom, weddings were occasions joining different families and even diverse tribes or ethnic groups in ways that obligated them far into the future.

The wedding feast was part of a larger set of events involving complex negotiations about females, which carried both economic and social importance. As Victor Matthews notes, bride-price, the dowry, the bride's virginity, provisions in the event of divorce, obligations linked to debt, and the inheritance rights of future children were all part of these discussions.[30] The wedding feast, which came at the conclusion of the negotiations, ratified and made public

---

30. Victor H. Matthews, *Judges and Ruth* (Cambridge: Cambridge University Press, 2004), 102–3.

the agreements affecting "social parity, economic advantage, and expansion of the kinship network."[31] In *Death and Dissymmetry*, Mieke Bal's central thesis is that the book of Judges is about the struggle among powerful men over the control of women.[32] Caleb offered his daughter Achsah to the warrior Othniel, Sisera hoped to return from battle with captured females (wombs), Jephthah presented his daughter to Yhwh in return for victory in war, the Levite's concubine and even the daughter of the Levite's host were offered to enemies in return for the personal safety of men, and wars between Benjamin and the other tribes were settled by the seizure of women. The account of Samson's wedding feast offers a window onto the conflict among men over women.

From the story of Samson's marriage to the woman from Timnah (Judges 14), we learn that it was common for young men to invite numerous guests to a feast lasting many days. Without doubt, the scale of the feast demonstrated the groom's wealth and largesse. By extension, this would have put on display the economic fortunes of the entire family, the father's house (*bêt 'āb* – בת אב). Besides eating and drinking, Samson's wedding celebration featured riddling and high-stakes wagering. While riddling and wagering were rituals intended to bond participants and set the prosperous apart from the less privileged members of society, such activities could be highly divisive games with the potential for great loss or gain. As with dueling or heroic competitions between individual champions on the battlefield, wagering and riddling were double-edged swords. To be invited to participate was to be acknowledged as an equal, but to be defeated could result in social humiliation.[33] In a duel or a fight

---

31. Ibid., 102.
32. Bal, *Death and Dissymmetry: The Politics of Coherence in the Book of Judges* (Chicago: University of Chicago Press, 1988).
33. Thus the Philistine warrior Goliath was greatly insulted when the Israelites put forward a young and poorly armed challenger.

on the field of battle, one risked injury or even death; in riddling or wagering one faced the possibility of substantial material loss. In the case of Samson's riddle, thirty fine garments and thirty sets of battle gear were at stake. Equally important, also at stake were the honor and reputation of the participants. The fact that Samson's story emphasized intrigue, threats, and brutal violence indicates that the riddle-based wager was far from an amusing competition among friends. The conclusion of the affair was the death of thirty Philistine warriors and the confiscation of their battle paraphernalia, the alienation of Samson's wife, the destruction of standing grain, vineyards, and olive groves, and the burning of the bride's entire house and its inhabitants. On a personal level, the tale is a reminder of how the unrestrained animal-like behavior of a young warrior could spiral out of control, threatening the very foundations of civilized life. At a societal level, the story of wagering, riddling, and revenge points to the high economic, social, and even political stakes involved in the institution of marriage.

The tension both camouflaged and expressed at wedding feasts was recalled by the humanist author writing long after the premonarchic period. In a carefully crafted story, the defeated sons of Benjamin faced ethnic extinction unless they could find a way to obtain wives (Judges 21). Because the laws of incest prevented them from marrying women from within their own kin group and because all the other tribes had vowed not to offer them wives, the men of Benjamin had to abduct girls dancing at the yearly festival to Yhwh at Shiloh. The preponderance of scholarly opinion is that the stylized account alludes to an ancient ritual in which eligible females danced seductively and young men symbolically seized their future brides. The message of the ritual was that women are highly valued, objects worth fighting for, and that their transfer to the family of non-kin represents an important loss for the girls' families.[34]

Although it contains no description of a feast, the tale of Jephthah's daughter offers a woman's perspective on the larger ritual of marriage (Judges 11). The story of Jephthah's sacrifice honors the strongman's willingness to uphold his oath and celebrates the unrestrained quality of his gift to Yhwh, but the story also recalls the personal loss experienced by a young girl given in marriage. Reviewing a range of literature from Greek plays to western European tales, Peggy Day and Susan Niditch suggest that the story of Jephthah's daughter represents the death of childhood and the beginning of marital and maternal responsibility.[35] Poignantly accepting her father's decision to offer her life to a male deity, thus symbolizing the transfer of her body and spirit to her husband, the daughter asked only that she, along with her companions, be allowed to spend time in the free and natural setting of the mountains where she could mourn the loss of her youth and waste of her virginity. Consistent with the stories of Achsah, the Levite's concubine, Samson's Timnite wife, Samson's lover Delilah, the women of Jabesh-gilead, and the daughters of Shiloh, the tale of Jephthah's daughter is but one account of how the lives of women were controlled by men. Women were used as tools to purchase the loyalty of subordinates, settle disputes, heal rifts between rivals, ensure the continuity of male lineages, gain access to the secrets of adversaries, satisfy male sexual desire, and win the favor of the divinity in war. However, the writers and storytellers in Judges also depict women as heroes. Achsah is described as a shrewd bargainer, Deborah as an authoritative diviner, Jael and Delilah as

---

34. As noted in chapter 4, similar rituals continue in twenty-first-century Africa. Among the Kikuyu of Kenya, the groom and his close kin engage in mock battles with the relatives of the bride.

35. Niditch, *Judges*, 134–35; Peggy L. Day, "From the Child Is Born the Woman: The Story of Jephthah's Daughter," in *Gender and Difference in Ancient Israel*, ed. Peggy L. Day (Minneapolis: Fortress Press, 1989), 58–74.

daring champions, and Abimelech's female killer as the hero ending the life of a heartless tyrant.[36]

A second tension-filled feast in Judges was the one organized by the lords of Shechem (Judg. 9:22–29). According to the bardic storyteller, the god El had sent an evil spirit between the strongman Abimelech and the lords of Shechem. The lords of Shechem then dealt treacherously with their leader by setting up ambushes against Abimelech on the mountains and by robbing travelers, thus undermining Abimelech's monopoly over "protecting" and taxing trade.[37] Shechem's revolt against Abimelech was formalized during the annual grape harvest festival. At the feast, held in the house of the town's deity, eating and drinking were accompanied by cursing and intrigue. By the end of the celebration, the lords of Shechem had pledged their loyalty to the rival house of Gaal and repudiated Abimelech. The atmosphere of scheming and duplicity was heightened by the fact that Abimelech's subordinate, Zebul, was an observer at the feast. As with Samson's wedding banquet, the grape harvest feast at Shechem ended in violence. While Samson's violent passion was personal, the armed revolt at Shechem was collective and political. Normally, harvest festivals were intended to reaffirm the existing political order, to honor the town leaders (*bĕʿālîm* – בעלים), to demonstrate the generosity of the elite, and to show respect to the gods. But, as seen in the example of Shechem, such celebrations could easily turn against the established authorities. Rather than an occasion where joyous townspeople ate and drank to a bountiful harvest, the feast at Shechem turned into a traitorous gathering engineered by conniving politicians plotting a coup.

---

36. Although Delilah would have been regarded by Israelites as despicable, from a Philistine perspective she would have been as gallant as Jael. See Niditch, *Judges*, 169.
37. Presumably the ambushes were not directed at Abimelech personally, but were intended to capture his sources of revenue.

The third feast in Judges is that of the Adon (lord) of Bezek's kingly table (Judg. 1:7). After being captured and humiliated by Judah and Simeon, the Adon of Bezek lamented the meals over which he had once presided. However, instead of describing the powerful officials and honored guests seated at his table, he spoke of the seventy defeated kings, big toes and thumbs cut off, who were forced to forage for scraps under the table. Treated like animals, these kings were the visible manifestation of an important function of feasting and gift giving. While generosity and good gifts to friends and allies extended approval and bestowed honor, gift giving could also express social distance and derision. At the table of the Adon of Bezek, where they received the gift of leftovers, the recipients' demeaning place under the table and their shameful disfigurement identified them as objects of scorn. While honored guests would have been seated next to the king and humbler guests placed at the foot of the table, there was an even lower place for contemptible enemies. Instead of being the subjects of laudatory speeches, these men would have been mocked and cursed. For them, the king's food and words were tools to humiliate and stigmatize.

Tales of plunder, tribute, and gifting underscore the fact that the accumulation, transfer, and preservation of wealth as described in the book of Judges took place outside of the marketplace. The realm of economics was deeply embedded in considerations of social standing, kin relationships, and the exercise of political power. While plunder, tribute, and gifting resulted in the increase or decrease of wealth, they were not purely or even primarily economic affairs that bore the marks of an impersonal market. When the protagonists in Judges did engage in explicitly commercial dealings, the judgment of the storytellers seems to be negative. After a career as a plunderer, Gideon turned his attention to managing a divination site, which became an important source of income for him and for his entire house.

Taking the spoils of plunder, Gideon made an ephod, which Gideon's house operated as an enormously popular wealth-creating venture and to which all Israel came. In reflecting on this, the story's narrator suggests this action was dishonorable.[38] Delilah's betrayal of Samson was the fruition of a heartless economic transaction, the Philistine lords' payment of eleven hundred pieces of silver. And Abimelech's relationship to his political backers in Shechem was based on money, not affection. In his bid for power, Abimelech hired worthless and reckless men (Judg. 9:4). Presumably, these are the followers who abandoned the house of Abimelech once the leader died.

The most obviously profit-motivated transactions in Judges were those involving Micah and the young Levite he engaged as a shrine priest (Judges 17–18). A devious man, who stole from his own doting mother, Micah hired the Levite, who served as a salaried functionary. The financial particulars of the arrangement are carefully spelled out by the humanist storyteller who listed the precise details of the wages paid to the Levite. The account also makes it clear that Micah regarded the Levite as an attractive pecuniary addition to his household shrine, which became an important source of income. What is most evident in the story is the lack of personal loyalty on the part of any of the characters. Micah had little loyalty toward his mother. Even though he called the Levite his son, he treated him as a worker. For his part, the Levite remained in Micah's employ only until he received a more lucrative offer. Furthermore, when leaving the service of the former thief Micah, the Levite stole the costly instruments of divination to be used in the operation of a more profitable rival shrine.

In summary, the stories in Judges about people engaging in economic dealings whose expressed purpose is profit present those

---

38. In the words of the storyteller, "And Gideon made an ephod and placed it in his town Ophrah. And all Israel prostituted itself after it and it was to Gideon and his house a snare" (Judg. 8:27).

actions in a negative light. The participants are portrayed as untrustworthy and easily turned aside by the hope of monetary gain. They have no sense of permanency, loyalty, or personal engagement. Accounts of their actions suggest that monetary payments do not win the services of loyal, honorable, or valiant followers. Seeking profit without risking oneself in heroic combat, without respecting the reciprocity of patronage, and without entering into the complications of gift giving was not valued by any of the storytellers in Judges. Even brutal plunderers like Gideon or Abimelech are accorded more honor than business-oriented individuals such as Delilah, Micah, or Micah's Levite.[39]

Celestial Transactions in Judges

In addition to describing the seizure or exchange of temporal wealth, the book of Judges gives detailed attention to economic dealings between the earth and heaven. These celestial transactions were shaped by temporal notions of patrimony and patronage. Thus the earthly social system of nested patronage units, built upon the concept of the father's house, was projected onto the realm of the supernatural. As the divine patron, Yhwh received gifts from his human clients and in return offered tangible blessings such as material prosperity or victory in battle. In the book of Judges the most powerful temporal clients were mighty warriors, the heads of prominent houses or important towns. Standing as intermediaries between their subjects and the supernatural realm, men of valor such as Jephthah were both clients and patrons. Their subordinate relationship as Yhwh's vassals gave them the right to claim the role of rulers over dependent warriors, houses, and towns.

---

39. Gideon was both a plunderer (a warrior) and an entrepreneur (the proprietor of a divining site). Only the former activity was honored by the storyteller.

Regarding the deity as the supreme patron was common in the ancient Near East. An address by Ramesses II following the famous 1288 BCE Battle of Kadesh between Egypt and the Hittites illustrates the way people understood the entangling relationships linking earthly leaders, their subjects, and the deity.[40] In his speech, Ramesses II pointedly identified himself as the obedient and loyal son of the god Amun. However, he also expressed frustration that his divine patron had not been sufficiently generous in response to Ramesses's many material gifts. Clearly, the assumption of reciprocity supplied the underpinning for the pharaoh's speech. Undoubtedly, Ramesses measured reciprocity by the help in battle he had anticipated from Amun and by the loyalty and honor Ramesses expected from his human followers.

As proof of his own fidelity, Ramesses gave an account of the gifts of tribute he had provided his supernatural lord. First, Ramesses recalled that he had filled Amun's temple with booty and that he had honored the deity with a magnificent chapel. In addition, he said that he had donated all of his property to the god, constructed impressive monuments, supplied the deity with trade goods from foreign lands, and offered lavish sacrifices of sweet-smelling herbs and tens of thousands of cattle. In proclaiming that he had been a faithful and generous client, Ramesses explicitly used patrimonial language. He referred to Amun as his "protector," "guardian in combat," "father," and "patron of battle." Ramesses went on to assert that Amun was far more useful to him than millions of soldiers or myriad chariots.[41]

---

40. For an extensive discussion of the address of Ramesses II after the Battle of Kadesh, see Scott Morschauser, "Observations on the Speeches of Ramesses II in the Literary Record of the Battle of Kadesh," in *Perspectives on the Battle of Kadesh*, ed. Hans Goedicke (Baltimore, MD: Halgo, 1985), 123–206. Morschauser identifies three separate addresses that make up the final poetic creation. One address is directed toward Amun, the other two to Ramesses's troops. Kadesh is located about one hundred kilometers north of Damascus.

41. Morschauser, "Speeches of Ramesses II," 141–44.

In describing his many gifts to Amun, Ramesses made it clear that his offerings deserved to be rewarded, specifically with victory in battle. Voicing displeasure, Ramesses recalled that the Egyptians had not prevailed in the fight with the Hittites. As a result, Ramesses's own standing and honor were diminished. Therefore, the pharaoh chided Amun for not upholding his side of the exchange. In spite of Ramesses's loyalty and liberality, Amun had not been a reliable patron or family head. Ramesses's expression of discontent must have mirrored the frustration earthly clients often felt toward their temporal patrons.

As Ramesses's address suggests, exchanges with the divine could be intensely entangling. Like Ramesses II, the men of valor in Judges presented gifts to their god in the expectation that their power, honor, and wealth would be enhanced. Through divination, through sacrifices of gratitude and importuning, and through votive offerings, the men of valor hoped to solidify their earthly patrimonial power. Their goal was to enhance their stature, increase the strength of their house, and multiply their wealth.

The protagonists and writers of Judges shared Ramesses's understanding of celestial exchanges. Earthly gains and losses were explained in terms of spiritual reality. A setback in battle was not just the result of inferior military equipment or strategy. Rather, victory or defeat depended on the strength and favor of supernatural forces that could be influenced not only by human behavior, but also by human gifts of material value. Communities might be destroyed as sacrificial gifts to the deity or they could be sold into the hands of enemies should they be disloyal to their divine sovereign. Because the political, social, and economic fortunes of people on earth were affected by the world of the gods, humans sought to gain the favor of heaven by the offer of material wealth. However, these transactions were never described as simple acts of buying and selling. As with earthly economic relations, material dealings involving the divine realm were clothed in layers of ritual, protocol, and ceremony. Humans in Judges presented gifts to the divinity in ritualized ceremonies, generally the feasts of a sacrifice, which were then accepted or rejected by the deity. Relational reality, not market forces, dominated the way humans interacted with the supernatural realm.

Consistent with the book of Judges' focus on the wealthy elite, bardic descriptions of dealings between humans and the world of the supernatural feature powerful individual protagonists. At times, men of valor approached the deity directly, at other times a peripatetic messenger of Yhwh acted as an intermediary. Unlike later times, there was no class of professional religious functionaries who carried out elaborate and meticulously prescribed rituals that challenged the role of a powerful political leader.[42] The mighty men of valor in Judges were not encumbered by limitations on their religious roles. While Saul was chastised by the seer-priest Samuel for offering a sacrifice without deferring to a professional operative (1 Samuel 15), big men such as Ehud, Gideon, Manoah, and Jephthah were free to consult the deity directly and to offer sacrifices on their own behalf. In every case, such gifts were provided in order to enhance the standing or power of the giver and to reap rewards greater than the value of the sacrifice.

By the time the Deuteronomistic editor and the humanist writer made their contributions to the book of Judges, attitudes had changed and men of valor had lost their religious role. Composed during the late monarchy, a Deuteronomistic story describes the entire people as weeping and offering sacrifice (Judg. 2:1–5). Written even later, the humanist's narrative contains many references to "all the people

---

42. Leviticus, written centuries after the time described in Judges, lays out rules for approaching the deity. These rules privilege the role of the priests and Levites.

inquiring of Yhwh" (Judges 1). However, no heroic man of valor is mentioned. What may be implied is that these inquiries were conducted by priests or Levites. Created years after the era of the judges, these stories reflect a time when nationhood had become the ideal and when professional religious figures monopolized dealings with the divine.

The big men described in Judges brought their gifts of sacrifice to Yhwh for three important reasons. First, they made sacrifices to determine the will of Yhwh. Second, they sacrificed to gain the help of the deity or to express gratitude for help in the past. Third, they offered a sacrifice to seal a contractual agreement. In no case did any man of valor in Judges make a sacrifice as a sign of regret for failure, as an act of repentance for his own misdeeds or the misdeeds of his followers, or as a means of religious cleansing. There is absolutely no evidence that the relationship with Yhwh had anything to do with later concepts of ethics, law, or religious purity. Thus the men of valor were not guided by the Hebrew values contained in the preaching of the prophets, the prescriptions of the Deuteronomic reformers, or the rituals cherished by the priests and Levites.

The sacrifice as a tool to determine the deity's will functioned much like the Urim and Thummim used by the professional divining class. Just as a diviner might cast lots, strongmen such as Gideon offered a sacred feast to read the mind of Yhwh. For the Israelites and their neighbors, a feast for the deity might consist of grain, meat, or fat. The meal was conveyed to the realm of heaven through fire whose flames and smoke sent the tasty repast upward. A fire that burned fiercely and consumed the feast completely was evidence of supernatural approval and support. As seen with the offerings of Gideon and Samson's father, Manoah, a fire whose ignition defied a natural explanation and whose intensity was extraordinary signaled an uncommonly strong endorsement from Yhwh. An affirmative response would have been reassuring to the big man and awe inspiring to others observing the sacrifice. But, as can be seen in the ninth-century competition between Elijah and the prophets of Baal, deities did not always accept a sacrifice (1 Kings 18). Such a response indicated either disapproval or divine impotence. Most likely, just as some divination specialists had trade secrets that enhanced the mechanics of their rituals, certain men of valor were renowned for their unusually dramatic sacrificial pyrotechnics.

The second reason for offering a sacrifice was to curry the favor of Yhwh or to give thanks for a gracious act on his part. In Judges, sacrifices were offered in gratitude for female fertility (Manoah and his wife) or for a military victory (Jephthah). A gift of great value and a gift offered without reservation reflected well on the giver. Thus the best sacrifice was a whole burnt offering, a feast that was consumed entirely by Yhwh and a feast where not even one morsel remained to be enjoyed by the human supplicants. While a meal of flour and goat meat was welcomed by Yhwh, a feast featuring a bull was even better. But finest of all was the sacrifice of a human being, the most precious offering anyone could make. In the case of Jephthah, the human being was his only daughter, his one hope for progeny. Although modern Christians and Jews have difficulty with this story, the original storyteller and his or her listeners admired Jephthah for his courage and generosity.

The third reason to sacrifice was to involve the gods as a party to a contract. Numerous passages in the Hebrew Bible refer to the practice of making an offering in conjunction with a pledge or vow. Also called peace offerings, these votive offerings were intended to cement or restore relationships. Written later than the events depicted in Judges, the books of Leviticus and Numbers contain references to and rules for such rituals. Unlike a whole burnt offering, which is given completely to Yhwh, a votive offering or peace offering is consumed by both the divine and human participants.[43] The fact that both parties eat the meat of sacrifice points to the collaborative nature of a vow or contract. Some vows were political, involving an entire community, others were more personal and private. Although not explicitly mentioned in Judges, it must be assumed that when Abimelech and Jephthah were installed as political leaders, a sacrifice was offered to enlist the deity as a witness and guarantor of the agreement. This votive feast would have been shared by the newly appointed leaders, the lords of the town, and the deity. In becoming a Nazirite warrior, Samson or his family would also have offered a sacrifice to seal his vow. The book of Numbers refers to the protocol for such a sacrifice (Num. 6:13-21).[44]

Offering a sacrifice—whether for the purpose of sealing a vow, for discerning God's will, for obtaining divine support for a battle, or for giving thanks after a victory—enhanced the prestige and authority of an ancient Israelite man of valor. Just as gifts exchanged among humans led to an entangling web of obligation and reciprocity, a gift to Yhwh might have been seen as ensnaring the deity in human affairs. Although as with temporal interactions the obligatory nature of the gift transaction was not stated explicitly, the more lavish the promise or more valuable the gift, the more probable a favorable response. As individuals with great wealth, the strongmen in Judges served as pivotal intermediaries between earth and heaven. They could generate divine support not available to men and women of more meager means. While the sacrifice of a bull or even a child was painfully expensive, that cost would have been more than outweighed by the reward in terms of political support or tribute from fearful or grateful followers.

43. See, for example, Lev. 7:16-17; 22:21; Num. 6:13-21.
44. Although both Numbers and Leviticus were compiled long after the time period depicted in Judges, it is safe to assume that protocols for sacrifices in Numbers and Leviticus reflected much earlier customs.

The sacrificial feast could also take the form of holy war (ḥērem – חרם). As Susan Niditch points out, many passages in the Hebrew Bible portray slaughter in war as an honorable way to make a choice offering to the deity. Just as an ancient god relished the savory animal fat ascending to heaven in the smoke of sacrifice, the same god would have delighted in an offering of human lives taken in battle. It was only late in the time of the monarchy, perhaps in the context of the Deuteronomic reform, that Hebrew thinkers came to challenge the morality of offering living humans—either those burned in sacrifice or slaughtered in war—to Yhwh. While Deuteronomistic writers condemned human sacrifice unequivocally, they nevertheless justified holy war as rightful punishment for idolatrous enemies.[45] Significantly, in Judges the only references to ḥērem or holy war are contained in the writings of the Deuteronomistic or humanist writers. The early bardic tales are more interested in relating the heroic exploits of combat or in sharing of the spoils among the warriors. However, the fact that one of the early storytellers celebrated human sacrifice would lead one to believe that sacrificing communities and towns to the deity would have been regarded as honorable.

Conclusions

In Judges, the exchange of wealth was an important vehicle for communicating deep social and political meaning. Economic dealings brokered, ratified, cemented, and healed the affairs of marriage, kinship, and politics. While marriage, kinship, and politics were valued for their material benefit, economic arrangements were at least equally important as relational tools in the service of family, kin, and community. Because of their social implications, economic

---

45. Susan Niditch, *War in the Hebrew Bible: A Study in the Ethics of Violence* (Oxford: Oxford University Press, 1993).

dealings were entangling. Tribute and gifting encumbered both the recipient and the donor. Whether carried out through plunder, tribute, or gift giving, the transfer of wealth was as much about honor, social position, and relative power as about material accumulation.

Even the act of plunder carried deep social and moral meaning. For the bardic writer, to be the victim of plunder was to be humiliated; to become the plunderer was a mark of glory. From the perspective of the humanist, to be plundered was to be impotent. The Deuteronomistic writer went even a step further. To be a casualty of plunder was to be the object of celestial reprobation, the most intense form of disapproval and dishonor. Tribute is different from plunder in the fact that with tribute the inferior party receives some benefit and has some leverage in bargaining. Tribute involves a lower level of violence, is less capricious, and may even be ratified by some type of covenant arrangement. However, the social and political inequality is symbolized by the fact that the flow of wealth is always unequal. The tribute collector becomes fat, the tribute giver is squeezed. In the stories of both Ehud and Abimelech, the most explicit accounts of tribute, the narrative ends with the death of the tribute monger. Although Ehud presented himself as a trusted confidant of King Eglon, Ehud assassinated the monarch. Supposedly the people of Shechem voluntarily elected Abimelech as their leader, but they conspired to overthrow him. And the inhabitants of another city in his tribute system ended his life. Thus, although veiled in the cloak of friendship and free election, the tribute system is exposed as predatory and adversarial, a system deeply resented by the tribute givers. Lurking beneath the surface of an association portrayed by the superior party as one of friendship and mutual benefit is a substratum of antipathy that constantly threatens the relationship.

Of the three types of economic exchange, gift giving is the most socially complex. Not surprisingly then, the book of Judges gives detailed attention to the intricacies of gifting. The Adon of Bezek's royal banquet, Achsah's dowry, Gideon's spectacular sacrifice, Samson's wedding feasts and reckless wagers, Jephthah's lavish gift to Yhwh, the unrestrained hospitality and inhospitality in the story of the Levite and his concubine, and the offering of wives to Benjamin are as much or more about social dynamics as about the transfer and consumption of wealth. Every aspect of gift giving was fraught with social complexity. While to be the object of plunder and tribute imposed inferiority on the victim, to receive a gift was to voluntarily accept a position of subordination or acknowledge an obligation of future reciprocity. Because of the entangling social and political dynamics, gift giving was often marked by tension. While the tensions could be limited (for example, when the tension was between friendly rivals), they also could be so deep as to lead to murder and war. Tensions of that magnitude could not be contained by the jubilant etiquette of feasting and festivals.

As individuals with comparatively great wealth, the men of valor in Judges were pivotal figures in all types of economic exchanges. All three writers—the bardic, Deuteronomistic, and humanist—described them as successful heroic plunderers or valiant protectors against plunder. Some of the men of valor, notably Ehud and Abimelech, also were powerful players in the tribute system. Both the bardic storyteller and the humanist devoted much attention to the exchange of gifts. As gift givers, the heroes in Judges presided at feasts and most likely offered hospitality to family and strangers. But more important than temporal gift giving was the act of offering a gift to Yhwh. The vows of Jephthah and Abimelech, when they were installed as political leaders, would have been ratified by a votive sacrifice. Gideon and Jephthah, two of the greatest heroes in Judges, offered spectacular and extravagant gifts, gifts that could not be matched by men and women of lower standing. Such gifts demonstrated their great power and established them as unparalleled intermediaries between the people and Yhwh.

6

Conclusions and Reflections

Neglected by secular scholars because of its religious content, reshaped by people of faith because its protagonists are morally offensive, and avoided by individuals committed to nonviolence because of its brutality, the book of Judges deserves to be taken more seriously. No other book in the Hebrew Bible mirrors the entire span of Israel's history as authentically as Judges. The main body of the book is a collection of premonarchic tales celebrating heroic champions, who competed for power in turbulent times. The book's sixth-century version reflects the tension between the priestly Deuteronomic reformers and the Deuteronomistic defenders of royal power.[1] In its final compilation Judges echoes the anxieties of the exilic and postexilic eras when the very existence of the nation was in doubt. The scope of the book and the debates embedded in its

---

1. My discussion in chapter 1 builds on Bernard Levinson's observation that the Deuteronomistic Historian challenged the ideals of the Deuteronomic reform, which attempted to limit the power of the king. See Bernard Levinson, "The Reconceptualization of Kingship in Deuteronomy and the Deuteronomistic History's Transformation of Torah," *Vetus Testamentum* 51, no. 4 (2001): 511–34.

content make Judges a potentially rich resource for social scientists, people of faith, and individuals concerned about peace and violence. Social scientists, especially those interested in the dynamics of patron-client politics, can learn much about Early Iron Age patrimonial systems. Jews and Christians should study Judges because, even if it seems to deny the tenets of any religion emphasizing forgiveness and reconciliation, members of both faiths consider it Scripture. For their part, students of nonviolence need to come to terms with a book in which martial values are celebrated so enthusiastically.

The Book of Judges for Social Scientists

Social scientists could benefit from studying Judges, a writing filled with information about political, economic, and social behavior in ancient Syria-Palestine. One need not accept the accounts in Judges as accurate records of real personages in order to mine the sagas for useful data. Even if figures such as Deborah, Jael, Gideon, and Jephthah are partially or wholly fictional, the fact that their stories were told in premonarchic times makes the tales valuable records of the actions and values of that age.[2] The narratives open a window onto the motives, strategies, and legacy of ancient patrimonial leaders. The evidence in Judges shows that leaders in Syria-Palestine were relentless in their pursuit of political power, that they employed methods other than the use of force or the distribution of wealth to achieve that power, and that they contributed both to the

---

2. Chinua Achebe's fictional stories of Igbo society in Nigeria are good examples of how imaginary accounts can be extraordinarily accurate representations of religion, family dynamics, social values, gender relations, farming, and governance. Chinua Achebe, *Things Fall Apart* (New York: Anchor Books, 1994). For a theoretical discussion of how fiction actually can explain reality more completely and accurately than a literalistic documentary depiction, see Paul Ricoeur, "The Function of Fiction in Shaping Reality," *Man and World* 12 (1979): 123–41. Ricoeur notes that even scientific observation relies on "analogies, models, and paradigms" to describe the world ("The Function of Fiction," 140).

development of an Israelite national consciousness and to the specific form of government used by later Israelite officials.

The tales in Judges demonstrate that the quest for political power preoccupied leaders in premonarchic Israel. Those leaders were not marching at the head of a peasant uprising, championing social justice, seeking to consolidate a nation, or encouraging spiritual conformity. Instead, the men and women of valor in Judges focused on maximizing power. Some were protecting their own houses, a few were acting as functionaries of a local or regional political elite, others were seeking to dominate in their own right. When they challenged Canaanite overlords, Philistine interlopers, and roving bandits from east of the Jordan, their primary goal was to advance their own political standing and strengthen their own houses. When they fought oppressors, their aim was not to liberate a subject people, but to usurp the oppressors. When men such as Ehud, Gideon, Abimelech, or Jephthah clashed with external predators, they did so with an eye to enhancing their own influence. When they offered sacrifices or consulted Yhwh, they were hoping to reap political, military, or economic benefits for themselves. As suggested by the stories of Gideon and Abimelech, because of their efforts to dominate, these men could themselves become the targets of resistance and revolt. When faced with opposition, the men of valor did not hesitate to employ the most brutal means to crush disobedience. Although the later Deuteronomistic editor reconstituted them as deliverers and liberators, the epic-bardic storyteller more accurately described them as ambitious political figures in pursuit of personal gain and glory.

While it is not surprising that the primary goals of ancient strongmen were political dominance and material riches, what is noteworthy is the multiplicity of strategies they employed to gain and maintain that power and wealth. Although the use of force and the redistribution of wealth were important instruments in their quest for control, Judges shows that leaders developed other subtler and more sophisticated methods to exert their rule. Foundational to their efforts was the practice of portraying themselves as protective patrons. Although frequently resorting to ruthless violence, they clothed their exercise of power in the language of family, loyalty, honor, generosity, and divine support. Regarded as patrimonial guardians, the heroes in Judges then consolidated their rule by using a variety of devices. One approach involved attracting or consulting individuals with exceptional expertise in the domain of indigenous knowledge. A person of valor could use that knowledge personally (for example, determining when and how to go to war) or might provide information to others in return for political or economic gain. Diviners like Gideon and Deborah achieved success by championing Yhwh as an especially reliable source of supernatural guidance. Individuals of valor also enhanced their political power by becoming known for steadfastness. A trustworthy patron was better able to retain the loyalty of subordinates and strike fear into the hearts of adversaries when those underlings and enemies had complete confidence in the leader's ability to keep his word. Although strongmen sought to ensure predictability by entering into formal public covenants, such contracts were frequently broken. More robust guarantees were needed. Thus a man of valor like Jephthah sealed his covenant with an oath to Yhwh and upheld that oath no matter the cost. Men of valor also convinced others to obey and follow by cultivating a reputation for honor, another key component of power. A leader regarded as honorable (consequential) was able to command obedience without resorting to coercion. Many of the heroes in Judges (for example, both Gideon and Samson) based their claim to honor on their relationship to Yhwh. It may be significant that Abimelech, who never acknowledged Yhwh, is remembered as having perished ingloriously. Finally, although gathering wealth through plunder and tribute collection was an important source of power for men of valor in Judges, giving gifts to Yhwh was another method to enhance their authority. Becoming known as someone whose sacrifices were both extravagant and well received in the celestial realm was a way in which the patrons in Judges gained the allegiance of their followers. All of these examples provide ample evidence that ancient strongmen and women depicted in Judges had a diverse set of political, social, economic, and religious tools to attract clients and to maintain their loyalty. All of these strategies were linked to an increasingly respected deity, Yhwh.

As shrewd and successful seekers after power, the men and women of valor in Judges contributed to the growth of Israel's ethnic and national awareness and to the development of Israel's system of government. While the heroic figures in Judges appear to have had little sense of Israelite unity, in fact little interest in regions outside their local domains, they did play a critical role in an emerging national consciousness that culminated in a unified monarchy.[3] This national consciousness was linked to Yhwh, the deity favored by the men and women of valor in Judges. There is strong evidence that the increasing allegiance to Yhwh was promoted by seers such as Deborah and by roving messengers of Yhwh. Capitalizing on the political ambitions of the men of valor, these prophets and peripatetic agitators promised that loyalty to their deity would give the strongmen a comparative political advantage. As can be seen in the persistence of identity politics, even in today's world, devotion to a single deity can be a powerful source and expression of cultural, ethnic, and national solidarity. To venerate a common god is to affirm unity at the deepest and most pervasive level. Seeking to

---

3. Men of valor like Gideon and Abimelech were concerned about outside invaders and they did engage in raids beyond the boundaries of their home base, but they expressed no desire to rule other regions of the land that later became Israel.

dominate earth by accessing heaven, the ambitious heroes in Judges were instrumental in moving Israel in the direction of ethnic and political unity. Elevating Yhwh over other deities was a way to distinguish Israel from the larger Canaanite culture and a first step in the direction of monotheism.

The strategies and values exhibited by the early leaders in Judges also had an important impact on the subsequent development of government. The first Israelite monarchs, Saul and David, were exceptionally successful mighty men, heads of dominant houses, who wielded extensive economic, military, religious, and political power. Although Solomon and later kings in Judah and Israel patterned themselves along the lines of conventional regional monarchs, the courts of Saul and David would have borne more resemblance to the establishments of Jephthah and Gideon. It is just as appropriate to think of the houses of Saul and David as it is to speak of the kingdoms of Saul and David. Saul and David may have been much more at home in the village of an African chief or in a pastoral warrior camp than in the urban palaces of King Ahab or Herod the Great.

As charismatic leaders, the men of valor in Judges represent one pole in the age-old tension between the desire for decisive individual action and the need for the predictability of bureaucracy, protocol, and law. Both the bardic storyteller and the Deuteronomistic Historian praised the dynamic heroic individual, who ruled on earth and who interceded with the celestial world. Other writings in the Hebrew Bible, notably Leviticus and Deuteronomy, advocated regulation and regularity. As is true for most societies, the history of Israel was marked by the contrast between an unconstrained individual ruler and a restrictive web of rules, laws, and procedures. The men and women of valor in Judges served as models for the robust leadership favored by later Israelite monarchs. Priests and

Levites, functionaries not celebrated by Judges, promoted a more predictable and routinized approach to the exercise of political power.

Although not their intention, the activities of the early heroes provided a shared collection of stories about heroes, battles, and enemies that could be used by later nationalistic writers and agitators to create a unified story of the past. Perhaps the earliest evidence of national awareness is the Song of Deborah, which contains the names of twelve Israelite tribes. The Song of Deborah, perhaps the oldest text in the Hebrew Bible, points to an emerging desire for cooperation among the peoples that later became a single nation. Composed a century or more prior to the kingdoms of Saul and David, the song expresses a poetic plea for tribal unity. Although Deborah's song acknowledges the fact that not all the tribes mobilized to defend against the Canaanites, the poem advocates such cooperation. The Song of Deborah suggests that poets and bardic singers were among the first champions of a common Israelite identity. The nationalist sentiments expressed in the words of musicians preceded the pronouncements of politicians, prophets, or law givers.[4]

The Book of Judges for People of Faith

Until this point, my book has not made assumptions about the faith of the reader. The previous five chapters have not approached the book of Judges differently than one would approach any ancient text. Nevertheless, most people reading Judges are interested in its religious content. Unlike social scientists, devout Jews and Christians regard the Hebrew Bible as God's authoritative word. Thus, they

---

4. The Song of Moses and Miriam in Exodus 15 is another example of bardic poetry promoting Israelite identity by celebrating a military victory. In modern times, bardic poets in the Horn of Africa have served as powerful voices to mobilize resistance against outside oppressors and to unify disparate peoples. See Said S. Samatar, *Oral Poetry and Somali Nationalism: The Case of Sayyid Mahammad Abdille Hasan* (Cambridge: Cambridge University Press, 1982).

come to Judges with the expectation that they will find moral or spiritual guidance. It is to those readers that I now turn my attention. While people of faith have frequently misinterpreted and misused Judges, as a person of faith myself I am convinced that this book, which records Israel's first steps toward devotion to Yhwh, has much to teach us about God, about religion, and about ourselves. What follows are some of my thoughts about those teachings.

Because the brutality, disregard for women, reliance on magic and divination, and celebration of aggressive warfare are all jarring to modern religious sensibilities, the book of Judges is too often ignored by people of faith. Even worse, modern Jews and Christians regularly transform the men and women of valor into something they were not and would not have wanted to be. This is an affront to them and to the Bible. The stories should be read as they were originally intended, as tales celebrating and memorializing the victories of premonarchic warrior heroes. Jews and Christians who claim the book of Judges contains a sacred message, an account of how God relates to mortals, and a reflection on the divine will for human beings, must study the text as it truly is, not as they might wish it to be. Present-day believers frequently say the Bible is to be read through the eyes of faith. When following that admonition many Jews and Christians then interpret the stories in Judges as an apology for building defenses against hostile social and political rivals, as lessons about the dangers of apostasy and cultural tolerance, as evidence of tribal unity willed in heaven, as accounts of supernaturally inspired saviors/deliverers, or as a divinely planned prelude to the later monarchy. Any Christian or Jew who has heard a sermon on Judges or read one of the faith-based commentaries cited in my book has heard one or more of those themes. While these interpretations may echo the perspectives of theologians promoting the Deuteronomic restoration (which came at least five hundred years after the time of the judges), of the

CONCLUSIONS AND REFLECTIONS

subsequent Deuteronomistic Historian, or of early Christian thinkers, they do not reflect the values and viewpoints of people dwelling in premonarchic Israel.

To treat the men and women in Judges honestly and respectfully, modern believers must accept them for who they were. No more than any other strong patron-client leaders in other preindustrial societies did people like Ehud, Gideon, Abimelech, or even Jephthah think of themselves as religious figures. They were ambitious and powerful political figures, pure and simple. Their aspirations were political, their roles were political, and their strategies were political. Of course they believed in divine power and, with the exception of Abimelech, in the power of Yhwh. But they were far more concerned about temporal power, honor, the distribution of wealth, and their reputation for reliability than they were anxious about any aspect of orthodox religion as later understood by the prophets of the Hebrew Bible or by the writers of the Christian Scriptures.

In reading the book of Judges, there is absolutely no indication that any character had even the slightest notion of Mosaic law. There is no mention of the Ten Commandments, no evidence of anyone actually dispensing codified legal judgments, and no suggestion that the ethics of the men and women of valor were much different from the ethics of other men and women of valor in the ancient Mediterranean world. In fact, within the frame of reference of the book itself, the most ethical act in the entire book of Judges was that of Jephthah sacrificing his own daughter. All of the evidence in Judges indicates that the book's protagonists emerged out of Canaanite culture; the most obvious example of this would be Abimelech. In every respect Abimelech is just another Canaanite petty potentate. Even men and women in Judges commonly held up as champions of the faith—Ehud, Deborah, Gideon, Jephthah, and Samson—would be considered theological and moral reprobates if judged by the standards of today. Although aware of the deity Yhwh, they thought of him in terms of his extraordinary power, not as a dispenser of ethical guidelines. When measured against the principles of accepted Jewish, Christian, or Muslim belief, the protagonists in Judges must be considered as individuals standing at the very raw and ragged edge of what later came to be regarded as orthodox religious faith.

Given these facts, anyone reading the Hebrew Bible must lay to rest the idea that the main purpose of the book of Judges was to describe moral heroes (at least in the way we understand morality) or to warn against a downward cycle of disobedience and apostasy. While those notions may be spiritually satisfying, they cannot be supported by the text. Too many exegetes, both Christian and Jewish, rely on the Deuteronomistic writer's commentary as a guide to all of the material in Judges. Thus, they present Othniel as Yhwh's ideal leader upholding covenant faithfulness and shape their description of each successive judge to suggest a path of degeneration and increasing unfaithfulness culminating with Jephthah and Samson.[5] Thus they interpret the ambiguous and noncommittal phrase "In those days there was no king, every man did what was right in his own eyes" as a tragic commentary on Israel's moral decline.[6] To measure the men and women in Judges according to the standards of Deuteronomic law and covenant faithfulness requires a fanciful and anachronistic tour de force. To write an analysis positing that people like Ehud, Deborah, Gideon, Jephthah, and the fictional Samson

---

5. Often the evidence cited for the moral decline is the Deuteronomistic editor's estimate of the length of time a man judged or the duration of the peace supposedly afforded by his rule. That is slim support indeed. Furthermore, except for the Deuteronomistic writer's assertion, there is no reason to believe that Othniel was anything other than a typical warrior big man. Only the brevity of his account allows modern readers to conclude that he was especially upright. For commentators to defend the interpretation of progressive covenantal infidelity they demonize Jephthah—the most faithful individual in Judges—as a rash and foolish man, unfit for leadership.
6. Susan Niditch says Judges 17–21 reflects a worldview "that is not messianic or apocalyptic, nor strongly pro-monarchic." The phrase "In those days there was no king in Israel" is simply "recalling a long-ago past." Niditch, *Judges* (Louisville: Westminster, 2008), 13.

understood anything resembling the Mosaic covenant or held to ethical values approximating those of the seventh century BCE is to create a novel noncanonical and nonexistent text. The irony of that innovation is that its makers generally regard themselves as faithful defenders of Scripture.

In taming and theologizing the men and women of Judges, modern people of faith domesticate God and deny human nature. Walter Brueggemann, who describes the faith of ancient Israel as complex, dynamic, and fluid, argues that the Hebrew Bible records an "on-going dialogic transaction in which all parties are summoned to risk and change."[7] That type of dynamic relationship is not possible if God is portrayed as static and immoveable or if humans in Scripture are regarded as saintly and unblemished. In Brueggemann's view, God, who is in an open-ended relationship with humans, is not a fixed, settled entity. Rather, "God is always emerging in new ways in response to the requirements of the relationship at hand."[8] In the book of Judges, we catch some of the first words in the conversation between a responsive God and a Hebrew people whose faith was in progress. Referencing the work of Morton Smith, Brueggemann notes that the people of Israel were entering a dialogue already begun by other people of faith. Building upon common concepts about divinity borrowed from other ancient Near Eastern religions, Israel based its understanding of Yhwh on a foundation of existing ideas. Among the notions constructed upon concepts borrowed from Canaanite religion were the beliefs that Yhwh is a High God, who is the power behind all human and natural phenomena; that Yhwh is a God active in the world and responsible for a moral order; that Yhwh exhibits anthropomorphic characteristics; that Yhwh is

---

7. Walter Brueggemann, *An Unsettling God: The Heart of the Hebrew Bible* (Minneapolis: Fortress Press, 2009), xii. *An Unsettling God* repeats the ideas first presented in Brueggeman's *Theology of the Old Testament: Testimony, Dispute, Advocacy* (Minneapolis: Fortress Press, 1997).
8. Brueggemann, *An Unsettling God*, 4.

powerful, just, and merciful; that Yhwh is a God connected to a particular people or region; and that Yhwh can be interpreted and represented by authoritative human agents.[9] Clearly, the heroes in Judges owed a debt to this Canaanite base.

The book of Judges provides unmistakable evidence that as theological neophytes, the early Israelites expressed ideas about God that would trouble modern sensibilities. Their God prized Samson's boldness, Jephthah's willingness to sacrifice his daughter, Gideon's manipulation of divination implements, Ehud's treachery, and Deborah's ecstatic prophecies. Their God showed too little concern for the victims of injustice, especially women. Israel's concept of God developed and was refined in a conversation over time. The men and women in Judges and the storytellers and writers who recorded their lives advanced that conversation. Nevertheless, the God depicted in Judges bore as much resemblance to Baal and El as to the Yhwh preached by Isaiah or the Abba described by Jesus.

Not only do many commentators domesticate God by failing to take into account the developmental nature of faith and the progressive nature of theological dialogue, they also reshape the men and women in the book of Judges. The protagonists in Judges are remade as people guided by principles that emerged centuries later. This reshaping violates the text, seeks to control God, and downplays the religious and moral struggles of God's earthly children. The transformation silences the human voice in the conversation between God and people. Ironically, modern readers might gain a more accurate picture of the men and women in Judges by watching episodes of the wildly popular HBO series, *The Sopranos*, than by reading the commentaries of pious exegetes. In *The Gospel according to Tony Soprano,* a short book written for laypeople, Pastor Chris Seay

---

9. Morton Smith, "The Common Theology of the Ancient Near East," *Journal of Biblical Literature* 71 (1952): 135–47, cited in Brueggemann, *An Unsettling God*, 2.

analyzes the social and moral struggles of the fictional mobster Tony Soprano, a man who displays all the characteristics required to rise to the top of the Mafia.[10] Exuberant in his embrace of life, Tony is a deeply flawed but fully human individual. Tony is a man capable of tender love and explosive anger. Totally committed to family (both the mob and his spouse and children), he mistreats his own teenagers and does not hesitate to kill his best friend. He adores his wife and is addicted to chasing other women. Utterly self-confident from all outward appearances, he suffers from regular debilitating panic attacks. A tough guy on the street, he displays vulnerability and tenderness in the office of his psychiatrist. A man with an unshakable belief in God and the church, at every turn his life violates the teachings of Scripture. Although a devout Catholic, he follows the moral rules of his profession, rules requiring him to murder, extort, and torture. Tony delights in his wealth but recognizes he lives in luxury because of the price paid by his victims.

Chris Seay suggests that Tony Soprano is a compelling figure because he reflects people as they are and life as it is, not how we pretend them to be. Personalizing the message of *The Sopranos*, Seay writes,

> The show actually sees me as I am. It pokes at my spirit with unsavory stories. And the stories it tells are pathetic. The characters take selfishness to a new level, selfishness that does not stop with subtle lies, lavish spending on momentary comforts, and a preoccupation with the admiration of others. It sinks to murder, theft, torture, extortion, adultery, and worse. I want to be sanctimonious and push these hideous characters away. But I cannot. We're just too much alike.[11]

---

10. Chris Seay, *The Gospel according to Tony Soprano: An Unauthorized Look into the Soul of TV's Top Mob Boss and His Family* (Lake Mary, FL: Relevant Books, 2002).
11. Ibid., xiii–xiv.

While Seay refers to an imaginary New Jersey gangster, he could have said the same things about Samson, Gideon, Ehud, Abimelech, Jael, and Jephthah. Seay believes people of faith can learn much about human nature and the search for God from Tony Soprano. Seay argues that unless we are honest about our own human shortcomings, we cannot enter into an authentic relationship with God. The ancient Hebrew storytellers model this honesty. In spite of their naïve faith and myriad moral faults, the imperfect heroes in Judges and the flawed Tony Soprano are people engaged in a realistic conversation with God. Moderns are at peril when they sanitize that exchange.

Both Tony Soprano and the characters in Judges are reminders that God created man and woman out of dust. According to the creation story in Genesis 2, dust is what God had to work with when first shaping human beings, who in turn fashioned civilization. The book of Judges suggests that all human culture, even orthodox religion, emerges from ideas and values that have a history and that are riddled with imperfection. However unsettling, accepting that reality can lead to gratitude and respect for the incomplete but important contributions of the heroes in Judges, men and women we take as our spiritual ancestors. The book of Judges may suggest that God values and uses all humans in spite of their theological or moral immaturity. From the divine perspective, the shred of virtuousness displayed by Jephthah's constancy may have outweighed the horrendous evil of his sacrifice. Jews, Christians, and Muslims might interpret this acceptance as an expression of divine grace and mercy.

The book of Judges invites us be tolerant of the faith of others, whether they are people from the distant past or our own contemporaries in different cultures. As we take an honest look at the men and women of valor in Judges, it is obvious that they were not virtuous people by modern standards—nor, at times, even by the standards of their own age. Certainly Yhwh/God/Allah is equally

CONCLUSIONS AND REFLECTIONS

aware of their flaws. Apparently, God wants us to acknowledge, without judgment it would seem, the divine work in all people. Early Christian missionaries to Africa, Asia, and the Americas deeply offended indigenous peoples by denigrating their religious ideas and practices. Those missionaries often relegated to perdition ancestors who died before having had access to the gospel. But were those ancestors any more pagan than the heroes of Judges? Why then should they be condemned and the men and women of valor in Judges honored? The same might be said of the Egyptian, Mesopotamian, Phoenician, and Canaanite religious thinkers whose ideas contributed to the faith of Israel.[12]

Recognizing that the conversation of faith is carried on between imperfect people and a gracious and responsive God calls for humility on our part. How can moderns be certain that our theology, philosophy, and ethics are qualitatively superior to those of the men and women of valor in Judges? Our abuse of the environment, our willingness to risk nuclear war in order to project national power or defend a political ideology, our readiness to sacrifice the poor, many of them children, so that shareholders can protect profits and so that the wealthy can reduce taxes, our appeal to freedom in order to obstruct meaningful restrictions on guns, and our commercialization of sex and violence are only some of the evils that people hundreds of years from now may look upon with disbelief.[13] Those of us who

---

12. The prophet Amos suggests that Yhwh values the Cushites, Philistines, and Arameans as much as Israel (Amos 9:7).
13. The renowned American diplomat, historian, humanist, and life-long Presbyterian George F. Kennan often expressed concern about the immature moral perspectives of people in the modern era. He was especially troubled by the ethical irresponsibility of stockpiling nuclear weapons and relying on defense strategies that risked the destruction of all civilization and nature. Kennan proposed complete nuclear disarmament and he went so far as to argue that defeat, which preserved the possibility of survival, was far preferable to a victory resulting in world annihilation. In a 1980 speech Kennan said, "For the love of God, of our children, and of the civilization to which you belong, cease this madness. You have a duty not just to the generation of the present—you have a duty to civilization's past, which you threaten to render meaningless, and to its future, which you threaten to render nonexistent. You are mortal men.

are people of faith and who read Judges theologically as well as analytically can only hope that God will grant us the same grace that was extended to the men and women of valor in premonarchic Israel. We must also admit that, like the heroes in Judges, we pay too little attention to the plight of the victims of all forms of violence.

In spite of the fact that the religious ideas of the men and women in Judges appear crude when measured against later standards, we should honor the contribution they made to later Hebrew religion.[14] The great ideas of the Hebrew faith did not spring only from a burning bush or from one man's encounter on Sinai. Nor did they emerge fully formed from the minds of the great Hebrew lawyers or prophets. It is possible that notions such as Yhwh's consistency and steadfast nature were built upon the values of trustworthiness cultivated by men like Jephthah. The belief that Yhwh is consequential and deserving of humans' highest esteem may have its roots in the concepts of honor celebrated during the time of Judges. The conviction that Yhwh is worthy of complete and undivided allegiance and thanks is consistent with primitive understandings of

---

You are capable of error. You have no right to hold in your hands—there is no one wise enough and strong enough to hold in his hands—destructive powers sufficient to put an end to civilized life on a great portion of our planet. No one should wish to hold such powers. Thrust them from you. The risks you might thereby assume are not greater—could not be greater—than those which you are now incurring for us all." George F. Kennan, diary, October 2, 1980, quoted in John Lewis Gaddis, *George F. Kennan: An American Life* (New York: Penguin, 2011), 645–46. Kennan's criticism of twentieth-century political morality was proved correct by the fact that the great majority of policy makers dismissed his ideas as irresponsible.

14. Surprisingly, Brueggemann pays scant attention to the religious role of people in Judges or to the storytellers, writers, and editors who recorded the tales in Judges. Brueggemann's focus is on covenant, grace, and justice, ideas that emerged later in the life of Israel. His *Theology of the Old Testament* contains only a few, rather tangential, references to the heroes in Judges. Although he mentions Gideon's call and alludes to those who hear the Song of Deborah, he says nothing about the efforts of Gideon or Deborah to communicate with Yhwh through divination. Furthermore, Brueggemann does not describe the thoughts or activities of any of the other men and women of valor in Judges. Brueggemann's *An Unsettling God* does not mention Judges even one time. Brueggemann's lack of attention to Judges is unfortunate since, as noted at the beginning of this chapter, more than any other book in the Hebrew Bible, Judges bears witness to Israel's entire faith journey.

whole burnt offerings ascending into the heavens. The practice of turning to Yhwh for guidance and support may have been shaped by the activities of diviners such as Gideon and Deborah, people who would have been very much at home in the company of an African or Canaanite "sorcerer." Also, as is evident in the story of Jephthah, the epic-bardic storyteller was fully aware of the painful moral dilemmas facing all human beings. Such intellectual sophistication may have laid the groundwork for future ethical musings by the authors of Jonah and Job. Certainly the writings of the humanist, who supplied the final chapters of Judges, reflect such moral contemplation. The preaching of the prophets would not have been possible without that kind of deep awareness of tragedy and moral complexity.

The Book of Judges for Adherents to Nonviolence

The book of Judges, along with Joshua and many other books in the Hebrew Bible, is deeply troubling for anyone committed to peace and nonviolence, both pacifists and those who take the principles of just war seriously. When learning about the violence in Judges, the most common responses of modern people are either to interpret the stories as a justification for military action (action whose defenders always present as a legitimate endeavor) or to say that the values in Judges should be ignored because they have been superseded by the teachings of the prophets and Jesus. These answers are typical of students in my peace studies classes and of the conservative or liberal faith traditions from which they come. Neither response is fair to Judges. If one relies on the book to excuse the practice of warfare, then could one not turn to Judges to defend genocide, human sacrifice, divination, pillaging and looting, seduction and assassination, burning the houses and families of deceitful opponents, rejoicing in the immolation of entire cities, and offering women as victims for rape? In fact, for someone trusting Judges for specific moral guidance, the story of Samson could be taken as permission for suicide bombing. In short, it is not morally or logically defensible to use Judges to legitimize war, but reject as barbaric and unethical the other practices celebrated in the book.

At first blush, there is little in the book of Judges to give comfort to a pacifist or a strict just-war theorist, even if the arguments of the preceding paragraph point out the difficulty of relying on Judges to make war acceptable. However, it should be noted that many of the stories acknowledge the high cost of violence. Certainly the tales of Ehud, Barak, Gideon, and Abimelech document the physical, economic, political, and social pain of war and pillaging. The legend of Samson recognizes that unrestrained violence can spiral out of control, threatening social stability and interethnic relations. And the tales of Jephthah and of the Levite's concubine mourn the deep suffering caused by violence.

In addition to acknowledging the price of violence, the book of Judges proves that the use of force was not the only political strategy employed by premonarchic leaders. As noted earlier, the heroes in Judges had a variety of nonmartial instruments to gain and retain power. They relied on the collection of information, their reputation for reliability, the attraction of their honor, and the renown of their generous sacrifices. All of these methods were used by the men and women of valor to consolidate their positions within their respective houses and communities. Clearly they were aware that violence alone was an expensive and unreliable political tool. Other strategies involved lower financial costs, carried less risk of inciting resistance, and prompted sentiments of loyalty and respect. While the bardic storyteller lauded violence, the bardic tales also contain ample evidence of alternative approaches that tempered the need to use force and that promised more permanency. For his or her part, the humanist writer suggested that violence resulted

CONCLUSIONS AND REFLECTIONS

in a downward spiral of conflict and chaos. With the humanist's stories, the book of Judges ends with a deeply pessimistic perspective about the utility of violence. Overall, the book of Judges stands as a critique of any assumption that violence could or should be the default mechanism for exercising power, resolving conflict, or responding to threat.

As suggested repeatedly, the book of Judges stands at the very beginning of a long journey by Jews, Christians, and Muslims toward greater ethical and spiritual maturity. The fact that later religious leaders accepted Judges as Scripture is proof that they honored the earliest Hebrew people to set foot on that journey. However, by way of contrast, Judges allows us to appreciate the great advancements made by the Bible's later prophets, poets, politicians, and creative writers, by Jesus of Nazareth, and by Mohammed. All emphasized peace, compassion, and forgiveness. The fact that so much progress has been made since the time of Judges challenges people in the twenty-first century to continue the journey. Moderns do a disservice to the men and women of valor in Judges when they regress to where the voyage of faith and ethics began. The Holocaust, the deployment and use of weapons of mass destruction, terrorism, and today's huge military expenditures represent such a return. The same is true of more subtle forms of structural violence that harm the environment, individuals at the bottom of the social and economic ladder, and people of other races, cultures, and religions. Consequently, moderns deceive themselves if they imagine they have achieved moral perfection. They dishonor the men and women of valor in Judges should they turn away from self-examination and suspend the quest for greater understanding.

I end this book on a note of hope and humility. We might take it that one message of the book of Judges is that a just, gracious, and patient God is willing to work with our imperfect capacity to understand and to conduct ourselves. In his *Institutes* and in his commentaries, John Calvin frequently acknowledged the reality of divine accommodation. Calvin held that God speaks and acts in ways that human beings can understand, even if the capacity to understand is imperfect. In a representative statement Calvin wrote that God never "appeared such as he actually is, but such as the capacity of men could receive." Nevertheless, this appearance, Calvin went on to say, is in "a manner as to cause some kind of mirror to reflect the rays of his glory."[15] A colleague, who is both a theologian and a Spanish professor, is fond of comparing the early Hebrews to his beginning language students. The students, he says, have much to learn. But rather than despair because their pronunciation is dreadful, their vocabulary limited, and their abuse of the subjunctive unremitting, my colleague takes delight because the students are making an effort. His pleasure, he says, may be similar to the divine perspective on human society. Along with the men and women of valor in Judges we ourselves struggle imperfectly with ethical subjunctives. The book of Judges reminds us that a gracious God is willing to accept our efforts.

---

15. John Calvin, *Commentary on the Book of the Prophet Isaiah*, trans. William Pringle (Grand Rapids, MI: Baker Book House, 1984), 1:200. Writing on John 3:12, Calvin suggests that God speaks to humans in childlike language, that "God prattles to us in Scripture in a rough and popular style." *Commentary on the Gospel According to John*, trans. William Pringle (Grand Rapids, MI: Baker Book House, 1984), 1:119. For an extended discussion of Calvin's concept of divine accommodation see Michael Tinker, "John Calvin's Concept of Divine Accommodation: A Hermeneutical Corrective," *Churchman* 118 (2004): 325–58.

Methodological Appendix

Relying on the usual strategies employed by historians, political scientists, anthropologists, sociologists, and biblical scholars, the first step in my research on the political culture of ancient Israel was to locate the men and women of Judges in the larger cultural, political, economic, and social contexts of Syria-Palestine in the Early Iron Age. I accept the scholarly consensus that the Israelites were one of many groups sharing a common Canaanite language, approaches to subsistence and family, political values, and religious understandings. To analyze the premonarchic Hebrew political culture depicted in the book of Judges, I turned to well-established theories about indigenous knowledge, patron-client political strategies, honor, and economics. My intent was to use those theories in a heuristic rather than a prescriptive manner. Hopefully, the theories provided categories that opened up avenues of inquiry, not filters which obscured or prejudiced data.

A guiding principle of my research was to keep in mind that ancient Syria-Palestine was a patrimonial society in which political and social arrangements as well as cultural similarities and differences were thought of in terms of family and kin relations. In patrimonial communities peaceful political relations and cultural resemblances are explained by genealogical proximity, while political antagonism and cultural distance are considered the result of an earlier family conflict or the lack of any kin link in the first place. High regard for the economy, politics, or religion of a neighbor might be expressed in the metaphors of journey, marriage, or borrowing. Political institutions that resemble those of neighboring peoples are frequently described as having been introduced by a remarkable innovator from that country's political elite. Admiration for a prestigious country often is expressed through claims of having migrated from that region. Sometimes these accounts include tales of the traveler/innovator marrying into a local family. Such stories can become the vehicle for explaining change, whether evolutionary or abrupt.

As can be seen in every chapter of this book, I have frequently drawn parallels between preindustrial Africa and Early Iron Age Syria-Palestine. While some may question this approach, all political scientists, anthropologists, and historians rely on parallels to understand and illustrate motives and actions. Game theory and the rational actor model are two common applications of parallelism. Consciously or unconsciously, scholars constantly ask how a rational person would behave in a given situation and what strategies that person might use to minimize cost and maximize rewards. For example, Westerners often assume that an overriding goal in the economic realm is to increase profit and personal gain, that class consciousness and class conflict drive social behavior, and that religious and social values are consistent with economic self-interest. By using examples from traditional Africa I hope to avoid the trap of assuming that the term "rational actor" defines rational and reasonable in the same way that a Western, post-Enlightenment individual would when thinking or acting. While rational people the world over strive for honor, manage material wealth, seek stability in life, turn to experts, and engage the fundamental forces of the temporal and spiritual worlds, there are many different "rational" ways of achieving those ends. Western concepts of status, economic motives, the place of the supernatural, or means to achieve stability may be quite different from those of people living in other cultures and other times. Turning to Africa for examples—as well as to Polynesia, sixteenth-century France, and ancient Ugaritic culture—can open our eyes to possible patterns in Palestinian hill-country society we might otherwise have overlooked.

In addition to the use of parallels, my study depends on extrapolation in order to arrive at a more general understanding. Judges contains a very limited number of major characters whose life stories provide some of the few literary records of Early Iron Age Israel. One must assume that these characters are representative of other comparable individuals and that the values displayed by those individuals were shared more widely. While Ehud is the only client-tribute gatherer described in Judges, it is safe to assume that he was one of many such individuals whose career paths were similar. While Samson is the only adolescent warrior depicted in Judges, his reckless exuberance would have been typical of other young men. While the strongman Barak is the only leader said to have turned to a female seer, the prophetess Deborah, his strategy would not have been unique. While both Abimelech and Jephthah engaged in tough negotiations with the political leaders who employed them, their situations would have been duplicated many times. Although the messenger of Yhwh is mentioned only three times in Judges, it seems reasonable to assume that such figures were not uncommon in the premonarchic era.

Besides the use of parallels and extrapolation, my study gives close attention to the meaning of clichés. As noted above, the book of Judges employs many clichés that act as a literary shorthand to convey a political or social message. Clichés are most easily identified by their formulaic and repetitive character. Statements about townspeople raping guests, warriors utterly destroying enemies, chariots being swept away in rising waters, individuals single-handedly destroying whole companies of opponents, heroes tearing lions apart with their bare hands, or warriors being killed by women may not tell us what literally happened. However, the tales should not be dismissed as irrelevant or fundamentally inaccurate. Instead of being considered as implausible and fanciful hyperbole, they should be understood as signposts to important events, processes, or values. As the historian Joseph Miller has noted, seemingly fanciful tales sometimes may be more accurate links to the past than the more "believable" and prosaic passages that later storytellers often add as narrative filler to make an account plausible, interesting, or coherent.[1]

One example of a Western political cliché would be the phrase "He threw his hat into the ring." While this cliché is of no interest to a haberdasher, it is an accurate reference to an actual political event. In Central Africa the cliché of drunkenness is used to assert that a chief was inept and the cliché "the chief refused to offer a feast" alleges that the tribute and patronage system had broken down.[2] Although it should not be assumed that the chief was inebriated or did not serve a meal, each cliché is a commentary about what people believe happened politically. The book of Judges is filled with clichés, which should not be read literally but which must be taken seriously. The following clichés are some of the most obvious: weeping as a literary symbol for seeking redress or reversal, "he said these words" as evidence that someone entered into a contract sealed by an oath, rape as an expression of humiliation and dishonor (sodomy, which treats a man as a woman being the most extreme form), and being killed by a woman or by a youth as a way to discredit an adversary's

---

1. Joseph C. Miller, *The African Past Speaks: Essays on Oral Tradition and History* (Dawson: Folkestone, 1980), 24–31.
2. Luc de Heusch, *The Drunken King, or the Origin of the State* (Bloomington: Indiana University Press, 1982).

warriorly reputation. Other common clichés such as being fat, riding on a donkey, having seventy sons, or ruling seventy cities are ways to suggest power and wealth. The cliché asserting that someone is a reckless and worthless fellow describes rootless warriors seeking a patron employer.

In spite of their historical value, clichés often attribute too much weight to external and extraordinary forces. Dramatic tales of wars, invasions, migrations, divine visitations, and journeys become clichés pointing to innovations and adjustments whose real causes may be more internal than external. Slow, internally generated social, religious, economic, and political transformations are not easily expressed by the intellectual models governing most traditional descriptions of the past. For one thing, gradual socioeconomic progress or the persistence of indigenous elements in later values and institutions often are incomprehensible and unnoticed by the men and women responsible for recounting the past. For another thing, novelty is often suspect, especially if it threatens central social or religious values. Acknowledging recent temporally induced theological or legal adjustments could undermine the legitimacy of existing principles and ideas. Therefore, stories of divine intervention or innovation by a larger-than-life founding figure become the only acceptable means of explaining change. In the absence of such intervention, current belief and practice are projected unchanged back in time. Accounts about earlier deviations from the contemporary norm are rationalized as apostasy or deterioration.

Another strategy to gain access to the political values of Early Iron Age Israel is through an analysis of Hebrew words. The fact that a word was used is irrefutable evidence that people consciously reflected on the concepts expressed by that word. As explained in chapter five of my book, we can be confident that the Israelites thought much about honor because the language of their stories contains so many words expressing and describing honor. The names used in Judges can also illuminate political perceptions and principles. As in the writings of the nineteenth-century English author Charles Dickens, the book of Judges sometimes gives the characters names suggesting their characteristics. Names such as Hacker, Bee, Bangles, Deception, Weeping, and Big Man all make evaluative statements about people and places. Some of these names may have been used by people living in premonarchic times, others were conferred later by the storytellers, editors, and authors of Judges. Some names were meant as honorific praise names, others were intended to disparage. Not just proper names, but also words referring to practices such as tribute and gifting provide a window into the material, religious, political, and social culture of the past. Terms suggesting strategies for battle, ways for gaining political office, or types of economic exchange also illuminate the past. Root words and their derivatives also can make us aware of and help us understand practices such as divination, the offering of sacrifices, and the nature of tribute systems.[3]

An additional way to gain access to ancient ideas is to give attention to tensions within and among stories. In part, this requires looking at differences expressed during the same time period. For example, the tensions implicit in irony can alert us to contending views about individuals, their deeds, and their values. Juxtapositions such as the contrast between the generosity of the Levite's father-in-law and of the old Ephraimite outsider, two men who had no obligation to extend assistance, and the outrageous behavior of the townsmen of Gibeah, people one would expect to offer comfort, help us understand the nature of hospitality and the obligation hospitality

---

3. Jan Vansina championed this methodology in his historical work on Central Africa. Two of the best examples of his approach are in *The Children of Woot: A History of the Kuba Peoples* (Madison: University of Wisconsin Press, 1978) and *Paths in the Rainforests: Toward a History of Political Tradition in Equatorial Africa* (Madison: University of Wisconsin Press: 1999).

placed upon a benefactor. Attention to tension also requires studying the historical evolution of the book of Judges. Not until the exile or soon after did people in Israel have access to Judges as a unified piece of literature. The dissimilar ways the bardic storyteller, the Deuteronomistic historian, and the humanistic editor describe the past help us understand shifting opinions about leadership, the relationship of humans to Yhwh, and the usefulness of violence. Like contrasting colors or textures, these differences clarify the political and social values that were important to the storytellers, editors, and writers.

Guiding all of the methodologies of my book has been the attempt to describe the past without deferring to preconceived notions of theological correctness or to explanations that privilege my own religion over another faith. Just as I would not assume that a magical snake actually created a bridge for African warriors to escape an enemy—although I would take the story seriously as an interpretive cliché—for purposes of research I do not take at face value the supernatural events described in Judges. It is not fair to attribute heavenly intervention to stories in one culture unless one extends the same interpretation to similar tales in other societies. Any attempt to theologize and acknowledge divine power must come after, not before, one has analyzed a given story from a social scientific perspective. To begin the theological exercise prematurely risks destroying the foundation of data upon which serious religious enterprise depends.

Bibliography

Achebe, Chinua. *Things Fall Apart*. New York: Anchor Books, 1994.

Ackerman, Susan. "The Personal is Political: Covenantal and Affectionate Love (*'āhēb, 'ahăbâ*) in the Hebrew Bible." *Vetus Testamentum* 52 (2002): 437–58.

Ahlstrom, G. W. *The History of Ancient Palestine from the Paleolithic Period to Alexander's Conquest*. JSOTSup 146. Sheffield: JSOT Press, 1993.

Arendt, Hannah. *The Human Condition*. Chicago: University of Chicago Press, 1958.

Arnold, Bill T. "The Love-Fear Antinomy in Deuteronomy." *Vetus Testamentum* 61 (2011): 551–69.

———. "Necromancy and Cleromancy in 1 and 2 Samuel." *Catholic Biblical Quarterly* 66 (2004): 199–213.

Bal, Mieke. *Death and Dissymmetry: The Politics of Coherence in the Book of Judges*. Chicago: University of Chicago Press, 1988.

Becker, Felicitas. "Traders, 'Big Men' and Prophets: Political Continuity and Crisis in the Maji Maji Rebellion in Southeast Tanzania." *Journal of African History* 45, no. 1 (2004): 1–22.

Boling, Robert G. *Judges: A New Translation with Introduction and Commentary*. Anchor Bible 6A. Garden City, NY: Doubleday, 1975.

Botterweck, G. Johannes, and Helmer Ringgren, eds. *Theological Dictionary of the Old Testament*. 11 vols. Grand Rapids, MI: Eerdmans, 1974.

Brettler, Marc. "The Book of Judges: Literature as Politics." *Journal of Biblical Literature* 108, no. 3 (1989): 395–418.

Bright, John. *A History of Israel*. Philadelphia: Westminster Press, 1959.

Brown, Francis, S. R. Driver, and Charles A. Briggs. *A Hebrew and English Lexicon of the Old Testament*. 1907. Reprint, Oxford: Oxford University Press, 1955.

Brueggemann, Walter. *Theology of the Old Testament: Testimony, Dispute, Advocacy*. Minneapolis: Fortress Press, 1997.

———. *An Unsettling God: The Heart of the Hebrew Bible*. Minneapolis: Fortress Press, 2009.

Bush, Frederic W. *Ruth, Esther*. Dallas: Word, 1996.

Calvin, John. *Commentary on the Gospel According to John, Volume First*. Trans. William Pringle. Grand Rapids, MI: Baker Book House, 1984.

———. *Commentary on the Book of the Prophet Isaiah. Volume First*. Trans. Rev. William Pringle. Grand Rapids, MI: Baker Book House, 1984.

Cohen, Ronald, and Elman Service, eds. *Origins of the State: The Anthropology of Political Evolution*. Philadelphia: Institute for the Study of Human Issues, 1978.

Cohen, Ronald, and Judith D. Toland, eds. *State Formation and Political Legitimacy*. New Brunswick, NJ: Transaction Books, 1988.

Coogan, Michael, ed. *The Oxford Encyclopedia of the Books of the Bible*. 2 vols. Oxford: Oxford University Press, 2011.

Crook, Zeba. "Honor, Shame, and Social Status Revisited." *Journal of Biblical Literature* 128, no. 3 (2009): 591–611.

Cross, Frank Moore. *Canaanite Myth and Hebrew Epic: Essays in the History of the Religion of Israel*. Cambridge, MA: Harvard University Press, 1973.

Dahood, Mitchell, SJ. *Psalms III: 101–150*. Anchor Bible 17A. Garden City, NY: Doubleday, 1970.

Davis, Natalie Zemon. *The Gift in Sixteenth-Century France*. Madison: University of Wisconsin Press, 2000.

Day, John. *Molech: A God of Human Sacrifice in the Old Testament.* Cambridge: Cambridge University Press, 1989.

Day, Peggy L. "From the Child Is Born the Woman: The Story of Jephthah's Daughter." In *Gender and Difference in Ancient Israel,* edited by Peggy L. Day, 58–74. Minneapolis: Fortress Press, 1989.

Dearman, J. Andrew. "The Tophet in Jerusalem: Archeology and Cultural Profile." *Journal of Northwest Semitic Languages* 22, no. 1 (1996): 59–71.

De Heusch, Luc. *The Drunken King, or the Origin of the State.* Bloomington: Indiana University Press, 1982.

De Tarragon, Jean-Michel. "Witchcraft, Magic, and Divination in Canaan and Ancient Israel." In *Civilizations of the Ancient Near East,* edited by Jack M. Sasson, 3:2071–81. New York: Charles Scribner, 1995.

Dever, William G. *What Did the Biblical Writers Know and When Did They Know It? What Archaeology Can Tell Us about the Reality of Ancient Israel.* Grand Rapids, MI: Eerdmans, 2001.

Exum, J. Cheryl. "Review of Robert H. O'Connell, *The Rhetoric of the Book of Judges.*" *Catholic Biblical Quarterly* 60 (1999): 537–38.

Finley, Moses. *The World of Odysseus.* New York: Viking, 1977.

Flanagan, James W. "Chiefs in Israel." *Journal for the Study of the Old Testament* 20 (1981): 47–73.

———. *David's Social Drama: A Hologram of Israel's Early Iron Age.* Sheffield: The Almond Press, 1988.

Frendo, Anthony J. *Pre-Exilic Israel, the Hebrew Bible, and Archeology.* New York: T&T Clark, 2011.

Frick, Frank S. *The Formation of the State in Ancient Israel: A Survey of Models and Theories. Social World of Biblical Antiquity* 4. Sheffield, UK: Almond, 1985.

———. *A Journey through the Hebrew Scriptures.* New York: Harcourt Brace, 1995.

Frolov, Serge. *Judges.* Grand Rapids, MI: Eerdmans, 2013.

Gaddis, John Lewis. *George F. Kennan: An American Life.* New York: Penguin, 2011.

Gay, John. *Africa: A Dream Deferred.* Northridge, CA: New World African Press, 2004.

Golden, Jonathan M. *Ancient Canaan and Israel: An Introduction.* Oxford: Oxford University Press, 2004.

Gottwald, Norman K. *The Tribes of Yahweh: A Sociology of the Religion of Liberated Israel, 1250–1050 B.C.E..* Maryknoll, NY: Orbis Books, 1979.

Guest, P. Deryn. "Can Judges Survive without Sources? Challenging the Consensus." *Journal for the Study of the Old Testament* 78 (1998): 43–61.

Gunn, D. M. *The Story of King David: Genre and Interpretation.* JSOTSup 6. Sheffield: JSOT Press, 1978.

Guyer, Jane I. "Wealth in People as Wealth in Knowledge: Accumulation and Composition in Equatorial Africa." *Journal of African History* 36 (1995): 91–120.

Halpern, Baruch. "The Assassination of Eglon: The First Locked-Room Murder Mystery." *Bible Review* 4, no. 6 (1988): 33–44.

Harms, Robert. *River of Wealth, River of Sorrow: The Central Zaire Basin in the Era of the Slave and Ivory Trade, 1500–1891.* New Haven: Yale University Press, 1981.

Harrelson, W. J. "Blessings and Curses." In *The Interpreter's Dictionary of the Bible*, 1: 446–48. Nashville: Abingdon, 1962.

Hauser, Alan J. "The 'Minor Judges': A Re-Evaluation." *Journal of Biblical Literature* 94 (1975): 190–200.

Heller, Roy. *Power, Politics, and Prophecy: The Character of Samuel and the Deuteronomistic Evaluation of Prophecy.* London: T & T Clark International, 2006.

Hutton, Rodney R. *Charisma and Authority in Israelite Society.* Minneapolis: Fortress Press, 1994.

Hyden, Goran. *Beyond Ujamaa in Tanzania: Underdevelopment and an Uncaptured Peasantry*. Berkeley: University of California Press, 1980.

Iliffe, John. *Honour in African History*. Cambridge: Cambridge University Press, 2005.

———. "The Organization of the Maji Maji Rebellion." *Journal of African History* 8 (1967): 495–512.

John of Salisbury. *The Statesman's Book*. Translated by John Dickinson. 1927. In *Great Political Thinkers: Plato to the Present*, edited by William Ebenstein and Alan Ebenstein, 199–217. New York: Harcourt, 2000.

Kapello, Powon Losuran. "Conflict among the Pastoralists in Kenya's North Rift Valley." Unpublished student paper, Daystar University, Nairobi, Kenya, 1998.

Klein, Lillian. *The Triumph of Irony in the Book of Judges*. Sheffield: Almond, 1988.

Knoppers, Gary N. "Rethinking the Relationship between Deuteronomy and the Deuteronomistic History." *Catholic Biblical Quarterly* 63, no. 3 (2001): 393–415.

———. "The Vanishing Solomon: The Disappearance of the United Monarchy from Recent Histories of Ancient Israel." *Journal of Biblical Literature* 116, no. 1 (1997): 19–44.

Koehler, Ludwig, and Walter Baumgartner. *The Hebrew and Aramaic Lexicon of the Old Testament*. 2 vols. Leiden: E. J. Brill, 2002.

Lapsley, Jacqueline E. "Feeling Our Way: Love for God in Deuteronomy." *Catholic Biblical Quarterly* 65, no. 3 (2003): 350–69.

Laswell, Harold. *Politics: Who Gets What, When, How*. Cleveland: Meridian Press, 1958. First published in 1935.

Lemche, Niels Peter. *Ancient Israel: A New History of Israelite Society*. The Biblical Seminar 5. Sheffield: JSOT Press, 1988.

———. "Kings and Clients: On Loyalty between the Ruler and the Ruled in Ancient Israel." *Semeia* 66 (1994): 119–32.

Levinson, Bernard M. "The Reconceptualization of Kingship in Deuteronomy and the Deuteronomistic History's Transformation of Torah." *Vetus Testamentum* 51, no. 4 (2001): 511–34.

Lind, Millard C. *Yahweh is a Warrior: The Theology of Warfare in Ancient Israel.* Scottdale, PA: Herald Press, 1980.

Logan, Alice. "Rehabilitating Jephthah." *Journal of Biblical Literature* 143, no. 4 (2009): 665–85.

Lopez, Rene A. "Identifying the 'Angel of the Lord' in the Book of Judges: A Model for Reconsidering the Referent in Other Old Testament Loci." *Bulletin for Biblical Research* 20, no. 1 (2010): 1–18.

Malamat, Abraham. "Charismatic Leadership in the Book of Judges." In *Magnalia Dei The Mighty Acts of God: Essays on the Bible and Archeology in Memory of G. Ernest Wright,* edited by Frank Moore Cross, Werner E. Lemke, and Patrick D. Miller, Jr., 152–68. Garden City, NY: Doubleday, 1976.

Marais, Jacobus. *Representation in Old Testament Narrative Texts.* Leiden: E. J. Brill, 1998.

Matthews, Victor H. *Judges and Ruth.* Cambridge: Cambridge University Press, 2004.

Mauss, Marcel. *The Gift: The Form and Reason for Exchange in Archaic Societies.* Translated by W. D. Hall. With a forward by Mary Douglas. New York: W. W. Norton, 1990. First published in French in 1923.

Meshel, Ze'ev. "Kuntillet 'Ajrud." In *Oxford Encyclopaedia of Archeology in the Near East,* 3:311–12. New York: Oxford University Press, 1997.

Migdal, Joel. *Strong Societies, Weak States.* Princeton: Princeton University Press, 1988.

Miller, Joseph C. *The African Past Speaks: Essays on Oral Tradition and History.* Folkestone, UK: Dawson, 1980.

Mobley, Gregory. "Judges." In *The Oxford Encyclopedia of the Books of the Bible*, edited by Michael D. Coogan, 1:516–31. Oxford: Oxford University Press, 2011.

Moran, William L., ed. and trans. *The Amarna Letters*. Baltimore: Johns Hopkins University Press, 1992.

———. "The Ancient Near Eastern Background of the Love of God in Deuteronomy." *Catholic Biblical Quarterly* 25 (1963): 77–87.

Morschauser, Scott. "Observations on the Speeches of Ramesses II in the Literary Record of the Battle of Kadesh." In *Perspectives on the Battle of Kadesh*, edited by Hans Goedicke, 123–206. Baltimore, MD: Halgo, 1985.

Muilenburg, James. "Gilgal." In *The Interpreter's Dictionary of the Bible*, 2:398–99. Nashville: Abingdon Press, 1962.

Niditch, Susan. *Judges: A Commentary*. Louisville: Westminster, 2008.

———. *War in the Hebrew Bible: A Study in the Ethics of Violence*. Oxford: Oxford University Press, 1995.

Noth, Martin. *The History of Israel*. New York: Harper, 1958.

O'Connell, Robert H. *The Rhetoric of the Book of Judges*. Leiden: E. J. Brill, 1996.

Olson, Mancur. *Power and Prosperity: Outgrowing Communist and Capitalist Dictatorships*. New York: Basic Books, 2000.

Olyan, Saul. "Honor, Shame, and Covenant Relations in Ancient Israel and Its Environment." *Journal of Biblical Literature* 115, no. 2 (1996): 201–18.

Peristiany, J. G., and Julian Pitt-Rivers, eds. *Honor and Grace in Anthropology*. Cambridge: Cambridge University Press, 1992.

Pitt-Rivers, Julian. "Honor." In *International Encyclopedia of the Social Sciences*, edited by David L. Sills, 6:503–11. New York: MacMillan Company, 1968.

Polanyi, Karl. *The Great Transformation: The Political and Economic Origins of Our Time*. Boston: Beacon Press, 2010.

Pritchard, James B., ed. *Ancient Near Eastern Texts Relating to the Old Testament.* Princeton: Princeton University Press, 1969.

Reefe, Thomas Q. *The Rainbow and the Kings: A History of the Luba Empire to 1891.* Berkeley: University of California Press, 1981.

Renfrew, Colin. *The Emergence of Civilization: Cyclades and the Aegean in the Third Millennium BC.* London: Methuen, 1972.

Reno, William. *Warlords and African States.* Boulder, CO: Lynne Reinner, 1999.

Ricoeur, Paul. "The Function of Fiction in Shaping Reality." *Man and World* 13 (1979): 123–41.

Roberts, J. J. M. "Does God Lie? Divine Deceit as a Theological Problem in Israelite Prophetic Literature." In *Congress Volume: Jerusalem 1986*, edited by John A. Emerton, 211–20. Leiden: E. J. Brill, 1988.

Sahlins, Marshall D. "Poor Man, Rich Man, Big-Man, Chief: Political Types in Melanesia and Polynesia." *Comparative Studies in Social History* 5 (1963): 285–303.

———. *Stone Age Economies.* Chicago: Aldine Publishing, 1972.

Samatar, Said S. *Oral Poetry and Somali Nationalism: The Case of Sayyid Mahammad Abdille Hasan.* Cambridge: Cambridge University Press, 1982.

Schattschneider, E. E. *The Semi-Sovereign People: A Realist's View of Democracy in America.* New York: Holt, Rinehart and Winston, 1960.

Schloen, J. David. "Caravans, Kenites and *Casus Belli*: Enmity and Alliance in the Song of Deborah." *Catholic Biblical Quarterly* 55, no. 1 (1993): 18–38.

———. *The House of the Father as Fact and Symbol: Patrimonialism in Ugarit and the Ancient Near East.* Winona Lake, IN: Eisenbrauns, 2002.

Seay, Chris. *The Gospel according to Tony Soprano: An Unauthorized Look into the Soul of TV's Top Mob Boss and His Family.* Lake Mary, FL: Relevant Books, 2002.

Seow, C. L. *A Grammar for Biblical Hebrew.* Nashville: Abingdon, 1995.

Sharp, Carolyn J. *Irony and Meaning in the Hebrew Bible.* Bloomington: Indiana University Press, 2009.

Shriver, Donald W., Jr. *An Ethic for Enemies: Forgiveness for Enemies.* New York: Oxford University Press, 1995.

Smith, Mark. *The Early History of God: Yahweh and Other Deities in Ancient Israel.* 2nd ed. Grand Rapids, MI: Eerdmans, 2002.

———. "Remembering God: Collective Memory in Israelite Religion." *Catholic Biblical Quarterly* 64 (2002): 631–51.

Smith, Morton. "The Common Theology of the Ancient Near East." *Journal of Biblical Literature* 71 (1952): 135–47.

———. *Palestinian Parties and Politics that Shaped the Old Testament.* London: SCM Press, 1987.

Smith, Patricia. "Infants Sacrificed? The Tale Teeth Tell." *Biblical Archeology Review* 40, no. 4 (July/August 2014): 54–56, 68.

Soggin, J. Alberto. *Judges: A Commentary.* Philadelphia: Westminster, 1981.

Stager, Lawrence E. "Forging an Identity: The Emergence of Ancient Israel." In *The Oxford History of the Biblical World,* edited by Michael D. Coogan, 90–131. New York: Oxford University Press, 1998.

Starbuck, Scott R. A. *Court Oracles in the Psalms: The So-Called Royal Psalms in Their Ancient Near Eastern Context.* Atlanta: Society of Biblical Literature, 1999.

Stewart, Frank Henderson. *Honor.* Chicago: University of Chicago Press, 1994.

Sunseri, Thaddeus. "Reinterpreting a Colonial Rebellion: Forestry and Social Control in German East Africa, 1874–1915." *Environmental History* 8, no. 3 (2003): 430–51.

Tinker, Michael. "John Calvin's Concept of Divine Accommodation: A Hermeneutical Corrective." *Churchman* 118, no. 4 (2004): 325–58.

Vansina, Jan. *The Children of Woot: A History of the Kuba Peoples.* Madison: University of Wisconsin Press, 1978.

———. *Paths in the Rainforests: Toward a History of Political Tradition in Equatorial Africa.* Madison: University of Wisconsin Press, 1999.

Volf, Miroslav. *Exclusion and Embrace: A Theological Exploration of Identity, Otherness, and Reconciliation.* Nashville: Abingdon Press, 1996.

von Oppen, Achim. *Terms of Trade and Terms of Trust: The History and Contexts of Pre-Colonial Market Production around the Upper Zambezi and Kasai.* Studien zur afrikanischen Geschichte 6. Münster: LIT Verlag, 1998.

Walzer, Michael. *In God's Shadow: Politics in the Hebrew Bible.* New Haven: Yale University Press, 2012.

Weber, Max. *Ancient Judaism.* Translated and edited by Hans H. Gerth and Don Martindale. New York: Free Press, 1952.

———. *Economy and Society: An Outline of Interpretive Sociology.* Edited by Guenther Roth and Claus Wittich. Berkeley: University of California Press, 1979.

Weinfeld, Moshe. "The Common Heritage of Covenantal Traditions in the Ancient World." In *I Trattati nel Mondo Antico: Forma, Ideologia, Funzione.* Saggi di storia antica 2, edited by Luciano Canfora, Mario Liverani, and Carlo Zaccagnini, 175–91. Roma: "L'Erma" di Bretschneider, 1990.

———. "The Loyalty Oath in the Ancient Near East." *Ugarit-Forschungen* 8 (1976): 379–414.

West, Harry. *Ethnographic Sorcery.* Chicago: University of Chicago Press, 2007.

Woods, Fred E. *Water and Storm Polemics Against Baalism in Deuteronomic History.* New York: Peter Lang, 1994.

Wright, G. Ernest. *Shechem: Biography of a Biblical City.* New York: McGraw Hill, 1965.

Wrong, Michela. *In the Footsteps of Mr. Kurtz: Living on the Brink of Disaster in the Congo.* London: Harper Collins, 1990.

Yoder, John C. *The Kanyok of Zaire: An Institutional and Ideological History to 1895*. Cambridge: Cambridge University Press, 1992.

Zevit, Ziony. "Three Debates about Bible and Archeology." *Biblica*, 83, no. 1 (2002): 1–27.

Index of Names and Subjects

Aaron, 28n54
Abdon, 131, 166n2
Abimelech: career and reputation as a mighty man at Shechem, 38, 42, 66, 55, 56, 87, 92–94, 103–4, 137, 141, 142n45, 147, 159, 177, 180n24, 192–95, 201, 203, 204, 209, 211, 215, 224, 229; elsewhere in scripture, 12, 20n39, 21n41; and honor, 118, 137–38, 147, 154–55, 160, 162; and Jotham's fable, 41n87, 99–100; and knowledge, 56. 72, 76; relation to Gideon, 11n19, 12, 37, 38, 93–95, 137–38, 147; and trust and treachery, 72, 81, 92–100, 102, 110, 111, 131, 142, 182, 192, 102, 109, 182, 192; and wealth, plunder, and tribute, 87, 160, 177–79, 181–82, 192, 194–95, 203, 204; and Yhwh, 21n4, 76, 77, 162, 178, 210, 215
Abraham, 21, 106, 108n32
Absalom, 35n75. *See also* Nazirite
Achebe, Chinua, 208n2
Achsah, 18, 38, 70, 76, 83, 116–17
Adoni-bezek (lord of Bezek), 82–83, 116
Adonijah, 89n9
Adrian IV, 82n4
Africa: cultural and political parallels with Syria-Palestine, *xiii–xiv*, 41, 30n59, 46–50, 52–53, 56n11, 57–58, 60–61, 59n32, 71n35, 73n37, 83n5, 93, 101n26, 120, 122, 142n47, 155, 156n60, 157n61, 166n2, 169n6, 169n7, 171n10, 181n25, 191n34, 212, 213n4; heuristic value for study of Syria-Palestine, *xiii, xiv,* 47–49,

247

52–53, 232; historical links to
    Syria-Palestine, *xiii*, 63
Ahab (king of Israel), 60, 62,
    108n32, 212
Ahaziah (king of Judah), 59
Ahlstrom, G. W., 5n6
altars: to Canaanite deities, 13, 41,
    64, 134–35, 176; as place of
    refuge, 90n9; to Yhwh, 65,
    90n9; as point of access to
    supernatural, 46, 51, 66. *See
    also* oak trees, sacrifice
Amalekites, 86, 87
Amarna Tablets, 26
Ammon and Ammonites, 31, 55,
    86, 87, 103–6, 179
Amnon (David's son), 129
Amorites, 104n29, 127
Amos, 221n12
amphictyony, 6n8
Amun (deity), 196–97
Antigone, 160
Apiru, 26
apostasy, 13–14, 18, 21, 174, 214,
    216, 231. *See also*
    Deuteronomistic School of
    Thought
Arabia, Arabian Peninsula, *xiii*
Arameans, 221n12
Arendt, Hannah, 44, 112–13
Aristotle, 141n44

Arnold, Bill T., 23–24, 59n19
Arnon River, 104
Asa (king of Judah), 60
Asher, 174n16
Asherah (Athirat): challenged by
    Israelites, 64, 134, 154; power
    and domain of, 58, 134;
    relation to El, 28, 33, 58–59,
    64, 134, 154; relation to Yhwh,
    62n25; revered by Canaanites,
    28, 58; revered by Israelites, 28,
    58, 59, 60
Ashkelon, 102
Assyria, 18, 20, 34, 36, 179
astrology, 59n19

Baal: challenged by Israelites, *xi*,
    12n23, 41–42, 60, 63, 64, 66,
    75, 77, 133, 134–37, 176, 200;
    and contracts/covenants, 51,
    93, 94; and human sacrifice,
    108n32; power and domain of,
    33, 60, 62, 69, 134–37; relation
    to other deities, 32–33; revered
    by Canaanites, 26, 131; revered
    by Israelites, 28, 58–59, 217
Baal Zebub of Ekron, 59
Babylon, 17, 59n20
Bal, Mieke, 8n14, 57n12, 61,
    91n12, 189

INDEX OF NAMES AND SUBJECTS

banditry, 26, 32, 87, 44, 167–68, 178, 209

Barak: career and reputation as a mighty man, 20, 37, 61, 66, 69, 89, 132, 141, 147, 157, 177; elsewhere in scripture, 20–21; and honor 56, 118, 132, 156–58, 160; and knowledge, 68–70, 76; reliance on Deborah, 56, 66–67, 75, 76, 81, 110, 117–18, 156–157, 224; and trust, 81, 110; and wealth, tribute, and plunder, 20, 21, 37; 176–78, 224; and Yhwh, 69, 111, 162

Bathsheba, 12, 20n39

Becker, Felicitas, 71n35, 73n77

Bedouins and honor, 119, 125, 151, 186

Beethoven, 29n58

Belial, 149, 150n55

Benjamnites, 86, 149, 174n16, 178, 204; conflicts with other tribes, 18n33, 37, 56–57, 108–9, 113, 130n30, 150–53, 161, 175, 187, 190; identification with Saul, 150; as renowned ambidextrous warriors, 7, 71, 86–87

besheth (shame), 12n23. *See also* Jerubbsheth and Gideon

Bet-ab (father's house), 31, 189. *See also* house/household

Bethel, 62, 84

Bethlehem, 148

Beth-millo, 95

betrayal, 85, 92, 100, 194. *See also* deception

Belial, 149, 130n55

blessings, and covenant ceremonies, 81, 96, 100; described and defined, 129–30; deuteronomistic theme, 13–14; examples of, 33, 39, 68, 96, 117, 156; and honor, 129–31; and oaths, 110–11. *See also* curses

Bochim, 41, 85. *See also* clichés; weeping/weepers

Boling, Robert G., 9n15, 36n81, 66n28, 95n17, 97n21, 116n1, 166n2

bravery, 22, 36, 81, 122, 123, 141

Brettler, Marc, 4n6

Bright, John, 20n38

Brown, Francis, S. R. Driver, and Charles A. Briggs, 126n23

Brueggemann, Walter, 44, 217, 222n14

Buganda, *xiii*

Bush, Frederic W., 19n35

249

Cain, 27
Caleb, 18, 70, 83–84, 116–17, 160, 179, 189
Calvin, John, 226
Canaanites: city states and political power of, 26–27, 63, 92, 179; conflict with Israelites, 2, 9, 16, 18, 20, 33, 83, 115–16, 127, 157, 158, 161–62, 173–75, 209, 212, 213; culture and religion of, 70, 111, 150; economy of, 177; relation to Egypt, 25, 30, 147; shared culture with Israelites, 16, 20, 28, 29n58, 31, 41, 58, 215, 217–18, 221, 223, 227
caravans, 27, 55, 63, 84, 87, 99, 162n2, 177, 181, 182
Carthage, 108n32
Central Africa, *xiv*
chariots, 34n70, 35, 157, 196, 230
charismatic authority: charismatic leaders, 8, 212; charismatic power, 16, 142; described and defined, 22, 23–25
Chemosh, 69, 70n32, 105
Chinnereth, Sea of (Sea of Galilee), 62, 73–74
Christians, 6–7, 22, 29n58, 200, 206, 213–16, 221, 225. *See also* people of faith

circumcision, 96–97, 101, 132, 143
city states, 9, 24–25
clichés: described and defined, 229–32; examples and use of, *xiv*, 29–30, 82, 108–9, 149–50, 157n61, 229–32; historical reliability of, 29, 229–31, 233
Cohen, Ronald, 9n15
Congo, *xii, xiii*
concubine: and gender violence, 113, 151–52, 175, 189, 224; as property, 61, 92n12, 151, 155, 189, 191; status of, 93, 125, 137, 148, 151, 154–55, 189; in story of Levite's concubine, 19n34, 108, 112–13, 149, 160, 185–86, 203
constancy, 79–113; as an alternative to violence, 79, 102–12, 224; deities as unreliable, 197; difficult to establish and maintain, 82–102, 105, 109–10; Jephthah an example of, 102–7, 112, 163, 164; and political power, xii, 20, 34, 36, 43–44, 79, 80–81, 111–12, 215, 224; and rigidity, 108–9, 110, 111–12; and Yhwh, 77, 107, 111, 112, 210. *See also* covenants

INDEX OF NAMES AND SUBJECTS

contracts. *See* covenants

covenants: and Baal, 51, 94, 98, 99, 111, 203, 210; as contracts, 55, 81, 93, 95–97, 101–11; covenant ceremonies, 95–96, 100, 103; as deuteronomistic theme, 13–16, 18, 41, 216, 222n14; failure of, 97–99, 100–102; and faithfulness/reliability, 22n43, 41, 84, 96, 126n23, 151; with humans, 95, 103–6; negotiating and ratifying, 95–96, 102–6; as personal relationships, 23–24; as political agreements, 95, 97, 103–6, 140, 176; and Yhwh, 13–14, 22n43, 41, 85, 106. *See also* constancy, oaths

Crook, Zeba, 120

Cross, Frank Moore, 28

curses, 33; and covenants, 81, 96, 100; and disgrace, 129–32, 138, 160, 162, 193; nature and power of, 110, 111, 129–31, 132, 160, 163; and trial by ordeal, 61. *See also* blessings

Cushites, 221n12

Cyprus, 31

Dagon, 42, 131, 139–40

Dahomey, *xiii*

Dahood, Mitchell, SJ, 28, 29n58

Dan, 18n33, 31, 37, 73–73, 84, 127, 174

dancing: to celebrate victory in battle, 106, 133, 156; of nubile girls, 109, 133, 153, 175, 190

David, 4n6, 12, 20n39, 21, 22n42, 24, 35, 37, 55n10, 95, 100n25, 124n20, 129, 150, 156n59, 174n16, 179, 212, 213

Davis, Natalie Zemon, 44, 167n3, 169, 183n27

Day, John, 70n33

Day, Peggy L., 191

Dearman, J. Andrew, 59n19, 108n32

Deborah, career and reputation as a diviner/seer, 42, 51, 56, 62, 64, 66, 68–70, 76, 157, 158, 160, 161, 191, 210, 215, 218, 229; elsewhere in scripture, 20; and honor and strength, 38, 68, 147, 117–18, 147, 154, 156–58, 160–162; as a judge, 33n67, 66–67; and knowledge, 64, 68–70; nature and age of her story, 10, 28, 208, 213; and war, 35n75, 56–57, 68–69, 76, 117–18, 177; and Yhwh 68–69, 162, 211, 216–17, 222n22, 223. *See also* Song of Deborah

251

deception/duplicity, 84, 96–102, 110. *See also,* Luz
deconstructionism, 7–8
Delilah, 11n18, 38, 91, 128, 130n29, 143, 144n52, 154, 161, 191, 192n36, 194–95
deliverers/deliverance, 13–14, 16, 17, 20–21, 22n43, 39, 41, 164, 176, 178, 209, 214
De Tarragon, Jean-Michel, 59n19, 62
Deuteronomic School of Thought: context and time period, 12–13, 164, 214; moral perspective of, 13–14, 108, 164, 199, 202, 214, 216; political perspective of, 14–15. *See also* apostasy, deliverers
Deuteronomistic School of Thought: context and time period, xi, 13, 5n7, 12–17, 82n2, 159, 164, 198; Deuteronomistic Historian/Editor, 10, 11n18, 13, 14–17, 66n29, 85, 128, 164, 233; moral perspective of, 13–14, 17, 41, 85, 108, 144n52, 146, 164, 173, 175–76, 178, 203, 214, 216; political perspective of, 14–17, 133, 174, 204, 207, 209

Deuteronomy, 12–13, 14–15, 50, 59n19, 212
Dickens, Charles, 97n21, 232
Dinah, 96–97
diplomacy, 76, 141
disgrace, 20, 116, 118, 128, 129, 136, 148, 150, 155, 158, 160, 162. *See also* grace, honor
divination: and advance of Yhwhism, 40–41, 66, 111, 135, 162, 210; in Africa, *xiii*–xiv, 41, 52–53, 57–58, 60–61, 69n32, 71n35; definition and description, 46, 50–69; as an economic enterprise, 63, 65, 70, 73–73, 75, 193, 194; in Israel, 20, 21, 33, 51, 59, 84, 105n30, 135, 232; tools and techniques, 6, 21, 46, 50, 51, 52, 53–54, 57, 65, 66, 73, 199–200; used by protagonists in Judges, 4, 6, 28, 51–55, 56, 64–71, 73, 75, 76, 111, 135–36, 158, 161, 162, 165, 191, 195n39, 197, 214, 218, 222, 223. *See also* Deborah; Gideon; Urim and Thummim
donkeys as sign of wealth, 67–68, 83, 117, 138, 165, 166n2, 183, 231

INDEX OF NAMES AND SUBJECTS

dowry, 83, 96, 148, 155, 179, 188, 204
drinking, 140, 143, 189, 192
dueling, 124–25, 136, 189

Early Iron Age/Iron Age I, 2, 25, 31, 147, 208, 227, 228, 229, 231
Early Israel, emergence in history, 28, 30; emergence of national consciousness, 29–30, 209; respect for El, 28n55; unity/disunity, 8, 32, 211–13
economic systems, 165–205; celestial economic transactions, 166, 171–72, 195–202; earthly economic transactions, 167–95; modern economic systems, 167–71; preindustrial economic systems, 167–71; protagonists in Judges as wealthy, 165–66; Syro-Palestinian economy, 26–27, 30; women as wealth, 20, 32, 37, 47, 61, 83, 87, 92, 93, 109, 117, 142, 146, 153, 155, 175, 177, 179–80, 190, 188. *See also* patronage; plunder; trade; tribute; gifts/gifting
Edom/Edomites, 30, 62, 156

Eglon, 6, 71–72, 76, 86–89, 180–82, 203
Egypt, *xiii*, 13, 26, 41, 63, 104, 147, 152, 176, 178n21, 184, 196–97, 221
Ehud: as a Benjaminite, 37, 71, 86, 15, 150; career and reputation as a mighty man, 71–72, 86–88, 141, 160, 162, 179–81, 198, 203, 209, 215, 224; and El, 71–72; and honor, 160; and knowledge, 71–72, 76; and plunder and tribute, 179–81, 203, 204; and trust/treachery, 6, 70–72, 86–88, 110, 181, 203, 218, 229; as a warrior, 7, 37, 86–87; and Yhwh, 72, 162, 198, 216
El: character of, 32; and covenants, 99; honored/recognized by Israelites, 11n19, 28, 35, 58, 71; power and domain of, 32, 62, 69; relation to other deities, 32–33, 77
Eli, 54, 77
Elijah, 60, 200
Elohim, 67, 116
Elon, 62
epic-bardic tales: context and time period, 10–12, 13, 20, 41, 159; literary characteristic of, 19, 28,

253

66n28; moral perspective of, 21n41, 106–8, 162, 164, 223; political perspective of, 10, 17, 38, 127, 146–48, 154, 209
ephod, 6, 51, 54, 73, 194
Ephraim, 72, 76, 88, 89n9, 149, 150, 151, 152, 174n16, 180–81, 186, 232
Ephraimite householder, 128, 149–52, 164. *See also* hospitality
Esau, 31, 183–84
ethnic consciousness, 28n55, 29–30
exile, 13n24, 17, 20, 21, 59, 233
exodus, the, 28n55, 29, 30n59
Exodus, book of, 40, 213n4
Exum, J. Cheryl, 8n14
Ezekiel, 59
Ezra, 19n35

family: as a political concept, 3, 22, 210, 227–28; structure in early Israel, 31–32, 91n12
fat, political meaning of, 72, 88, 181, 203, 231. *See also* clichés
feasts: at celebrations and festivals, 91, 101–2, 138, 172, 175, 187–92, 204; as political clichés, 82, 193, 130; as

sacrifice, 134, 139, 175, 198, 199. *See also* clichés
Finley, Moses, 122, 142
Flanagan, James W., 9n15, 22n42
forgiveness, 112–13, 184, 208, 225
Frendo, Anthony J., 2n2, 5n6, 25, 28n55
friendship (as an economic and political concept), 3, 81, 167, 171n10, 184, 203

Gaal ben Ebed, 97–99, 138, 182, 192
Gabriel, 35
gambling and games, 81, 101–2, 123, 124, 140, 172, 189. *See also* Samson
Gates, Bill, 166n2
Gay, John, 52–53
Gibeah, 149–52, 175–87, 232
gibbor/gibborim, 1, 35, 37, 86, 133, 136. *See also* men of valor
Gideon: career and reputation as an aggressive mighty man, 1, 7n11, 10, 36–37, 38, 42, 60, 64, 66, 75, 118, 134–37, 141, 142n45, 147, 204–5, 208, 209, 215; as a diviner/seer, 51, 62, 63, 64–66, 71n36, 193–94, 198, 210, 218; elsewhere in scripture, 12, 20, 21; and

INDEX OF NAMES AND SUBJECTS

honor, 133, 137, 160, 162; and knowledge, 64, 70, 75; and trust, 110, 142; and wealth, plunder, tribute, 75, 136–37, 154, 165, 193–94, 195, 211n3, 224; and Yhwh, 7, 11n19, 39–40, 41, 63, 64, 66, 75, 134–37, 199, 204, 216–17, 222, 223

gifts/gifting: described and defined, 167–70, 183–95; gifts to and from deities, 171–72, 195–202; gifts among humans, 183–95. *See also* economic systems

Gilead, 55, 95n18, 103–5, 178, 182

Gilgal, 41, 71

Goliath, 35, 89n33, 124n20

Gomorrah, 149

Gottwald, Norman K., 9n15, 13m 26n53, 36n81

grace, 116, 118–19, 128, 131, 148. *See also* disgrace, honor

Greece, 6n8, 31, 122, 141

Guest, P. Deryn, 4n6

Guyer, Jane I., 43, 47–50, 58, 63

Hacker, 7, 64, 177, 232. *See also* Gideon

Hamor, 96, 138, 184. *See also* Abimelech; Gaal ben Ebed; Shechem; Zebulon

Harms, Robert, 93n15

Harrelson, W. J., 129

Hauser, Alan J., 10n18

ḥāyil – חיל (mighty, prosperous), 1, 38, 133, 136, 165n1

Heber, 89n9

Hebron, 55n10, 89n9, 95. *See also* Kiriath-arab

Heller, Roy, 13n24, 51n6, 54n9

herem. *See* holy war

Hillel, 132

Hiram of Tyre, 179

Hittite, 84, 196–97

holy war, 173, 202

Homer/Homeric Greece, 10, 122, 141, 147

Hongo (African deity), 41

honor/honorable, 115–54; code of honor, 120–22, 133–34, 147, 151, 159; described and defined, 118–25; Hebrew words for, 126–33; for householders, 123, 148–51, 160, 164; and the law, 121, 125; for mighty men, 100, 159–60; political value of, 136–37; situational and contested nature of, 120–21,

255

125, 147, 154–58, 159; for warriors, 122–23, 133–34, 160; for women, 123, 154–58, 160, 161
Horn of Africa, *xiii,* 213n4
Hosea (prophet), 24
Hosea (king of Syria), 179
hospitality, 20, 90, 105n30, 108, 148–51, 171n10, 184–87, 204, 232
house/household: of deities, 51, 62, 84, 94, 98, 99, 111, 192; duties of to protect, 148, 150–51, 158, 160–61, 164, 186; as a family unit, 6, 51, 23, 31–32, 35, 140, 154, 165; honor of, 135, 148–50, 157, 160, 163, 186; management of, 39, 63, 77, 120, 123, 140, 154, 260; outside threats to, 84, 88, 91, 96, 99, 100, 108, 110, 134; political importance of, 1, 4, 24, 82, 93, 96, 127, 132, 195, 197, 209, 212, 224; religion of, 32, 48, 58, 65, 72n192; rivalry within, 75, 94, 103, 134–35, 137, 161–62, 194; wealth of, 10n18, 64, 65, 75, 76, 136, 154, 165, 188–89, 193, 194
human sacrifice, 21, 33, 59, 70n33, 81, 102, 106–9, 202

Humanist writer: context and time period, 12n22, 17–20, 28n54, 84, 92n12, 148, 159, 173, 175, 185, 190; literary characteristics of, 19, 73n38, 82, 92n12, 153–54; moral perspective of, 18, 44, 108, 113, 151–54, 164, 174–75, 148, 174, 186, 223; political perspective of, 18, 133, 147–48, 173–74, 176, 199, 202–4, 224–225
Hyden, Goran, 169n6

Igbo, 208n2
Iliffe, John, 120, 122
indigenous knowledge. *See* knowledge
insults, 123, 124, 143, 152, 189n33. *See also* disgrace; dueling; taunts
irony, 84, 120n10, 143–47
Isaiah, 19n35

Jabbok River, 104
Jabesh-gilead, 109, 153–54, 191
Jabin (king of Hazor), 89
Jacob, 183–184, house of, 96–97
Jael: as a cunning warrior, 38, 90, 158, 161, 191–92; as honorable, 7, 147, 157–58, 161, 163; as an ideal woman, 90; as

INDEX OF NAMES AND SUBJECTS

treacherous, 89–90, 91, 185; and Yhwh, 7
Jebus, 149. *See also* Jerusalem
Jephthah: career and reputation as a mighty man, 37, 55, 81, 87, 103–7, 137, 147, 156n59, 160, 162, 177–78, 180n24, 182, 195, 209, 216; elsewhere in Scripture, 21, 201n27; and honor, 133, 160–62; and human sacrifice, 106–7, 108n33; and knowledge, 76; as a misunderstood moral champion, 6–7, 44, 102–7, 151, 153, 163–64, 191, 200, 210, 215, 216, 220, 222, 223; and trust and reliability, 81, 102–7, 108–12, 163–64, 191, 210; and wealth, plunder, and tribute, 177–78, 180n24, 182; and women, 133, 151, 154, 160, 189, 191; and Yhwh, 21, 105, 106–7, 111–12, 162, 178, 191, 198, 200, 210, 215, 218, 222
Jephthah's daughter, 6, 102, 106–7, 133, 151, 154, 160, 163–64, 189, 191, 200, 215, 216
Jeremiah, book of, 24, 128
Jericho, 34, 86. *See also* Palm City, 86

Jeroboam, 36, 87n8, 141n43
Jerubbaal, 12, 75, 135, 138. *See also* Gideon
Jerubbesheth, 12n23. *See also* Baal; Gideon
Jerusalem, 17, 34, 59, 82n2, 108n32, 116, 149. *See also* Jebus
Jehoshaphat (king of Judah), 179
Jesus, 112, 113, 218, 223, 225
Jews. *See* people of faith
Jezebel, 60
Jezreel Valley, 62
Joab, 12, 90n9
Joash, 65, 134–36
John of Salisbury, 82n4
Jonah, 19n35, 223
Jonathan, 24
Joseph, 184; tribe/house of, 84, 127, 174n16
Joshua, 34, 83; book of, 18, 29, 30n59, 174, 179, 113
Josiah (king of Judah), 12–13, 15, 50, 82n2
Jotham's fable, 41n87, 99–100, 127, 151
Judah: kingdom of, 11n21, 59, 60, 73, 89n9, 179, 212; tribe of, 8n14, 83, 115–16, 161, 173, 174n16

257

judges, protagonists in Judges
    mislabeled as judges, 22, 33

kabod, 126–28, 157
Kadesh, Battle of, 196n40
Kenites, 27, 63, 84, 257
Kennan, George F., 221n13
Kenya, *xiii,* 101n26, 142, 155n58,
    166n2, 191n34
Kiriath-sepher, 70, 116–17
Kish, 67
Klein, Lillian, 144n52
knowledge, 45–77; as an
    alternative to violence, 65;
    celestial knowledge, 68–69,
    71n36, 76; collecting,
    gathering, controlling, 47, 48,
    49–58, 64, 70, 71–72, 74;
    complexity and elusive nature
    of, 48, 58–64, 74–75, 76;
    demand for, 51, 61–62;
    distributing, dispensing, using,
    64–66, 75; indigenous
    knowledge, 43, 46, 48, 50,
    53–54; knowledge specialists,
    47, 52–54, 58, 60, 61; political
    importance of, 48–49, 63–74;
    suppression of, 49–50, 60;
    temporal knowledge, 48,
    54–57, 68–69, 76
Kuntillet 'Ajrud, 62

Kynes, Will, *ix*

Laish, 74, 176n18
Laswell, Harold, 122n15
Late Bronze Age, 28n55, 31
Leah, 96
left-handedness of ambidextrous
    warriors, 7, 37, 71, 86
Lemche, Niels Peter, 2–3, 5, 172
Levites, 18, 19, 28n54, 63, 84, 162,
    198–99, 213
Levite and his concubine, 73, 74,
    92n12, 108, 112–13, 128,
    148–53, 134, 135, 160, 164,
    175, 185–86, 189, 191, 194–95,
    204, 224, 232
Leviticus, 198n42, 200, 210n44,
    212
Levinson, Bernard M., 207n1,
    15–16
Liberia, *xiii,* 52–53
Logan, Alice, 108n32
Lopez, Rene A., 40n85
Lot, 149
lots, casting of, 6, 18, 51, 52, 53,
    59n19, 199. *See also* Urim and
    Thummim
Luz, 84. *See also* deception

Maasai, 101n26, 166n2
Machiavelli, 140n40

Maji Maji Rebellion, 32, 71n35
Manasseh, king of Judah, 50; tribe of, 174n16
Manoah, 57n12, 127, 139, 198–200
Marais, Jacobus, 8n14
Marx, Karl, Marxism, 9, 47, 162
matrilineal societies, 8n14, 91n12, 181. *See also* patrilineal societies
Matthews, Victor H., 6n9, 19n35, 188
Mauss, Marcel, 44, 69
Melanesia, 169n7
men of valor, *xi–xii*, 1–3, 10, 33–38, 73–74; attributes and appearance of, 22, 35, brutality of, 5, 7, 64, 110, 122, 163, 185, 190, 195, 207, 209, 214; elite status and wealth of, 22, 36, 118, 136, 165–66, 172–78, 204; martial qualities of, 34–35, 147, 177; mislabeled as judges, xi, 22, 33; preoccupation with power, *xi–xii*, 4, 97–99, 209; and subordinates, 87, 142; and Yhwh, 22, 195–99, 201, 210–11
Menahem (king of Israel), 36
mercenaries, 19n34, 26, 37, 70–72, 76, 84, 86–88, 94n16, 97, 142n45, 165, 181
Merneptah Stele, 30
messenger of Yhwh, *xii*, 1, 13, 27, 28n54, 33, 39–42, 57, 65, 85, 127, 128n27, 137, 139, 144n52, 154, 162, 165, 185, 198, 211, 229
Micah: career and reputation as a big man, 73, 74, 131, 155; and honor, 131, 195; and knowledge, 72–73, 74, 76; as proprietor of divination site, 73, 74, 51, 194; story as a literary creation, 18–19, 73, 148; and treachery, 19n34, 131, 155, 176, 194; and wealth, 73–74, 194–95; and Yhwh, 73
Midian and Midianites, 16, 20, 27, 39, 41, 63, 64–65, 84, 134–35, 177
Migdal, Joel, 43, 80
Miller, Joseph C., 30, 230
minimalists, 4, 5n6, 5n7
minor judges, 6n8, 10n18, 131–32, 166n2
Miriam, 213n4
Mizpah, 103, 108–9

Moab and Moabites, 16, 31, 70n33, 71, 72, 76, 86, 89. *See also* Eglon; Ehud
Mobutu Sese Seko, *xii*, 169n7
Mohammed, 225
Molech, 69, 70n33
morality: ancient standards offensive to moderns, *ix*, 159, 207, 214–16, 218, 224; immaturity and inconsistency of modern moral standards, 221n3, 224, 225; Israelite awareness of moral ambiguity, 108, 113, 145–46, 152, 153, 163, 164, 223; moral standards of Israelites, *ix*, 105, 125, 144n52, 159, 175, 178, 202, 203, 217, 222–23, 225; moral struggles of all humans, 218–20
Morschauser, Scott, 196n40
mosaic law, 215, 216–17
Moses, 21, 28n54, 34, 36, 39, 40, 41, 213n4
Muslims, 216, 220, 225. *See also* people of faith

Naphtali, 89, 174n16
Nazi Germany, 29n58
Nazirite, 35n75, 142–43, 201. *See also* Absalom; Samson
necromancy, 33. *See* divination

Nehemiah, book of, 19n35
Neo-Assyrian Empire, 20. *See* Assyria
Nephilim, 35
New Testament, 17, 21, 102n27
Niditch, Susan, *xiv*, 9, 10, 12, 17, 19, 20n37, 44, 142, 143, 156n59, 161n62, 177n20, 191, 202, 216n6
Nigeria, 208
Nimrod, 35
Noah, 130
Noam, 132
nonviolence, 223–26
North Africa, *xiii*, 30
Noth, Martin, 6n8, 10n18
nuclear weapons, 221
Numbers, 200–201

oak trees, as sacred places, 46, 51, 55, 62, 66, 67, 89n9, 95
oath, 21, 33, 55n10, 81, 95, 96, 103, 106–11, 152, 153, 191, 210, 230. *See also* covenant; vows
O'Connell, Robert H., 8n14
oil: and anointing a king, 68; and honor, 100, 117
Olson, Mancur, 44, 167–68
Olyan, Saul, 126n23
Operation Iraqi Freedom, 69n32

INDEX OF NAMES AND SUBJECTS

Ophrah, 11n19, 62, 93, 94, 99, 194n38

Oppen, Achim von, 171n10

oracles. *See* divination

oral history, 4, 30n59, 43, 64, 133, 21n181

Othniel: career and reputation as a client warrior, 70, 83–84, 117, 141, 176, 179, 180, 188–89, 216; regarded as an ideal leader, 216; story of added by Deuteronomistic and Humanist editors, 10n17, 17n31, 18, 176, 179

Pacific Islands, 168n6, 169

pacifism/peace studies, *xi*, 208, 223–25

Palm City, 86. *See also* Jericho

pastoralists, *xiii*, 27, 69n32, 122, 156, 166n2, 212

patrilineal societies, 8n14, 31, 91n12, 93n14. *See also* matrilineal societies

patrimonialism, *xi, xii*, 1, 23–25, 26n51, 32, 169n6, 196, 197, 208, 227

patronage and patron-client polities: described and defined, *xi*, 1–3, 11n21, 43–44, 22–25, 119, 124, 195–96, 211, 227, 231; instability and cost of, 43, 83, 102, 124, 169, 179, 185, 197, 210; judgments about, 5, 17, 82n4, 164n65; kings and deities as patrons, 108n13, 195–97; pervasiveness of, *xiii*; and protagonists in judges, 1–5, 17, 22–24; and redistribution, *xii*, 43–46, 82–83, 168n6, 169, 172–73, 179, 183, 185, 195

Paul, 21

Paul Bunyan, 57, 141

peasant revolution and discontent, 9, 26, 27, 66, 162, 209

people of faith, *xi*, 207–8, 213–23

Peristiany, J. G., 44, 118–19, 126

Phinehas, 63

Phoenicians, 31, 220. *See also* Tyre

Philistines, 2, 16, 31, 39, 41, 84n6, 91, 101–2, 130n29, 131, 139–40, 144, 146n54, 161, 221n12

Pitt-Rivers, Julian, 44, 118–20, 124, 126, 158

place of refuge, 27, 89–90

Plato, 141n44

plunder: described and defined, 16, 20, 26, 44, 83n3, 167–68, 172–77, 182, 193; and honor, 203, 204; relation to tribute,

261

89, 97, 180, 181n25, 182; protagonists of Judges as plunderers, 74, 83, 89, 97, 99, 101, 160, 177–78, 182, 194, 211; spoils of plunder, 22, 65, 69n32, 79, 82, 102, 165, 177, 178, 194. *See also* economic systems; Olson, Mancur; roving bandits

Pokot, 69n32

Polanyi, Karl, 44, 168, 170

politics, definition of, 4n5

prophets: early prophets, 1, 55, 66–67, 69n31, 76, 211, 229; false and foolish prophets, 29, 54; late prophets, 17, 59, 112, 113, 199, 213, 215, 221n12, 222, 223, 225; non-Yhwhistic prophets, 50, 60, 200. *See also* Deborah

Proverbs, 38–39

Psalms, 17, 28, 29n58, 131

Rahab, 21, 84n6

Ramah. *See* Gilead

Ramesses II, 196–97

rape, 7, 96, 97, 150, 152, 156, 186, 223, 230. *See also* clichés; honor; hospitality

rational actor model, 228

Rebekah, 67

Red Sea, *xiii*

redistribution. *See* economic systems; patronage; tribute

reliability. *See* constancy

Renfrew, Colin, 9n15

Reno, William, 80n1

respect, 119, 122n15, 103, 132, 159, 170, 192. *See also* honor

revenge, 7, 27, 60, 80, 89n9, 112, 134, 136, 140, 141, 152, 153, 154, 190

Rhodesia, 29n58

Ricoeur, Paul, 208n2

riddles. *See* games and riddles

Romulus and Remus, 94

roving bandits, 44, 167–68, 178. *See also* Olson, Mancur; plunder

Ruth, 19n35

sa'al (to ask or inquire), 50, 51, 56, 68, 115. *See also* divination

sacrifice: for divination, 46, 51, 65–66, 68, 199–200; expression of rulers' power and wealth, 21, 44, 88, 136, 165, 167–69, 172, 191, 196–97, 198, 201, 209, 211, 224; as a feast for a deity, 139, 154, 196, 198–99, 202; holy war as, 173, 174, 197, 202; human sacrifice, 6, 21, 33,

59, 70n33, 81, 102, 106–7, 108nn32 33, 163–64, 191, 200, 202, 215, 218, 220, 223; offered by men of valor, 44, 65–66, 106–7, 139, 154,198; offered to influence or obligate a deity, 166, 196–97, 198; offered by specialists, 46, 67–68, 154, 198; for repentance/remorse, 41, 99, 198; to seal an oath or covenant, 96, 107, 108n33, 163–64, 191, 197, 199, 200–201, 204; smoke and pyrotechnics of, 40, 139, 199, 202; to thank or honor a deity, 68, 106, 139, 197, 199, 200; as tribute to deity/patron, 196–98, 200, 201. *See also* holy war

Sahlins, Marshall D., 168–69

Samaria, 11n21, 62, 179

Samatar, Said S., 213n4

Samson: career and reputation as a youthful warrior, 7, 35n75, 37, 38, 201, 229, 140–47; elsewhere in scripture, 21; and honor/dishonor, 118, 120n10, 127–28, 130, 137, 138–47, 160–61, 190, 210; and knowledge, 56–58, 72, 76; as a Nazirite, 35n75, 142–43, 201; story as a literary creation, 10, 11, 38, 57, 91, 100, 120n10, 141, 143–47, 216, 224; and strength, 7, 57, 91, 128, 139, 140, 144; and trust/treachery, 72, 76, 81, 91, 100–102, 110, 194; as an untamed beast, 139–42, 144n52, 190, 229; and violence, 102, 150, 144, 190, 192, 224; and wealth, 166n2, 187–90, 204; and women, 91, 101, 110, 128, 154, 188–90, 191, 194; and Yhwh, 7, 39–40, 41, 57, 127, 130, 139, 140, 144n52, 154, 162, 199, 210, 215–17, 218. *See also* Nazirite

Samuel, 21, 52n7, 54, 67–68, 71n36, 77, 198; book of, 11–12, 13, 15

Sarah, 21

Saul, 4n6, 18n33, 22n42, 24, 36, 52n7, 67–68. 71n36, 100n25, 150, 198, 212, 213

Schattschneider, E. E., 162n63

Schiller, Fredrich, 29n58

Schloen, J. David, 23–24, 31n61, 31n63, 32n64

Sea of Galilee. *See* Chinnereth, Sea of

Sea Peoples, 31. *See also* Dan; Philistines

Seay, Chris, 218–20

263

seer, *xii*, 33n67, 52n7, 54, 57, 67–68, 69n32, 73, 76, 198, 211, 229. *See also* Deborah; prophets; Samuel
segmentary lineage system, 8, 9n15, 152, 160
Semitic cultural group, *xiii*, 30, 31
Service, Elman, 9n15
seventy, 116, 137, 193, 231. *See also* clichés
Shaka the Zulu, 56n11
shalom, 89n9, 106, 116
shame, 12n23, 20, 110, 116, 118, 125, 126n23, 136n34, 139, 151, 157, 186n28, 193. *See also* disgrace
Sharp, Carolyn J., *ix*, 143n51, 145–46
Shechem, 51, 55, 56, 89n9, 92–99, 103, 110, 131, 137–38, 181–82, 184, 188, 192, 194, 203
Shiloh, 133, 153, 155, 175, 190, 191
Shimei, 100n25
shrines, 28, 48, 51, 52, 58, 60, 61, 62, 65, 66, 70, 73–74, 75, 137, 165, 194
Shriver, Donald W., Jr., 44, 112–113
Simeon, 115–16, 173, 174n16, 193
Sinai, 62, 69, 118, 151, 186

Sisera, 38, 87, 89–90, 117n5, 118, 157–58, 177, 185, 189
slaves, 16, 23, 26, 32, 37, 47, 139, 165, 174
Smith, Mark, 2n2, 8n13, 28n55, 57n12
Smith, Morton, 58–59, 217
Smith, Patricia, 108n32
social science, 8, 42, 168, 208–13, 233
social stratification, 26, 32, 37, 53–54, 66, 70, 118, 120, 123–24, 125, 127–28, 148, 159, 162, 166, 170, 183, 188–89, 193, 203, 225
Sodom, 149
Soggin, J. Alberto, 20n5
Solomon, 22n42, 36, 90n9, 179, 212
Song of Deborah, 28, 35n75, 69, 106n31, 130n30, 132, 133n31, 142–43, 154, 156–58, 161, 163, 166n2, 163, 176–77, 213, 222n14
spies, 56, 74, 80, 84, 93
Stager, Lawrence E., 31n61
Starbuck, Scott R. A.. *ix*, 11n21, 55n10, 95
stationary bandits, 44, 168, 178. *See also* Olson, Mancur; tribute; plunder

Stewart, Frank Henderson, 44, 119–21, 124–25, 126, 127, 151, 153, 158, 159, 186
Succoth, 137, 185, 187
suicide bombing, 224
Syria, 62, 178

Tabor, battle of, 36
Tamar, 129
Tanganyika, 41–42
Tanzania, *xiii*, 73n37, 143, 166n2
taunts, 10, 56, 118, 131, 132–33, 137–39, 163
temples, 27, 46, 51, 59, 61, 95n17, 118, 131, 140, 196
teraphim, 73
Thebes, 34
Thebez, 99
Tiglath-pileser III, 20n38. *See also* Assyria
Timnah, 91, 154, 189
Tinker, Michael, 226n15
Tony Soprano, 218–20
tophet, 108n32. *See also* human sacrifice
trade, xiii, 27, 30, 48, 55, 70, 84, 87, 96, 112, 170, 192, 196. *See also* tribute
treachery. *See* deceit
trial by ordeal, 52–54, 61–62

tribute: compared to plunder, gifting, and market economics, 167, 170, 178–82; described and defined, 2–3, 166, 167, 168–70, 172–73, 178–82; protagonists of Judges as tribute collectors, 16, 22, 71–72, 76, 86, 89, 172, 179–82, 204, 229. *See also* economic systems; gifts/gifting; patronage; plunder; stationary bandits
trust/trustworthiness. *See* constancy
Tyre, 108n32, 178

Ugaritic, 23n44, 28, 29n58, 229. *See also* Canaanite
unwalled hamlets (*perazon*), 27, 74, 177, 179, 181
Uriah, 12
Urim and Thummim, 6, 51, 54, 199. *See also ephod*
Uzziah, 179

valiant mighty men. *See* men of valor
Vansina, Jan, 83n5, 232
vengeance. *See* revenge
virginity, 106–7, 109, 151–53, 154, 155, 164, 186, 188, 191

visions. *See* dreams
Voice of the Theologian. *See* Deuternomistic School of Thought, Susan Niditch
Volf, Miroslav, 44, 112–13
von Oppen, Achim, 171n10
votive offerings, 200–201, 204. *See also* vows
vows, 3, 96, 102–4, 106–11, 172, 175, 190, 200–201, 214. *See also* covenant; oath; votive offerings

wagers. *See* gambling
Walzer, Michael, 2n2
warlord, *xi*, 1, 7, 80n1, 164. *See also* men of valor
wealth. *See* economic systems
Weber, Max, 3, 8, 9, 22–24, 169n6
weeping/weepers (technical religious and legal term), 41, 67, 85, 199, 198, 230, 232. *See also* Bochim
West, Harry, 46
whole burnt offering, 200, 222. *See also* holy war; sacrifice
women: abuse of, 5, 8n14, 214, 218, 223; barrenness, fertility, and childbearing, 40, 61–62, 70, 123, 139, 151, 154, 155, 187; challenging traditional gender roles of, 38, 70, 117, 120, 156–58, 161, 191–92; as economic producers, 47, 188; fidelity and chastity of, 61–62, 122, 151, 154; and honor, 117–18, 122, 123, 154; as household managers, 123, 155, 188; as property and booty, 20, 32, 37, 61, 83, 87, 92, 93, 109, 117, 142, 146, 153, 155, 175, 177, 179–80, 190; regarded as unreliable, 89–92, 101, 102, 110, 139, 139, 154; status of, 106n31, 151, 154–55, 160, 189, 191; as warriors, 56, 155, 157. *See also* Deborah; dowry; Jael; virginity; women of valor
women of valor, 38–39, 158. *See also* Deborah, Jael.
Woods, Fred E., 60n22, 69n31
worthless fellows (mercenaries), 36, 84, 94, 138, 141, 147, 180, 194, 231
Wright, G. Ernest, 96
Wrong, Michela, 169n7

Yhwh: competition with Baal, 60, 63, 66, 69, 75, 134–137, 162; covenants and vows, 13–14, 21, 41, 81, 85, 106–7, 111–12, 191, 210; Deuteronomistic understanding of, 12–17, 85, 176; epic-bardic understanding of, 178; humanist writer's understanding of, 18–20; as a divine patron, 195–97, 199; and national consciousness, 22n43, 28n55, 211, 212; power and domain of, 62–63, 69; promoted by men of valor, 11n19, 41–42, 66, 75, 111, 134–37, 162; relation to other deities, 50, 62n25, 105, 162, 217–18; revered by Israelites, 33, 162, 190, 198, 199, 200, 211; and sacrifice, 173, 200–202, 204; as source of supernatural knowledge, economic and political power, 51, 73, 77, 199, 216; as a warrior and ally in war, 56, 68–69, 73, 106, 111, 156, 179, 189. *See also* messenger of Yhwh

Yhwh of Shomron, 62
Yhwh of Teman, 62
Yoder, Perry, *ix*

Zebulon, 132, 174n16
Zepath, 173
Zevit, Ziony, 5n6
Zion, 34

Index of Scripture References

HEBREW BIBLE
Genesis
2…..220
6:4…..35n73
8:8…..130
8:11…..130
10:8-9…..35n73
32…..183
33…..183
33:8…..183
33:9…..184
33:16-20…..184
34…..96
34:29…..34n72
35:8…..67
43…..184
43:28…..184
47:6…..34n71

Exodus
3…..39
3:9…..178n21
14:9…..34n70, 35n76
14:17…..34n70, 35n76
14:19…..34n70
14:28…..34n70, 35n76
15…..213n4
18:21…..34n71, 36n78
18:25…..36n78
21:12-14…..89n9

Leviticus
7:16-17…..201n43
22:21…..201n43

Numbers
5:11-34…..61
6:5…..142n49
6:13-21…..201
27:21…..59n19
31:1-34…..89n9
31:9…..34n72
35:1-34…..89n9

Deuteronomy
7:14-20…..15
7:22…..14n26
8:17…..34n72
8:18…..34n72
13:1-5…..50
17:14-20…..14, 15
18:9-14…..59n19
18:20-22…..54n9
19:1-13…..89n9
20…..15
26:7…..178n21
32:42…..142n49

Joshua
6:2…..34n70
9:12…..85n7
10:7…..34n70
15:15-19…..179n23
15:16-19…..18
20:1-9…..89n9
20:7…..89n9

Judges. *See below*

1 Samuel
2:18-20…..54
3:1…..54
9…..67
9:6…..67
10:18…..178n21

10:26…..36n80
12:3-5…..54
14:48…..175n17
15…..198
16:18…..35n77
17:51…..35m74
17:53…..175n17
18:7-8…..106n31
23:1…..175n17
28…..52n7
28:6…..59n19
31:12…..36n79

2 Samuel
5…..95
5:3…..95
5:23…..95
8:2…..179n22
8:6…..179n22
11…..20
11:14-17…..12
11:19-21…..12
13:13…..129
16…..100n25
22:5-6…..150n55
23…..95
23:3-4…..95
23:8-39…..37

1 Kings
1:50…..89n9

INDEX OF SCRIPTURE REFERENCES

2:28…..89n9
5:1…..179n22
18…..60, 200
19…..60
20:23…..62
20:28…..62

2 Kings
1:2-17…..59
6:14-15…..35n76
13:4…..178n21
13:22…..178n21
16:3…..108n32
17:3…..179n21
21:1-9…..59n19
22…..12

1 Chronicles
12:2…..86
12:8…..35
19…..12n22

2 Chronicles
13:7…..87n8, 141n43
17:5…..179n21
26:8…..179n22

Job
20:21…..34n69
31:25…..34n72

Psalms
18:4-5…..150n55
18:32…..34n72
18:39…..34n72
33:17…..34n69
44:10…..175n17
48:13…..34n68
83…..20
89:42…..175n17
106…..20
122:7…..34n68

Proverbs
31…..39
31:10-31…..38

Isaiah
8:4…..34n72
8:19…..67
10:14…..34n72
13:16…..175n17
17:14…..175n17
19:20…..178n21
30:6…..34n72
36:2…..34n70
42:24…..175n17

Jeremiah
14:21…..128
15:13…..34n72
30:16…..175n17

30:20.....178n21

Ezekiel
18.....59n20
38:11.....177n20
44:20.....142n49

Daniel
11:24.....82n3

Hosea
13:15.....175n17

Amos
9:7.....221n12

Micah
4:13.....34n72

Nahum
3:8.....34n68

Habakkuk
2:8.....175n17

Zechariah
2:8.....177n20
14:14.....175n17

Zephaniah
1:13.....175n17

CHRISTIAN NEW TESTAMENT

John
3:12.....226n15

Acts
13:20.....21

Hebrews
11:32-34.....21
11:32.....102n27

JUDGES

Sources
Epic Bardic Source.....chapters 3:16—16:31
Deuteronomistic Editor.....chapters 2, 3:1-15; editorial inserts in chapters 3–16
Humanistic Writer.....chapters 1, 17–21

Protagonists
Abimelech.....9:1-57
Achsah, Calab, and Othniel.....1:11-15; 3:7-11
Adon of Bezek.....1:5-7
Barak, Deborah, and Jael.....4:2—5:31
Ehud and Eglon.....3:12—5:1

Gideon…..6:1—8:35
Jephthah…..10:6-12:7
Levite and
   Concubine…..19-1-19:30
Micah…..17:1-18:31
Minor Judges…..10:1-5; 12:7-15
Samson…..13:1-16:31

Tribe of Benjamin…..20:1-21:5

www.ingramcontent.com/pod-product-compliance
Lightning Source LLC
Chambersburg PA
CBHW071151070526
44584CB00019B/2752